W9-BUQ-349

Steps to Writing Well

Steps to Writing Well

A Concise Guide to Composition

SECOND EDITION

JEAN WYRICK
Colorado State University

HOLT, RINEHART AND WINSTON

New York   Chicago   San Francisco   Philadelphia
Montreal   Toronto   London   Sydney
Tokyo   Mexico City   Rio de Janeiro   Madrid

Library of Congress Cataloging in Publication Data

Wyrick, Jean.
  Steps to writing well.

  Includes index.
  1. English language—Rhetoric. I. Title.
PE1408.W93 1984   808'.042   83-18573
ISBN 0-03-062207-7

Copyright © 1984 by CBS College Publishing
Copyright © 1979 by Holt, Rinehart and Winston
Address correspondence to:
383 Madison Avenue
New York, N.Y. 10017
All rights reserved
Printed in the United States of America

Published simultaneously in Canada

  6 7   059 9 8 7 6

CBS COLLEGE PUBLISHING
Holt, Rinehart and Winston
The Dryden Press
Saunders College Publishing

This book is dedicated to
David
and
Sarah
and
Kate

To the Teacher

This second edition of *Steps to Writing Well* was written, as was the first edition, for teachers of composition who have had trouble finding a text that is accessible to their students. Too many texts on today's market, these teachers rightfully complain, are still unnecessarily complex, sophisticated, or massive for the majority of students. Written simply in an informal, straightforward tone addressed to the student, this text was designed to provide a clear step-by-step guide to writing a 500-to-800 word essay. The combination of concise, practical advice, some student and professional essays, and a brief handbook should provide more than enough helpful information for students enrolled in a one-semester or one-quarter course without intimidating them with more material than they can possibly master.

Although many parts of the book have been revised and updated, its organization remains essentially the same: Part One offers advice on "The Basics of the Short Essay"; Part Two discusses the "Modes and Strategies"; and Part Three presents "A Concise Handbook." An Appendix containing information on finding and incorporating research material as well as sample footnote forms and bibliographic entries is new to this edition. Those familiar with the first edition will note, however, that the text still begins with the essay "To the Student," which not only argues that students can learn to write better with practice and dedication but also gives them a list of practical reasons why they *should* learn to write better.

Part One, now expanded to seven chapters, moves students sequentially through the process of writing the short essay. Chapter 1, on prewriting, stresses finding the proper attitude ("the desire to communicate"), presents practical suggestions for selecting a subject, and then offers several techniques for helping students move from large subjects to more manageable topics. Explanation and a student sample of looping, a useful pre-writing exercise that incorporates both freewriting and the skill of focusing, have been added to this edition. After finding focused topics for their essays, students are then ready for Chapter 2, devoted almost entirely to discussion of the thesis statement. Unlike many texts, this book stresses the importance of a clearly defined stance or purpose by using over two dozen examples to illustrate advice discussing what a good thesis is and isn't; also included in this chapter is explanation of the "essay map," an organizational tool that can help students outline their essays and plan their body paragraphs.

Chapter 3 discusses in detail the requirements of good body paragraphs: topic sentences, unity, order and coherence, adequate development, use of specific detail, and logical sequence. Over forty paragraphs—many of them new to this edition—illustrate both strengths and weaknesses of student writing. These paragraphs are not complex literary or professional excerpts but rather well-designed, precise examples of the principles under examination, written on subjects students can understand and appreciate. Some sections in this chapter have been slightly expanded in this edition; additional advice on specific development, paragraph unity, and idea hooks between paragraphs should prove helpful.

Chapter 4 explains how to write good introductions, conclusions, and titles, and Chapter 5, on effective sentences, emphasizes the importance of clarity, conciseness, and vividness. Nearly one hundred and fifty sample sentences illustrate the chapter's advice, and new sentence combining models and exercises have been included in this edition for additional practice. Chapter 6, on word choice, presents practical suggestions for selecting accurate, appropriate words that are specific, memorable, and persuasive. The chapter also contains a section on tone often omitted in other texts.

Chapter 7, "Revising Your Drafts," is new to this edition. Because too many students still think of "revision" as merely proofreading their essays rather than as an integral part of composing, an entire chapter has been devoted to explaining the revision process and to stressing the necessity of revision in all good writing. These pages guide the students through the various stages of revision, carefully cautioning novice writers against trying to analyze and revise too many parts of their papers at once. The chapter also includes hints for overcoming writer's block, a checklist for essays, and two student essays for revision practice.

Each chapter in Part One contains both exercises and assignments, many new to this edition. As before, the "Practicing What You've Learned" exercises follow each major section in each chapter so that both teacher and students may quickly discover if particular material needs additional attention. Moreover, by conquering small steps in the writing process, one at a time, the students should feel more confident and should learn more rapidly. The assignments, which also follow each major section in these chapters, suggest class activities and frequently emphasize "peer teaching," a useful method that asks students to prepare appropriate exercises for classmates and then to evaluate the results. Such assignments, operating under the premise that "you don't truly learn a subject until you teach it," provide engaging classroom activity for all the students and also remove from the teacher some of the burden of creating additional exercises.

Part Two concentrates on the four rhetorical modes: exposition, argumentation, description, and narration. Chapter 8 on exposition is divided into separate discussions of the expository strategies: example, process, comparison/contrast, definition, classification, and causal analysis. Each discussion in Chapter 9 and each of the chapters on argument, description, and narration follow a similar format by offering the students (a) a clear definition of the mode (or strategy), explained with familiar examples, (b) practical advice on developing each essay, (c) warnings against common problems, (d) suggested essay topics on subjects that appeal to students' interests and capabilities, (e) a sample student essay with marginal notes, (f) a professional essay followed by questions on content, style, and structure, and a vocabulary list. The advice on developing the essay and the section on common problems are both explained in easy-to-understand language accompanied by numerous examples. The nine student essays—the majority new in this edition—should encourage student writers by showing them that others in their situation can indeed compose organized, thoughtful essays. The student essays that appear here are not perfect, however; consequently, teachers may use them in class to generate suggestions for still more improvement. The nine professional essays were also selected to spur class discussion and to illustrate the rhetorical principles presented in this text. The four professional essays most popular with users of the first edition were retained in this revision; five new essays replace outdated readings.

Part Three contains a concise handbook with non-technical explanations and easy-to-understand examples showing how to correct the most common errors in grammar, punctuation, and mechanics. This edition also includes nine sets of exercises over the grammar and punctuation rules. Instead of following each and every rule with five or ten simplistic sentences containing the error in question, this text offers a series of exercises systematically placed so that the students may practice applying several rules at one sitting, just as they must do when they write their own prose. The interesting facts and humor found in these exercises may also make doing them less of a chore than usual.

Once again, this edition of *Steps* contains a list of grading symbols with page references on the inside front and back cover of the text to help students identify and review their errors.

Finally, an updated Instructor's Manual with suggestions for teaching and answers to the exercises and essay questions is available from the English Editor, Holt, Rinehart and Winston, 383 Madison Avenue, New York, NY 10017.

Although a second edition of this text has allowed its author to make a number of changes and additions, the book's purpose remains the same, as summarized in the original preface: "While there are many methods of teaching composition, *Steps to Writing Well* tries to help inexperienced writers by offering a clearly defined sequential approach to writing the short essay. By presenting simple, practical advice directly to the students, this text is intended to make the demanding jobs of teaching and learning the basic principles of composition easier and more enjoyable for everyone."

I would like to thank former Associate English Editor Anne Boynton-Trigg for her tireless efforts and good counsel during the revision of this text. I am also grateful to Professor Richard S. Beal for his work on the original manuscript, to former English Editor Nedah Abbott for her support, and to the following teachers for their thoughtful advice on this new edition: Stephen Baar, Westminster College; Professor Thomas J. Campbell, University of Oregon; Lois Friesen, Butler County Community College; Nancy Ann Gidden, Georgia College; Doreen Grandy, Portland Community College; Sandra Sellers Hanson, LaGuardia Community College; Sydney M. Harrison, Manatee Junior College; Donald Keesey, San Jose State University; Stephen H. Martin, Pace University; James Ruppert, University of New Mexico; Warren Wedin, California State University; Ray M. Zercher, Messiah College.

Special thanks to composition students at Colorado State University who allowed me to publish their work and to many of my colleagues there who offered valuable suggestions that helped me revise this text.

Finally, I want to express my gratitude once again to my husband, David Hall, not only for his contributions to the first edition of this book, but also for his continued support and encouragement during its revision.

Jean Wyrick
Director of Composition
Fort Collins, Colorado   *Colorado State University*

To the Student

Finding the Right Attitude

If you agree with one or more of the following statements, we have some serious myth-killing to do before you begin this book:

1. I'm no good in English—never have been, never will be.
2. Only people with natural talent for writing can succeed in composition class.
3. My composition teacher is a picky, comma-hunting liberal/conservative/ hippie freak/old fogey/whatever, who will insist I write just like him or her.
4. I write for myself, not for anyone else, so I don't need this class or this book.
5. Composition classes are designed to put my creativity in a strait jacket.

The notion that good writers are born, not made, is a widespread myth that may make you feel defeated before you start. But the simple truth is that good writers *are* made—simply because *effective writing is a skill that can be learned.* Despite any feelings of insecurity you may have about composition, you should realize that you already know many of the basic rules of good writing; after all, you've been writing since you were six years old. What you need now is some practical advice on composition, some coaching to sharpen your skills, and a strong dose of determination to practice those skills until you can consistently produce the results you want. Talent, as the French writer Flaubert once said, is nothing more than long patience.

Think about learning to write well as you might consider your tennis game. No one is born a tennis star. You first learn the basic rules and movements and then go out on the court to practice. And practice. No one's tennis will improve if he or she stays off the court; similarly, you must write regularly and receive feedback to improve your composition skills. Try to see your teacher not as Dr. Frankenstein determined to reproduce his or her style of writing in you, but rather as your coach, your loyal trainer who wants you to do the very best you can. Like any good coach, your teacher will point out your strengths and weaknesses; she or he will often send you to this text for practical suggestions for improvement. And while there are no quick, magic solutions for learning to write well, the most important point to remember is this: with this text, your own common sense, and determination, *you can improve your writing.*

Why Write?

"OK," you say, "so I can improve if I try—but why should I bother? Why should I write well? I'm not going to be a professional writer."

In the first place, writing helps us explore our own thoughts and feelings. Writing forces us to articulate our ideas, to discover what we really think about an issue. For example, let's suppose you're faced with a difficult decision and that the arguments pro and con are jumbled in your head. You begin to write down all the pertinent facts and feelings, and suddenly, you begin to see that you do, indeed, have stronger arguments for one side of the question than the other. Once you "see" what you are thinking, you may then scrutinize your opinions for any logical flaws or weaknesses and revise your argument accordingly. In other words, writing lays out our ideas for examination, analysis, and thoughtful reaction. Thus when we write, we (and the world at large) see who we are, and what we stand for, much more clearly. Moreover, writing can provide a record of our thoughts that we may study and evaluate in a way that conversation cannot. In short, writing well enables us to see and know ourselves—our feelings, ideas, and opinions—better.

On a more practical level, we need to write effectively to communicate with others. While a part of our writing is done solely for ourselves, the majority of it is created for others to share. In this world, it is almost impossible to claim that we write only for ourselves. We are constantly asked to put our feelings, ideas, and knowledge in writing for others to read. In four years of college, no matter what your major, you will repeatedly be required to write essays, tests, reports, and exercises (not to mention letters home). Later, you may need to write formal letters of application for jobs or graduate training. And on a job you may have to write numerous kinds of reports, proposals, analyses, and requisitions. To be successful in any field, you must make your correspondence with business associates and co-workers clearly understood; remember that enormous amounts of time, energy, and profit have been lost because of a single unclear office memo.

There's still a third—more cynical—reason for studying writing techniques. Once you begin to improve your ability to use language, you will become more aware of the ways others write and speak. Through today's mass media, we are continually bombarded with words from politicians, advertisers, scientists, preachers, and teachers. We need to understand and evaluate what we are hearing, not only for our benefit but also for self-protection. Language is frequently manipulated to manipulate us. For example, some defendants preferred us to see Watergate as an "intelligence information gathering mission" rather than as simple breaking and entering, and some politicians now claim to merely "misspeak themselves" when caught in lies. Advertisers frequently try to sell us "authentic reproductions" that are, of course, fakes all the same; the television networks treat us to "encore presentations" that are the same old summer reruns.

By becoming better writers ourselves, we can learn to recognize and reject the irresponsible, cloudy, and dishonest language of others before we become victims of their exploitation.

A Good Place To Start

If improving writing skills is not only possible but important, it is also something else: hard work. H. L. Mencken, American critic and writer, once remarked that "for every difficult and complex problem, there is an obvious solution that is simple, easy and wrong." No composition text can promise easy formulas guaranteed to improve your writing overnight. Nor is writing always fun for anyone. But this text can make the learning process easier, less painful, and more enjoyable than you might anticipate. Written in plain, straightforward language addressed to you, the student, this book will suggest a variety of practical ways for you to organize and write lucid, lively prose. Because each of your writing tasks will be different, this text cannot provide a single, simple blueprint that will apply in all instances. Later chapters, however, will discuss some of the most common methods of organizing essays, such as development by example, definition, classification, causal analysis, comparison/contrast, and argument. As you become more familiar with, and begin to master, these patterns of writing, you will find yourself increasingly able to assess, organize, and explain the thoughts you have about the people, events, and situations in your own life. And while it may be true that in learning to write well there is no free ride, this book, along with your own willingness to work and improve, can start you down the road with a good sense of direction.

J.W.

Contents

PART TWO: MODES AND STRATEGIES

PART THREE: A CONCISE HANDBOOK

Steps to Writing Well

THE BASICS OF THE SHORT ESSAY

In the first section of this text, you will read about the main parts of the short essay, the kind you are most likely to encounter in composition class and in other college courses. Chapters 1 and 2, on prewriting and the thesis statement, will help you organize your thoughts and plan the design of your essay; Chapter 3, on paragraphs, will show you how to write the body or middle section; Chapter 4 will help you complete your essay; Chapters 5 and 6 will present advice on selecting the words and composing the sentences in your rough drafts. Chapter 7 will offer suggestions for revising and polishing your writing.

Prewriting

GETTING STARTED, OR SOUP-CAN LABELS CAN BE FASCINATING

For many writers getting started is the hardest part. You may have noticed that when it is time to begin a writing assignment, you suddenly develop an enormous desire to defrost your refrigerator, water your plants, or sharpen your pencils for the fifth time. If this situation sounds familiar, you may find it reassuring to know that many professionals undergo these same strange compulsions before they begin writing. Jean Kerr, author of *Please Don't Eat the Daisies*, admits that she often finds herself in the kitchen reading soup-can labels—or anything—in order to prolong the moments before taking pen in hand. John C. Calhoun, vice-president under Andrew Jackson, insisted he had to plow his fields before he could write, and Joseph Conrad, author of *Lord Jim* and other novels, is said to have cried on occasion from sheer dread of sitting down to compose his stories.

In order to spare you as much hand-wringing as possible, this chapter presents some practical suggestions on how to begin writing your short essay. Although all writers must find the methods that work best for them, you may find some of the following ideas helpful.

But no matter how you actually begin putting words on paper, it is absolutely essential to maintain two basic ideas concerning your writing task. Before you write a single sentence, you should always remind yourself that

1. you have some valuable ideas to tell your reader, and
2. more than anything, you want to communicate those ideas to your reader.

These reminders may seem obvious to you, but without a solid commitment to your own opinions as well as to your reader, your prose will be lifeless and boring. If *you* don't care about your subject, you can't very well expect anyone else to. Have confidence that your ideas are worthwhile and that your reader genuinely wants, or needs, to know what you think.

Most importantly, however, you must have a strong desire to tell others exactly what you are thinking. The single most serious mistake inexperienced writers make is writing for themselves only. The very act of composing an essay demonstrates that you have ideas about your subject; the point is to communicate your opinions to others clearly and persuasively. Whether you wish to inform your readers, change their minds, or stir them to action, you cannot accomplish your purpose by writing so that only you understand what you mean. Remember that the burden of communicating your thoughts falls on *you*, not the reader, who is under no obligation at all to struggle through confused, unclear prose, paragraphs that begin and end for no apparent reason, sentences that come one after another with no more logic than lemmings following one another into the sea. Therefore, before you begin writing, commit yourself to becoming more sensitive to the feelings of your reader. Ask yourself as you revise your writing, "Am I making myself clear to others, or am I merely jotting down a conversation with myself?" Other chapters in this book will give you concrete advice on ways to make your writing clearer, but for now, at the jumping-off point in the writing process, the goal is to become *determined to communicate with your readers*.

SELECTING A SUBJECT

Once you have decided that communicating with others is your primary goal, you are ready to select the subject of your essay. Here are some suggestions on how to begin:

Start Early. Writing teachers since the earth's crust cooled have been pushing this advice, and for good reason. It's not because teachers are egoists competing for the dubious honor of having the most time-consuming course; it's because few writers, even experienced ones, can do a good job when rushed. You need time to mull over ideas, organize your thoughts, revise and polish your sentences. Rule of thumb: always give yourself twice as much time as you think you'll need to avoid the four-A.M.-why-did-I-come-to-college panic.

Select Something in Which You Currently Have a Strong Interest. If the essay subject is left to you, think of something fun, fascinating, or frightening you've done or seen lately, something perhaps you've already told a friend about. The subject might be the pleasure of a new hobby, the challenge of a recent book or movie, or even the harassment of registration—anything in which you are personally involved. If you aren't enthusiastic enough about your subject to want to spread the word, pick something else. Bored writers write boring essays.

Don't feel you have nothing from which to choose your topic. Your days are full of activities, people, joys, and irritations. Essays do not have to be written on lofty intellectual or "poetic" subjects—in fact, some of the world's best essays have been written on such subjects as china teacups, roast pig, and chimney sweeps. Think: what have you been talking or thinking about lately? What have you been doing that you're excited about? Or what about your past? Reflect a few moments on some of your most vivid memories—special people, vacations, holidays, childhood hideaways, your first job or first date—all of which are possibilities. If a search of your immediate or past personal experience doesn't turn up anything inspiring, you might try looking in the campus newspaper for stories that arouse your strong feelings; don't skip the "Letters to the Editor" column. What are the current topics of controversy on your campus? How do you feel about open admissions? Dorm hours and restrictions? Compulsory class attendance? Consider the material you are studying in your classes—information on spies during the Civil War might lead to a thought-provoking essay comparing nineteenth-century espionage to the modern methods of the CIA or FBI. Finally, your local newspaper or a national news magazine might suggest essay topics to you on local, national, or international affairs that affect your life. In other words, when you're stuck for an essay topic, take a closer look at your environment: your own life, past, present, and future; your hometown; your college town; your state; your country; and your world. You'll probably discover more than enough subjects to satisfy the assignments in your writing class. (One last tip: many professional writers carry small notebooks so they can jot down ideas and impressions for future development. You might try a similar tactic, or try keeping a brief daily journal as a springboard for essay topics.)

Make Sure Your Topic Is of a Manageable Size. Once you've selected a subject, you may find that it is too broad for effective treatment in a short essay; you may therefore need to narrow it somewhat. Suppose, for instance, you like to work with plants and have decided to make them the subject of your essay. The subject of "plants," however, is far too large and unwieldy for a short essay, perhaps even for a short book. Consequently, you must make your subject less general. "Houseplants" is more specific, but, again, there's too much to say. "Minimum-care houseplants" is better, but you still need to pare this large, complex subject further so that you may treat it in depth in your short essay. After all, there are many houseplants that require little attention. After several more tries, you might arrive at more specific, manageable topics such as "four houseplants that best thrive in dark areas" or "growing the easy-care Devil's Ivy."

Then again, let's assume you are interested in sports. A 500—800-word essay on "sports" would obviously be superficial, since the subject covers so much ground. Instead, you might divide the topic into such categories as "sports heroes," "my years on the high school tennis team," "the new role of women in sports," "my love of jogging," and so forth. Perhaps several of your categories would make good short essays, but after looking at your list, you might decide that your real interest at this time is jogging and that it will be the *subject matter* of your essay.

Let Your Interest and Knowledge Guide You to Your Central Purpose. What can be said about jogging? What's the point or purpose of this essay? Part of your problem may be solved by your assignment; that is, your teacher may ask you to compare two subjects (tennis and jogging), to explain a process (how to jog properly), or to analyze an effect (the results of daily jogging). The various methods of developing essays will be discussed in specific detail in Part 2 of this book; if, however, the essay organization is your own decision, your interest and knowledge can guide you to a central purpose. Don't become frustrated if you have to discard several ideas before you hit the one that's right. For instance, you might first consider writing on how to select running shoes and then realize that you know too little about the shoe market, or you might find that there's just too little of importance to say about jogging paths to make an interesting 500-word essay.

FINDING A FOCUS

If you become stuck at this point—if you have a subject but no direction, no focus—don't panic. Try jotting down all the ideas that pop into your head about your subject. Free associate; don't hold back anything. A list on jogging might look like this:

> jogging—fun
> > sometimes painful
> > healthy
> > good exercise
> > good for heart
> > relieves tension
> > strengthens leg muscles
> > increases stamina
> > gives a sense of accomplishment
> > tightens stomach muscles
> > good for lungs
> > persons of almost any age can run
> > both sexes can enjoy it
> > improves circulation
> > no complex equipment needed

As you read over the list, look for a large idea that encompasses several of the smaller ones. Here, the predominant idea focuses on health matters: exercise, heart, circulation, lungs, stomach, and leg muscles, etc. Therefore, you decide that the main purpose of your essay is to discuss the physical benefits of jogging.

Another way to discover a focus for your essay is called *looping*.* Let's suppose you've been assigned that old standby subject, "My Summer Vacation." Obviously you can't discuss every aspect of your latest vacation; you must narrow your focus. First, take out several sheets of paper, and at the top of page 1 write your general subject— "summer vacation." Then begin to write whatever comes into your mind on this subject (this activity is called "freewriting"). Take any direction you wish; don't worry about form, style, organization, or mechanics. Write without stopping for at least ten minutes. Do not change, correct, or delete anything. At the end of this period read over what you've written and try to identify a central idea that has emerged. This idea may be an important thought that occurred to you in the middle or at the end of your writing, or perhaps it was the

*This technique is suggested by Peter Elbow in *Writing Without Teachers* (New York: Oxford University Press, 1975).

idea you liked best for whatever reason. It may be the idea that was pulling you onward when time ran out. In other words, look for the thought that stands out, that seems to indicate the direction of your thinking. Put this thought or idea into one sentence called the "center-of-gravity sentence." You have now completed loop one.

To begin loop two, use your "center-of-gravity sentence" as a jumping-off point for another ten minutes of freewriting. Stop, read what you've written, and complete loop two by composing another "center-of-gravity sentence." Use this second sentence to start loop three. You should write at least three loops and three "center-of-gravity sentences." At the end of three loops, you may find that you have focused on a specific topic that might lead to a good essay. If you're not satisfied with your topic at this point, by all means try two or three more loops until your subject is sufficiently narrowed and focused.

Here's an example of one student's looping exercise:

SUMMER VACATION

Loop One

I think summer vacations are very important aspects of living. They symbolize getting away from daily routines, discovering places and people that are different. When I think of vacations I think mostly of traveling somewhere too far to go, say, for a weekend. It is a chance to get away and relax and not think about most responsibilities. Just have a good time and enjoy yourself. Vacations can also be a time of gathering with family and friends.

Center-of-gravity Sentence

Vacations are meant to be used for traveling.

Loop Two

Vacations are meant for traveling. Last summer my family and I drove to Yellowstone National Park. I didn't want to go at first. I thought looking at geysers would be dumb and boring. I was really obnoxious all the way up there and made lots of smart remarks about getting eaten by bears. Luckily, my parents ignored me and I'm glad they did, because Yellowstone turned out to be wonderful. It's not just Old Faithful—there's lots more to see and learn about, like these colorful boiling pools and boiling patches of mud. I got interested in the thermodynamics of the pools and how new ones are surfacing all the time, and how algae make the pools different colors.

Center-of-gravity Sentence

Once I got interested in Yellowstone's amazing pools, my vacation turned out great.

Loop Three	Once I got interested in the pools, I had a good time, mainly because I felt I was seeing something really unusual. I knew I'd never see anything like this again unless I went to Iceland or New Zealand (highly unlikely!). I felt like I was learning a lot, too. I liked the idea of learning a lot about the inside of the earth without having to go to class and study books. I really hated to leave—Mom and Dad kidded me on the way back about how much I'd griped about going on the trip in the first place. I felt pretty dumb. But I was really glad I'd given the Park a closer look instead of holding on to my view of it as a boring bunch of water fountains. I would have had a terrible time, but now I hope to go back someday. I think this experience made me more open-minded about trying new places.
Center-of-gravity Sentence	My vacation this summer was special because I was willing to put aside my expectations of boredom and learn some new ideas about the strange environment at Yellowstone.

At the end of three loops, this student has moved from the general subject of "summer vacation" to the more focused idea that her willingness to learn about a new place played an important part in the enjoyment of her vacation. Although her last center-of-gravity sentence still contains some vague words ("special," "new ideas," "strange environment"), the thought stated here may well lead to an essay that will not only say something about this student's vacation but may also persuade the readers to reconsider their approach to taking trips to new places.

Once you have found the main purpose of your essay and have focused on a specific idea, you are ready to compose the *thesis statement*, a vitally important part of your essay discussed in great detail in the following chapter.

Practicing What You've Learned

A. Some of the subjects listed below are too broad for a 500–800-word essay. Identify those topics that might be treated in short papers and those that still need to be narrowed.

1. The role of the modern university
2. My first (and last) experience with cross-country skiing
3. The characters of William Shakespeare
4. Nature
5. Collecting Indian arrowheads
6. The commercialism of Christmas
7. Down with throwaway bottles

8. Computers
9. The best teacher I've ever had
10. Selecting the right bicycle

B. Select two of the large subjects below and, through looping or listing details or some prewriting technique of your own invention, find focused topics that would be appropriate for essays of 500–800 words.

1. music
2. cars
3. education
4. dorms
5. television commercials
6. politics
7. drugs
8. childhood
9. pollution
10. gambling

TWO MORE TIPS: AUDIENCE AND VOICE

Before you begin writing your thesis statement and first draft, you should consider two other important aspects of good writing. First, decide to whom you are writing. Who will be the specific *audience* of your essay? (Again, this aspect of your assignment may be designated by your teacher.) Are you addressing fellow students? A general audience of adults? A professional or special-interest group?

Determining your audience before you begin will help you choose an appropriate style, tone, and content for your essay. Suppose, for example, you are attending a college organized on the quarter system, and you want to argue for a switch to the semester system. If your audience is composed of classmates, your essay will probably focus on the advantages to the student body, such as better opportunities for in-depth study in one's major, the ease of making better grades, and the benefits of longer mid-winter and summer vacations. On the other hand, if you address the Board of Regents, you might emphasize the power of the semester system to attract more students, cut registration costs, and use professors more efficiently. If your audience is composed of townspeople who know little about either system, you will have to devote more time to explaining the logistics of each one and then discuss the semester plan's advantages to the local merchants, realtors, restaurateurs, etc. In other words, such factors as the age, education, profession, and locale of your audience can make a difference in determining which points of your argument to stress or omit, what aspects need additional explanation, and what kind of language to adopt.

Focusing on your audience provides another enormous benefit for your writing. Imagining specific readers will help you stick to your goal of communicating with others. Forgetting that they have an audience of real people often causes writers to address themselves to their typing paper, a mistake that usually results in dull or stilted prose.

A last bit of advice refers to what some writers call finding the proper *voice*. Too often inexperienced writers feel they must sound especially scholarly, scientific, or sophisticated for their essays to be convincing. In fact, the contrary is true. When you assume a tone that is not yours, when you pretend to be someone you're not, you don't sound believable at all—you sound phony. *You should not assume another personality when you write.* Your readers want to hear what *you* have to say, and the best way to communicate with them is in your own natural voice.

You may also believe that to write a good essay it is necessary to use a host of unfamiliar, unpronounceable, polysyllabic words gleaned from the pages of your thesaurus. Again, the opposite is true. (This common misconception may have arisen from the enthusiasm of high school teachers who, bless their overworked and underpaid hearts, encouraged the use of "big words" while trying to build student vocabularies.) Our best writers agree with Mark Twain, who once said, "Never use a twenty-five-cent word when a ten-cent word will do." In other words, avoid pretension in your vocabulary and writing just as you do in everyday conversation. Select simple, direct words you know and use frequently; keep your tone natural, sincere, and reasonable. (For additional help on choosing the appropriate words and level of your diction, turn to Chapter 6.)

The Thesis Statement

AFTER SELECTING YOUR SUBJECT

The famous American author Thomas Wolfe had a simple formula for beginning his writing: "Just put a sheet of paper in the typewriter and start bleeding." For a few writers, the "bleeding" method works fine. Most of us, however, need a more structured approach. Without a clear notion of our essay's main purpose or a definite plan of how to begin and where to go, we may often find ourselves drifting aimlessly through ideas, starting with "x," trudging through "y," and concluding with several layers of wadded paper balls strewn about our feet. To avoid the problem of roaming from one unrelated idea to another, you first need to formulate a *thesis statement*.

WHAT DOES A THESIS DO?

The thesis statement declares the main purpose or controlling idea of your entire essay. Most frequently located at the beginning of a short essay, the thesis briefly answers the questions "What is my opinion on subject 'x'?" and "What am I going to argue (or illustrate, define, or explain) in this essay?" Your essay on jogging, for instance, might contain this thesis statement: "Jogging is an excellent way to improve physical health." Such a thesis asserts an opinion about your subject— that it is a good way to keep fit—and suggests to the reader what the essay will do —discuss the ways in which jogging improves health.

A thesis statement, prepared before you begin your first rough draft, is perhaps your single most useful organizational tool. Once you know your essay's specific purpose, you can arrange the rest of your paper to explain and back up your

11

thesis statement. In other words, *everything in your essay supports your thesis.* Consequently, if you write your thesis statement at the top of your first draft and refer to it often, your chances of drifting away from your purpose are reduced. Furthermore, a clearly stated thesis alerts your readers to what the essay will discuss and what you are trying to accomplish.

WHAT IS A GOOD THESIS?

A Good Thesis States the Writer's Clearly Defined Opinion on Some Subject. You must tell your reader what you think. Don't dodge the issue; present your opinion specifically and precisely. For example, if you were asked to write a thesis statement expressing your position on legalizing abortion on demand, the first three theses listed below would not be acceptable:

Poor: People have a variety of opinions on whether abortion on demand should be legalized, and I agree with some of them. [The writer's opinion is not clearly asserted.]

Poor: The abortion question is a difficult one to decide. [The writer still avoids presenting a statement of opinion on the issue.]

Poor: I want to discuss my view on abortion. [What is the writer's opinion?]

Better: Abortion on demand should be legalized only in cases of rape or when the mother's life is endangered. [The writer clearly states an opinion.]

Better: Abortion on demand should be legal for everyone who desires one. [The writer clearly presents an opinion.]

A Good Thesis Asserts One Main Idea. Many essays drift into confusion because the writer is trying to explain or argue two different issues in one essay. You can't effectively ride two horses at once; pick one idea and explain or argue it in convincing detail. At this point, you may recall from your high school days a rule about always expressing your thesis in one sentence. Writing teachers often insist on this to help you avoid the double-thesis problem. While not all essays have one-sentence theses, many do, and it's a good habit to strive for at this stage of your writing.

Poor: Marijuana is a harmless drug, and besides, the laws against it are unfair. [These two assertions require two different kinds of supporting evidence.]

Better: Marijuana causes no physical damage to its users. [This is a clear stand on one issue.]

Better: The laws concerning penalties for possession of less than one ounce of marijuana in this state are unjust. [This represents another clear stand on one issue.]

Poor: Biology class had too much lab work, and the instructor was a confusing lecturer. [Again, these two assertions require two different kinds of supporting evidence.]

Better: My biology instructor was a confusing lecturer. [This is a clear stand on one issue.]

Better: My biology course required too much work in the laboratory. [This is another clear stand on one issue.]

A Good Thesis Has Something Worthwhile To Say. Although it's true that almost any subject can be made interesting with the right treatment, some subjects are more predictable and therefore more boring than others. Before you write your thesis, think hard about your subject: does your position lend itself to trite, shallow, or overly obvious ideas? For example, most readers would find the theses below tiresome unless the writers had some original method of developing their essays:

Poor: Dogs have always been man's best friends. [This essay might be full of ho-hum clichés about dogs' faithfulness to their masters.]

Poor: Friendship is a wonderful thing. [Again, watch out for tired truisms that restate the obvious.]

Poor: Food in my dorm is horrible. [While this essay might be enlivened by some vividly repulsive imagery, the subject itself is ancient.]

In other words, try to select a subject that will interest, amuse, challenge, or enlighten your readers; if your subject itself is commonplace, try to find a unique approach or an unusual, perhaps even controversial, point of view. A good thesis should encourage the reader to read on with enthusiasm rather than invite a groan of "not this again" or a shrug of "so what?"

A Good Thesis Is Limited To Fit the Assignment. Your thesis should show that you've narrowed your subject matter to an appropriate size for your essay. Don't allow your thesis to promise more of a discussion than you can adequately deliver in a short essay. You want an in-depth treatment of your subject, not a superficial one. (For a review of how to narrow your subject, see pp. 5–8.)

Poor: The parking permit system at this university should be completely revised. [An essay calling for the revision of the parking permit system would probably involve discussion of permits for various kinds of students, faculty, administrators, staff, visitors, delivery personnel, handicapped persons, and so forth. Therefore, the thesis is too broad for a short essay.]

Better: Students without a "B" average should be not allowed to purchase campus parking permits. [This thesis is narrowed enough to be discussed thoroughly in a short essay.]

Poor: Black artists have contributed much to American culture. ["Black artists," "culture," and "much" cover more ground than can be dealt with in one short essay.]

Better: Scott Joplin, a black musician, was a major influence in the development of the uniquely American music called ragtime. [This thesis is more specifically defined.]

A Good Thesis Is Clearly Stated in Specific Terms. More than anything, a vague thesis reflects lack of clarity in the writer's mind and almost inevitably leads to an essay that talks around the subject but never makes a coherent point. Try to avoid words whose meanings are imprecise or those that depend largely upon personal interpretation, such as "interesting," "good," and "bad."

Poor: The Women's Movement has been good for our country. [How is it good? For whom?]

Better: The Women's Movement has worked to ensure the benefits of equal pay for equal work for both male and female Americans. [This tells who will benefit and how—clearly defining the thesis.]

Poor: Registration is a big hassle. [No clear idea is communicated here. How much trouble is a "hassle"?]

Better: Registration's alphabetical fee-paying system is inefficient. [The issue is specified.]

Poor: My sister taught me many things about growing up. ["Things" and "growing up" are both too vague—what specific ideas does the writer wish to discuss?]

Better: My sister taught me how to give and take criticism. [The thesis is clearly defined.]

A Good Thesis Is Clearly Located, Usually in the First Paragraph. Many students are hesitant to spell out a thesis at the beginning of an essay. To quote one student, "I feel as if I'm giving everything away." Although you may feel uncomfortable "giving away" the main point so soon, the alternative of waiting until the last page to present your thesis can seriously weaken your essay. Without an assertion of what you are trying to prove, your reader does not know how to assess the supporting detail your essay presents. For example, if your roommate comes home one afternoon and points out that the roof on your apartment leaks, the rent is too high, and the closet space is too small, you may agree but you may also be confused. Does your roommate want you to call the owner, or is this merely a gripe session? How should you respond? On the other hand, if your roommate first announces that he or she wants to move to a new place, you can put the discussion of the roof, rent, and closets into its proper context and react accordingly. Similarly, you write an essay to have a specific effect on your readers. You won't have a chance of producing this effect unless the readers understand what you are trying to do. Although a few essays whose position is unmistakably obvious from the outset can get by with a strongly implied thesis, most profit from a clear statement of the paper's main idea. It is, after all, your responsibility to make your purpose clear, with as little expense of time and energy on the reader's part as possible. No readers should be forced to puzzle out your essay's main point—it's your job to tell them. Remember: an essay is not a detective story. Don't keep your reader in suspense until the last minute. Put your brief but clearly worded thesis statement near the beginning of your essay.

AVOIDING COMMON ERRORS IN THESIS STATEMENTS

Here are five mistakes to avoid when forming your thesis statements:

1. **Don't** make your thesis merely an announcement of your subject matter or a description of your intentions. State an attitude toward the subject.

> Poor: The subject of this theme is my experience with a pet boa constric-
> tor. [This is an announcement of the subject, not a thesis.]
>
> Poor: I'm going to discuss boa constrictors as pets. [This represents a
> statement of intention, but not a thesis.]
>
> Better: Boa constrictors do not make healthy indoor pets. [The writer states
> an opinion that will be explained and defended in the essay.]
>
> Better: My pet boa constrictor, Sir Pent, was a much better friend than my
> dog, Fang. [The writer states an opinion that will be explained and
> illustrated in the essay.]

2. **Don't** clutter your thesis with expressions such as "in my opinion," "I believe," and "in this essay I'll argue that . . ." These unnecessary phrases weaken your thesis statement because they often make you sound timid or uncertain. This is your essay; therefore, the opinions expressed are obviously yours. Be forceful; speak directly, with conviction.

> Poor: My opinion is that the federal government should devote more
> money to solar energy research.
>
> Poor: My thesis states that the federal government should devote more
> money to solar energy research.
>
> Better: The federal government should devote more money to solar energy
> research.
>
> Poor: In this essay I will give you lots of reasons why horse racing should
> not be legalized in Texas.
>
> Better: Horse racing should not be legalized in Texas.

3. **Don't** be unreasonable. Making irrational or oversimplified claims will not persuade your reader that you have a thorough understanding of the issue. Don't insult any reader; avoid irresponsible charges, name-calling, and profanity.

Poor: Only rednecks and racists are against busing to achieve integration.
Better: Busing is the most effective method of achieving racial balance in our schools.

Poor: Busing is a stupid policy supported only by knee-jerk liberals with children in private schools.
Better: Busing will weaken the quality of public school education.

4. **Don't** merely state a fact. A thesis is an assertion of opinion that leads to discussion. Don't select an idea that is self-evident or dead-ended.

Poor: The hottest day of the summer registered 107°. [OK, now what?]
Better: Nuclear testing is causing our weather to become warmer. [This thesis will lead to a discussion in which supporting evidence is presented.]

Poor: Governor John Doe was reared in the country. [Who wants to argue this fact?]
Better: Governor John Doe's rural boyhood makes him overly sympathetic to the problems of the farmers. [This thesis leads to a discussion.]

5. **Don't** express your thesis in the form of a question, unless the answer is already obvious to the reader.

Poor: Why should every college student have to take two years of foreign language?
Better: Math majors should be exempt from the foreign language requirement.

Practicing What You've Learned

A. Identify each of the following theses as adequate or inadequate. If the statement is weak or insufficient in some way, explain why.

1. My essay will show why everyone should join Operation Help.
2. Living in a co-ed dorm is really something else.
3. Why don't Americans do something about the energy crisis?
4. During the fall term, final examinations should be held before Christmas, not after.
5. It is evident that there is a great deal of difference between a sailboat and a motorboat, but there are many similarities also.
6. Gun-control laws are highly controversial.
7. Freshman composition should be required of all students entering this university, regardless of their entrance or placement scores.
8. I have lived near the ocean all my life.

9. Having been both an "independent" and a member of a fraternity, I have two views of Greek life.
10. Death is a word that carries a very heavy meaning for some people.

B. Rewrite the sentences below so that each one is a clear thesis statement. Be prepared to explain why you changed the sentences the way you did.

1. Spending my summer vacation in Los Angeles turned out to be weird.
2. Some people see many advantages to having motorcycle helmet laws, but others see many disadvantages.
3. High school dress codes are unconstitutional and usually outdated.
4. In this essay I will discuss the benefits of having a part-time job while in college.
5. Religion is a confusing subject to write on.
6. Dieting is hard to do and can be dangerous.
7. I love to water-ski.
8. In *Huckleberry Finn*, Mark Twain makes some really interesting points about brotherhood and human relationships.
9. In my opinion, country music is no good.
10. My essay asks whether cigarettes cause cancer or not.

Assignment

Narrow the subject and write one good thesis sentence for each of the following topics:

1. capital punishment
2. high school
3. a recent movie or book
4. fast-food restaurants
5. parents
6. a hobby
7. grades
8. vacations
9. football
10. a current fashion

USING THE ESSAY MAP*

Many thesis sentences will benefit from the addition of an *essay map*, a brief statement in the introductory paragraph introducing the major points to be discussed in the essay. Consider the analogy of beginning a trip by checking your

*I am indebted to Professor Susan Wittig for this useful concept, introduced in *Steps to Structure: An Introduction to Composition and Rhetoric* (Cambridge, Mass.: Winthrop Publishers Inc., 1975), pp. 125–126.

map to see where you are headed. Similarly, an essay map allows the readers to know in advance where you, the writer, will be taking them in the essay. For example, after reading the thesis statement "Daytona Beach is an exciting place to vacation," the reader knows that Daytona is an excellent vacation spot but still doesn't know *why* Daytona is exciting nor what points the essay will cover. With an essay map added, the reader has a brief but specific idea of where the essay is going and how it will be developed:

Thesis	Daytona Beach is an exciting place to spend Spring
Essay Map	Break. The beautiful beaches, the temperate weather,
(underlined)	and the inexpensive entertainment attract students
	from as far away as Maine and Oklahoma.

Thanks to the essay map, the reader knows that the essay will consider beaches, climate, and entertainment.

Here is another example of a thesis and essay map:

Thesis	*The Maltese Falcon* is one of the best movies of the
Essay Map	1940s. The witty dialogue, fast-paced direction, and
(underlined)	excellent acting make it an unforgettable thriller.

After reading the introductory paragraph, the reader knows the essay will discuss the movie's script, direction, and acting. In other words, the thesis statement defines the main purpose of your essay, and the essay map indicates the route you will take to accomplish that purpose.

The essay map is often inserted after the thesis, but it can also appear before it. It is, in fact, frequently tacked onto the thesis statement itself, as illustrated in the following examples:

Essay Map	Beautiful beaches, temperate weather, and inexpen-
(underlined)	sive entertainment make Daytona Beach an ideal
	place for Spring Break.

Essay Map	*The Maltese Falcon* is one of the best movies of the
(underlined)	1940s because of its witty dialogue, fast-paced direc-
	tion, and excellent acting.

Essay Map	Because of its witty dialogue, fast-paced direction, and
(underlined)	excellent acting, *The Maltese Falcon* is one of the best
	movies of the 1940s.

In addition to suggesting the main points of the essay, the map provides two other benefits. It will provide a set of guidelines for organizing your essay, and it will help keep you from wandering off into areas only vaguely related to your thesis. A clearly written thesis statement and essay map provide a skeletal outline for the sequence of paragraphs in your essay, with one body paragraph frequently devoted to each main point mentioned in your map. (Chapter 3, on paragraphs, will explain in more detail the relationships among the thesis, the map, and the body of your essay.) Note that the number of points in the essay map may vary, although three or four may be the number found most often in 500–800-word essays.

One warning: avoid a tendency to make your essay map sound too repetitive or mechanical; try to link the thesis and map as smoothly as possible.

> Poor: Daytona has many advantages for college students. These many advantages are the following: beautiful beaches, good weather, inexpensive entertainment.
>
> Better: Beautiful beaches, temperate weather, and inexpensive entertainment make Daytona an ideal vacation spot for college students.

Practicing What You've Learned

Identify the thesis and the essay map in each of the following items by underlining the map.

1. This county should not vote to legalize the sale of liquor. Such a move will raise the number of crimes and automobile accidents as well as increase the number of alcoholics on the welfare rolls.
2. Apartment living is preferable to dorm living because it's cheaper, quieter, and more luxurious.
3. His patience, understanding, and generosity make Chuck Byrd the best friend I've ever had.
4. The Civil Rights Movement of the 1960s has profoundly changed the nature of America's work force: more minority persons are being hired for a wider variety of jobs and more are being promoted to executive positions than ever before.
5. Because it builds muscles, increases circulation, and burns harmful fatty tissue, weight lifting is a sport that benefits the entire body.
6. My stylish, roomy, maintenance-free Stallion was the perfect car for me to buy.
7. Not everyone can become an astronaut. To qualify, a person must have intelligence, determination, and courage.
8. Senator Elizabeth Dripwater won passage of her antipollution bill by arguing with relevant testimony, arresting statistics, and persuasive hypothetical examples.
9. Avocados make excellent plants for children. They're inexpensive to buy, easy to root, quick to sprout, and fun to grow.
10. Through use of symbolic settings and grotesque characters in her

short story "A Good Man Is Hard to Find," Flannery O'Connor effectively argues that no one is safe from harm in an absurd, irrational world.

Assignment

Review the thesis statements you wrote for the Practice exercise on page 17. Write an essay map for each thesis statement. You may place the map before or after the thesis, or you may attach it to the thesis itself. Identify which part is the thesis and which is the essay map by underlining the map.

The Body Paragraphs

PLANNING THE BODY OF YOUR ESSAY

The middle or *body* of your essay is composed of paragraphs that support the thesis statement. By presenting details, explaining causes, offering reasons, and citing examples in these paragraphs, you supply enough specific evidence to persuade your reader that the opinion expressed in your thesis is a sensible one. Each paragraph in the body usually presents and develops one main point in the discussion of your thesis. Generally, but not always, a new body paragraph signals another major point in the discussion.

To plan the body of your essay, look at your introduction. The main points mentioned in your essay map will frequently provide the basis for the body paragraphs of your essay. For example, recall the thesis and essay map regarding Daytona: "The beautiful beaches, temperate climate, and inexpensive entertainment make Daytona an ideal choice for Spring Break." Your plan for developing the body of your essay might look like this:

Body paragraph one: discussion of beaches
Body paragraph two: discussion of climate
Body paragraph three: discussion of inexpensive activities

Adding details to your plan makes your <u>outline</u> appear this way:

  I. Beaches
    A. Large number
    B. Clean
    C. Free
 II. Climate
    A. Temperature range
    B. Always sunny

III. Entertainment
  A. Restaurants
  B. Cultural events
  C. Night spots

Of course, a three-part essay map does not always mean you will write an essay with only three body paragraphs. You might discover, for example, that you have too much to say about Daytona's entertainment and consequently need two (or more) paragraphs to present a complete discussion.

The sort of plan shown above can be turned into a more formal sentence or topic outline if you or your teacher so desire. But regardless of whether you are required to turn in an outline of your essay, you should always jot down some sort of plan you can follow to avoid drifting away from the discussion promised by your thesis and essay map.

ORGANIZING THE BODY PARAGRAPHS

There are many ways to develop body paragraphs. Paragraphs developed by such common patterns as definition, example, comparison, and so forth will be discussed in specific chapters in Part Two; at this point, however, we can make some comments about the general nature of all good paragraphs that should help you write the first draft of your essay.

Most of the body paragraphs you will write require a *topic sentence*. In addition, every paragraph should have *unity*, *coherence*, and adequate *development*.

THE TOPIC SENTENCE

Each body paragraph presents one main point in your discussion, expressed in a *topic sentence*. The topic sentence of a body paragraph has three important functions:

1. It supports the thesis by clearly stating a main point in the discussion.
2. It announces what the paragraph will be about.
3. It controls the subject matter of the paragraph. The entire discussion—the examples, details, explanations—in a particular paragraph must directly relate to and support the topic sentence.

Think of a body paragraph (or a single paragraph) as a kind of mini-essay in itself. The topic sentence is, in a sense, a smaller thesis. It too asserts one main idea on a limited subject that the writer can illustrate or argue in the rest of the paragraph. And, like the thesis, the topic sentence should be stated in as specific language as possible. A vague, fuzzy, or unfocused topic sentence most often leads to a paragraph that drifts aimlessly around the surface of its subject or that wanders away from the writer's main idea. On the other hand, a topic sentence that is focused narrowly and stated precisely will not only help the reader to understand the point of the paragraph but will also help you select, organize, and develop your supporting details. (As you practice writing topic sentences, you may wish to review pp. 12–16, the advice on composing good thesis statements.)

Study these body paragraphs and their topic sentences (underlined):

Essay Thesis: Mandatory age-based retirement laws should be abolished.

Topic sentence of the paragraph	<u>Instead of becoming unproductive, many people over sixty-five make significant contributions to their professions.</u> Anthropologist Margaret Mead, for example,
1. The topic sentence supports the thesis by stating a main point (one reason why retirement laws should be abolished).	was an active lecturer and author at seventy-five. Millions of music lovers adored Arthur Fiedler, who conducted the Boston Pops Orchestra into his mid-eighties, while others enjoyed the music of Pablo Casals, who was still giving cello concerts at eighty-eight. At eighty-nine Albert Schweitzer headed a hos-
2. The topic sentence announces the subject matter of the paragraph (contributions of persons over sixty-five).	pital in Africa, and at eighty-five Coco Chanel ran a successful fashion-design firm. And, of course, Grandma Moses, who didn't even begin her craft until she was over eighty, was still painting at age one hundred. The talents of these and other persons over sixty-five would have been lost had mandatory retirement laws been enforced for them.
3. The topic sentence controls details (each example supports the claim of the topic sentence).	

Essay Thesis: When I was growing up, my hometown was an excellent place for parents to raise children.

Topic sentence of the paragraph	<u>McKinney's small size made it a safe place for children to grow up.</u> It was safe, for example, for kids to ride
1. The topic sentence supports the thesis by stating a main point (one reason why this town was a good place to raise children).	bicycles, since there were so few cars on the streets and the drivers of those cars were well aware that children rode bikes freely throughout the town and were always watching out for them. A child roaming about McKinney was also not likely to become lost, as even the grade schoolers knew all the streets and neighborhoods by heart. There was little chance that a

2. The topic sentence announces the subject matter of the paragraph (the safety afforded by the town's small size).

3. The topic sentence controls details (each example supports the claim of the topic sentence).

child would stray into a nasty part of town because, again, the town was familiar enough that it was easy to avoid such neighborhoods. For instance, everyone in McKinney—from children to adults—knew that the mill area across the tracks was a hazardous place because of the dangerous equipment. Consequently, nobody ventured there. In short, McKinney's parents could count on the city's smallness to help protect their children—the town itself was a trusted baby-sitter.

Placing Your Topic Sentence

While the topic sentence most frequently occurs as the first sentence in the body paragraph, it also often appears as the second or last sentence. A topic sentence that directly follows the first sentence of a paragraph usually does so because the first sentence provides an introductory statement or some kind of a "hook" to the preceding paragraph. A topic sentence frequently appears at the end of a paragraph that first presents particular details and then concludes with its central point. Here are two paragraphs in which the topic sentences do not appear first:

Topic sentence

Baseball cards once belonged only to small boys devoted to bubble gum. Today, however, the baseball card craze is in full swing, with a new breed of serious adult collectors who see the cards as an investment as well as a hobby. Of the more than one hundred thousand collectors in the United States, some make as much as twenty thousand dollars a year selling and trading their cards. Meeting at the twelve annual trading conventions, the collectors might pay up to four thousand dollars for a 1910 card of Pittsburgh Pirate shortstop John Peter ("Honus") Wagner or nineteen hundred dollars for the 1910 Sweet Caporal card of Philadelphia Athletics pitcher Eddie Plank. Other collectors, not so interested in individual cards, buy in order to complete a series printed by one company in a particular year.

In the previous paragraph, the first sentence serves as an introduction leading into the topic sentence; in the following paragraph, the writer places the topic sentence last to make a general comment about the benefits of natural habitats for zoo animals.

In the past, zoo animals were usually confined to cramped cages, where they were bored to the point of neurosis. Their boredom was often shared by visitors to the zoo, who came expecting to see "wild" creatures but found only dejected wolves and tigers with nothing to do all day but eat, sleep, and pace aimlessly back and forth. In today's modern San Antonio zoo, however, long-legged birds stroll exotically among the big dusty rhinos—just as they do on the savannahs of Africa. And in Milwaukee, mountain goats leap from rock to rock, while down below lions romp with their young and exchange meaningful glances with excited

Topic sentence   zoo visitors. Zoo officials around the country now tend to agree: when efforts are made to simulate the animals' natural habitats, both animals and humans benefit.

As you can see, the position of topic sentences largely depends on what you are trying to do in your paragraph. However, if you are a beginning writer, you may want to practice putting your topic sentences first for a while in order to help you organize and unify your paragraphs.

Some paragraphs with a topic sentence near the beginning also contain a concluding sentence that makes a final general comment based on the supporting details. The paragraph below, for example, first presents a topic sentence to assert that Saturday night in a small town is a time for young love; sentences two, three, and four provide examples of young love in action; and the last sentence wraps up the paragraph with a general comment on the innocently romantic nature of small-town Saturday nights.

Topic sentence   Saturday night in a small town is often a time for young love. Where I grew up, for instance, lucky couples sat hand in hand in the local theater, eagerly anticipating a slow moonlight drive later down some dark country road. And for those of us without partners, male and female alike, there was always the auto promenade up and down the main street, everyone giving a tantalizing look at everyone else. Then we'd all meet at a hospitable hamburger joint to boast and flirt and try to line up something for the next Saturday night. Romance in that setting, though not high-powered, was nevertheless never taken for granted—and Satur-

Concluding sentence   day nights were exciting in a way that only innocence could make them.

Practicing What You've Learned

A. Point out the topic sentences in the following paragraphs; identify those paragraphs that also contain concluding sentences.

Of all nature's catastrophes, tornadoes cause the most bizarre destruction. Whirling out of the sky at speeds up to three hundred miles per hour, tornadoes have been known to drive broom handles through brick walls and straws into tree trunks. In one extreme case, a Kansas farmer reported that his prize rooster had been sucked into a two-gallon distilled-water bottle. More commonly, tornadoes lift autos and deposit them in fields miles away, or uproot trees and drop them on lawns in neighboring towns. One tornado knocked down every wall in a house but one— luckily, the very wall shielding the terrified family. Wherever a tornado touches the earth, spectacular headlines are sure to follow.

Denim is one of America's most widely used fabrics. It was first introduced during Columbus' voyage, when the sails of the Santa Maria were made of the strong cloth. During our pioneer days, denim was used for tents, covered wagons, and the now-famous blue jeans. Cowboys found denim an ideal fabric for protection against sagebrush, cactus, and saddle sores. World War II also gave denim a boost in popularity when sailors were issued jeans as part of their dress code. Today, denim continues to be in demand as more and more casual clothes are cut from the economical fabric. In 1981, for example, a record 612 million jeans were sold in the U.S., averaging nearly three pairs per person. Because of its low cost and durability, manufacturers feel that denim will continue as one of America's most useful fabrics.

Want to win a sure bet? Then wager that your friends can't guess the most widely sold musical instrument in America today. Chances are they won't get the answer right—not even on the third try. In actuality, the most popular instrument in the country is neither the guitar nor the trumpet, but the lowly kazoo. Last year alone, some three and one-half million kazoos were sold to music lovers of all ages. Part of the instrument's popularity arises from its availability, since kazoos are sold in variety stores and music centers nearly everywhere; another reason is its inexpensiveness—it ranges from the standard thirty-nine-cent model to the five-dollar gold-plated special. But perhaps the main reason for the kazoo's popularity is the ease with which it can be played by almost anyone—as can testify the members of the entire Swarthmore College marching band, who have now added a marching kazoo number to their repertoire. Louie Armstrong, move over!

When you're in love, the bills you receive in the morning mail seem suddenly trivial compared to the letters from your beloved. The careless driver who runs the stop sign and nearly smashes you can now be forgiven. The grumpy boss who constantly criticizes your work is to be pitied and treated kindly. All along the street, the workers rushing to offices appear not as strangers but as fellow humans, returning your smile much more often than before. Even the broken T.V. set doesn't faze you, as you'd rather spend your time thinking about your lover. In short, when you're in love, the world just seems a better place.

Every Saturday morning I'm awakened by my neighbor's lawnmower. If I look out the window, I can spot a smile on his face as he runs his mower over the grass. Why he enjoys it is a mystery to me. Tending a lawn is hard work. First you have to pick up all hoses and trash scattered over the yard. Then you push a noisy machine back and forth over the grass until your arms are aching. Meanwhile, you're about to pass out from the gasoline fumes rising from the overheated motor as you try to watch for half-buried rocks and sticks that could bend your blade or send a sharp fragment into your shin. Finally, you have to get out your electric edger to trim all the tall grass your mower couldn't reach. In the end, all you've got to show for your exhaustion is a crew-cut yard that looks like all the others in the neighborhood.

B. Add topic sentences to the following paragraphs:

Vegetarians who eat strictly vegetables, fruits, and nuts are called vegans. Lactovagans also eat vegetables, fruits, and nuts, but supplement their diets with milk and milk products, which supply more calcium, protein, and amino acids. By far the largest group is the lacto-ovo-vegetarians, who add eggs, dairy products, and sometimes fish to their basic vegetarian diet.

When successful playwright Jean Kerr once checked into a hospital, the receptionist asked her occupation and was told, "Writer." The receptionist said, "I'll just put down 'housewife.' " Similarly, when a British official asked W. H. Auden, the late award-winning poet and essayist, what he did for a living, Auden replied, "I'm a writer." The official jotted down "no occupation."

A coin no more than fifty or sixty years old may well be worth more than one minted over a century ago. For instance, a 1909 Lincoln penny can bring its lucky owner a hundred dollars or more, while a silver dollar issued in the 1800s may be worth little more than face value, simply because fewer pennies were made then, thus making them rarer. Any gold coin is certainly worth a considerable amount, but one particular gold coin, an 1819 double eagle, recently sold at an auction for nearly thirty thousand dollars. The secret of its success is merely that out of several thousand made that year, only about twenty can be accounted for.

The divorced are twice as likely to develop lung cancer or suffer a stroke; divorced white males develop cirrhosis of the liver seven times more often and tuberculosis ten times more often. The heart attack rate among widows between twenty-five and thirty-four is five times higher than among married women of the same age.

C. Write a topic sentence for a possible paragraph for each of the following subjects:

1. job interviews
2. natural food
3. airplanes
4. money
5. selecting a major
6. clothes
7. co-ed dorms
8. dreams
9. dentists
10. children

Assignment

1. Review the thesis statements with essay maps you wrote for the practice exercise on p. 20. Choose four, and from each thesis create three topic sentences for possible body paragraphs.
2. Write two paragraphs, with each one containing at least five sentences; underline your topic sentences.

UNITY

Every sentence in a body paragraph should directly relate to the main idea presented by the topic sentence. A paragraph must stick to its announced subject; it must not drift away into another discussion. In other words, a good paragraph has *unity*.

Examine the unified paragraph following; note that the topic sentence clearly states the paragraph's main point and that each sentence thereafter supports the topic sentence.

(1)Frank Lloyd Wright, America's leading architect of the first half of the twentieth century, believed that his houses should blend naturally with their building sites. (2)Consequently, he designed several "prairie houses," whose long, low lines echoed the flat earth plane. (3)Built of brick, stone, and natural wood, the houses shared a similar texture with their backgrounds; (4)large windows were often used to blend the interior and exterior of the homes. (5)Wright also punctuated the lines and spaces of the houses with greenery in planters to further make the buildings look part of nature.

The first sentence states the main idea, that Wright thought houses should blend with their location; the other sentences support this assertion:

Topic sentence: Wright's houses blend with their natural locations
              2. long, low lines echo flat prairie
              3. brick, stone, wood provide same texture as location
              4. windows blend inside with outside
              5. greenery in planters imitates the natural surroundings

Now look at the next paragraph, in which the writer strays from his original purpose:

(1)Cigarette smoke is unhealthy even for people who don't have the nicotine habit themselves. (2)Secondhand smoke can cause asthmatics and sufferers of sinusitis serious problems; (3)doctors regularly advise heart patients to avoid confined smoky areas because coronary attacks might be triggered by the lack of clean air. (4)Moreover, having the smell of smoke in one's hair and clothes is a real nuisance. (5)Even if a person is without any health problems, exhaled smoke doubles the amount of carbon monoxide in the air, a fact that may cause lung problems in the future.

Sentence four refers to smoke as a nuisance and therefore does not belong in a paragraph that discusses smoking as a health hazard to nonsmokers.

Sometimes a large portion of a paragraph will drift into another topic. In the paragraph below, did the writer wish to focus on her messiness or on the beneficial effects of her engagement?

I have always been a very messy person. As a child, I was a pack rat, saving every little piece of insignificant paper that I thought might be important when I grew up. As a teenager, my pockets bulged with remnants of basketball games, candy bars, gum wrappers, and other important articles from my high school education. As a college student, I became a boxer—not a fighter, but the kind who cannot throw anything away and therefore it winds up in a box in my closet. But my engagement has changed everything. I'm really pleased with the organization in my life, and I owe it all to my fiancé. My overall outlook on life has changed because of his influences on me. I'm much much more cheerful, and I'm even getting places on time like I never did before. It's truly amazing what love can do.

This writer may wish to discuss the changes her fiancé has inspired and then use her former messiness, tardiness, and other bad habits as examples illustrating those changes; however, as presented here, the paragraph is not unified around a central idea. On the contrary, it first seems to promise a discussion of her messiness but then wanders into comments on "what love can do."

Also beware a tendency to end your paragraph with a new idea. A new point calls for an entirely new paragraph. For example, the last sentence of the following paragraph should be omitted or moved to the beginning of the next paragraph:

Of all the nineteenth-century photographers who made their reputations during the Civil War, none is more famous than Mathew Brady. With a crew of fifteen, Brady moved from battlefield to battlefield, traveling in a cumbersome wagon that also was used for on-the-spot developing of negatives. Despite the great personal risk involved in photographing a war, Brady left a comprehensive record of the conflict, with pictures including combat scenes, the hanging of a deserter, and a portrait of Lee in surrender. Before the war, Brady specialized in portraits.

Think of paragraph unity in terms of the diagram below:

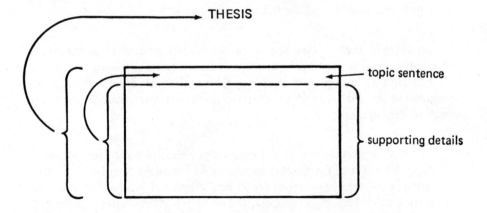

The sentences in the paragraph support the paragraph's topic sentence; the paragraph, in turn, supports the thesis statement.

Practicing What You've Learned

In each of the following examples, delete or rewrite any information that interferes with the unity of the paragraph:

In the Great Depression of the 1930s, American painters suffered severely because few persons had the money to spend on the luxury of owning art. To keep our artists from starving, the government ultimately set up the Federal Art Project, which paid then little-known painters such as Jackson Pollock, Arshile Gorky, and William de Kooning to paint murals in post offices, train stations, schools, housing projects, and other public places. During this period, songwriters were also affected by the depression, and they produced such memorable songs as "Buddy, Can You Spare a Dime?" The government-sponsored murals, usually depicting familiar American scenes and historical events, gave our young artists an opportunity to develop their skills and new techniques; in return, our country obtained thousands of elaborate works of art in over one thousand American cities. Sadly, many of these art works were destroyed in later years, as public buildings were torn down or remodeled.

The best time of year for a day at the lake is undoubtedly early spring. As you lie on your back on a beach towel, you can let your eye wander over a scene as yet unspoiled by the hordes of summer. The sky overhead is crystal and deep, the invisible breeze still cool and refreshing. The trees around you are green; the flowers have begun to bloom red and yellow and pink after the long cold winter. Personally, however, even the prettiest of flowers aggravates my allergies, but my doctor says a new drug will be on the market soon. The water is pure and blue, unpolluted by the gasoline-powered speedboats that will soon arrive by the hundreds. Even the beach itself is clean and sparkling, reclining innocently before the summer's deluge of beer cans and broken bottles and sandwich wrappers turns it into a garbage dump.

The quality of frozen dinners has improved dramatically over the past few years. Not long ago, you had a choice of either tasteless beans and franks or soggy chicken legs and shriveled peas. Now, however, you can choose from among such elegant entrees as beef Stroganoff, sweet and sour shrimp, chicken divan, and mushroom crepes. Canned delicacies have become more popular, too, so that vichyssoise soup and artichoke hearts are becoming more common items in the grocery basket. The improvement in frozen foods may be a result of manufacturers finally realizing that because of inflation more and more people are eating at home, but that they still want something to excite the tastebuds. After all, if you can enjoy a romantic meal of quick-thaw quiche Lorraine for just a few bucks in front of your own fireplace, why go out?

Living in a college dorm is a good way to meet people. There are activities every weekend such as dances and parties, where one can get acquainted with all kinds of students. Even just sitting by someone in the cafeteria during a meal can start a friendship. Making new friends can teach students how to get along better with people from foreign countries. A girl on my dorm floor, for example, is from Peru, and I've learned a lot about the customs and culture in her country. She's also helping me with my study of Spanish.

After complaining in vain about the quality of food in the campus restaurant, University of Colorado students are having their revenge after all. The student body recently voted to rename the grill after Alferd Packer, the only American ever convicted of cannibalism. Packer was a Utah prospector trapped with an expedition of explorers in the southwest Colorado mountains during the winter of 1874; the sole survivor of the trip, he was later tried by a jury and sentenced to hang for dining on at least five of his companions. Colorado students are now holding an annual "Alferd Packer Day" and have installed a mural relating the prospector's story on the main wall of the restaurant. Some local wits have also suggested a new motto for the bar and grill: "Serving our fellow man since 1874." Another incident of cannibalism occurred in the winter of 1846, when the Donner party, a wagon train of eighty-seven California-bound immigrants, became trapped by ice and snow in the mountains south of the Great Salt Lake.

COHERENCE

In addition to unity, *coherence* is essential to a good paragraph. Coherence means that all the sentences and ideas in your paragraph flow together to make a clear, logical point about your topic. Your paragraph should not be a confusing collection of ideas set down in random order. The readers should be able to follow what you have written and see easily and quickly how each sentence grows out of, or is related to, the preceding sentence. To achieve coherence, you should have a smooth connection or transition between the sentences in your paragraphs.

There are five important means of achieving coherence in your paragraphs:

1. a natural or easily recognized order
2. transition words and phrases
3. repetition of key words
4. substitution of pronouns for key nouns
5. parallelism

These transition devices are similar to the couplings between railroad cars; they enable the controlling engine to pull the train of thought along as a unit.

A Recognizable Ordering of Information

Without consciously thinking about the process, you may often organize paragraphs in easily recognized patterns that give the reader a sense of logical movement and order. Discussed below are four common patterns of ordering sentences in a paragraph:

The Order of Time

Some paragraphs are composed of details arranged in chronological order. You might, for example, explain the process of changing an oil filter on your car by beginning with the first step, draining the old oil, and concluding with the last step, installing the new filter. Here is a paragraph on black holes in which the writer chronologically orders his details:

> A black hole in space, from all indications, is the result of the death of a star. Scientists speculate that stars were first formed from the gases floating in the universe at the beginning of time. In the first stage in the life of a star, the hot gas is drawn by the force of gravity into a burning sphere. In the middle stage—our own sun being a middle-aged star—the burning continues at a regular rate, giving off enormous amounts of heat and light. As it grows old, however, the star eventually explodes to become what is called a nova, a superstar. But gravity soon takes over again, and the exploded star falls back in on itself with such force that all the matter in the star is compacted into a mass no larger than a few miles in diameter. At this point, no heavenly body can be seen in that area of the sky, as the tremendous pull of gravity lets nothing escape, not even light. A black hole has thus been formed.

The Order of Space

When your subject is a physical object, you should select some orderly means of describing it: from left to right, top to bottom, inside to outside, and so forth. For example, you might describe a sculpture as you walk around it from front to back. Below is a paragraph describing a cowboy in which the writer has ordered the details of his description in a top-to-bottom pattern:

> Harry was every inch a cowboy. On his head he wore, even indoors, a dusty, broad-brimmed black hat with a band made of genuine rattlesnake skin. His leathery face was weathered to a deep reddish brown from spending day after hot day riding the Wyoming ranges. A bright yellow bandana was tied snugly around his hard-muscled neck. His blue cotton work shirt sporting pearl buttons was tucked into well-worn, faded Levi's held up by a wide leather belt with his name on the buckle. Harry's feet seemed forever encased in the same pair of scratched and colorless old boots that looked like they might have been

handed down to him by the first cowboy ever to ride into a lonesome Western sunset.

Deductive Order

A paragraph ordered deductively moves from a generalization to particular details that explain or support the general statement. Perhaps the most common pattern of all paragraphs, the deductive paragraph begins with its topic sentence and proceeds to its supporting details, as illustrated in the example below:

If 111 ninth graders in Honolulu are typical of today's teenagers, spelling and social science teachers may be in for trouble. In a recent experiment, not one of the students tested could write the Pledge of Allegiance correctly. In addition, the results showed that the students apparently had little understanding of the pledge's meaning. For example, several students described the United States as a "nation under guard" instead of "under God," and the phrase "to the Republic for which it stands" appeared in several responses as "of the richest stand" or "for Richard stand." Many students changed the word "indivisible" to the phrase "in the visible," and over nine percent of the students, all of whom are Americans from varying racial and ethnic backgrounds, misspelled the word "America."

Inductive Order

An inductive paragraph begins with an examination of particular details and then concludes with a larger point or generalization about those details. Such a paragraph often ends with its topic sentence, as does the following paragraph on Little League baseball:

At almost every Little League baseball game, one or another adult creates a minor scene by yelling obscenely at an umpire or a coach. Similarly, it is fairly common to see such adults arguing loudly with each other in the stands over whose child should have caught a missed ball. Perhaps the most astounding spectacle of all, however, is an irate father or mother yanking a child off the field after a bad play for a humiliating lecture in front of the whole team. Sadly, Little League baseball today often seems intended more for childish parents than for the children who actually play it.

Transition Words and Phrases

Some paragraphs may need transition words to help you move smoothly from one thought to the next so that your ideas do not appear choppy or jerky.

Here is a list of common transition words and phrases and their uses:

giving examples:	for example, for instance, specifically, in particular, namely
comparison:	similarly, not only . . . but also, in comparison
contrast:	although, but, while, in contrast, however, though, on the other hand
sequence:	first . . . second . . . third, and finally, moreover, also, in addition, next, then, after, furthermore
results:	therefore, thus, consequently, as a result

Notice the difference the use of transition words makes in the paragraphs below:

> Working in the neighborhood grocery store as a checker was one of the worst summer jobs I've ever had. In the first place, I had to wear an ugly, scratchy uniform cut at least three inches too short. My schedule of working hours was another inconvenience; because my hours were changed each week, it was impossible to make plans in advance, and getting a day off was out of the question. In addition, the lack of working space bothered me. Except for a half-hour lunch break, I was restricted to three square feet of room behind the counter and consequently felt as if I were no more than a cog in the cash register.

The same paragraph rewritten without transition words sounds choppy and childish:

> Working in the neighborhood grocery store as a checker was one of the worst summer jobs I've ever had. I had to wear an ugly, scratchy uniform. It was cut at least three inches too short. My schedule of working hours was inconvenient. My hours changed each week. It was impossible to make plans in advance. Getting a day off was out of the question. The lack of working space bothered me. Except for a half-hour break, I was restricted to three square feet of room behind the counter. I felt like a cog in the cash register.

While transition words and phrases are useful in bridging the gaps between your ideas, don't overuse them. Not every sentence needs a transition phrase, so use one only when the relationship between your thoughts needs clarification. It's also a mistake to place the transition word in the same position in your sentence each time. Look at the paragraph below:

> It's a shame that every high school student isn't required to take a course in first aid. *For example*, you might need to treat a friend or relative for drowning during a family picnic. Or, *for instance*, someone might break a bone or receive a snakebite on a camping trip. *Also*, you should always know what to

do for a common cut or burn. *Moreover*, it's important to realize when someone is in shock. *However*, very few people take the time to learn the simple rules of first aid. *Thus*, many injured or sick people suffer more than they should. *Therefore*, everyone should take a first aid course in school or at the Red Cross Center.

As you can see, a series of sentences each beginning with a transition word quickly becomes repetitious and boring. To hold your reader's attention, use transition words only when necessary to avoid choppiness, and vary their placement in your sentences.

Repetition of Key Words

Important words or phrases (and their synonyms) may be repeated throughout a paragraph to connect the thoughts into a coherent statement:

One of the most common, and yet most puzzling, phobias is the *fear* of *snakes*. It's only natural, of course, to be afraid of a poisonous *snake*, but many people are just as frightened of the harmless varieties. For such people, a tiny green grass *snake* is as terrifying as a cobra. Some researchers say this unreasonable *fear* of any and all *snakes* is a legacy left to us by our tree-dwelling ancestors, for whom these *reptiles* were a real and constant danger. Others maintain that the *fear* is a result of our associating the *snake* with the notion of evil, as in the Garden of Eden. Whatever the reason, the fact remains that for many otherwise normal people, the mere sight of a *snake* slithering through the countryside is enough to keep them city dwellers forever.

The repeated words "fear," "snake," and the synonym "reptile" help tie one sentence to another so that the reader may follow the ideas easily.

Pronouns Substituted for Key Nouns

A pronoun is a word that stands for a noun. In your paragraph you may use a key noun in one sentence and then use a pronoun in its place in the following sentences. The pronoun "it" often replaces "shark" in the description below:

[1]The great white shark is perhaps the best equipped of all the ocean's predators. [2]*It* can grow up to twenty-one feet and weigh three tons, with two-inch teeth that can replace themselves within twenty-four hours when damaged. [3]The shark's sense of smell is so acute *it* can detect one ounce of fish blood in a million ounces of water. [4]In addition, *it* can sense vibrations from six hundred feet away.

Sentences two, three, and four are tied to the topic sentence by the use of the pronoun "it."

Parallelism

Parallelism in a paragraph means using the same grammatical structures in several sentences to establish coherence. The repeated use of similar phrasing helps tie the ideas and sentences together. Below, for example, is a paragraph predominantly unified by its use of grammatically parallel sentences:

> The weather of Texas offers something for everyone. If you are the kind who likes to see snow drifting onto mountain peaks, a visit to the Big Bend area will satisfy your eye. If, on the other hand, you demand a bright sun to bake your skin a golden brown, stop in the southern part of the state. And for hardier souls, who ask from nature a show of force, the skies of the Panhandle regularly release ferocious springtime tornadoes. Finally, if you are the fickle type, by all means come to Central Texas, where the sun at any time may shine unashamed throughout the most torrential rainstorm.

The parallel structures of sentences 2, 3, and 5 ("If you" + verb) keep the paragraph flowing smoothly from one idea to the next.

Using a Variety of Transition Devices

Most writers use a combination of transition devices in their paragraphs. In the following example, three kinds of transition devices are circled. See if you can identify each one.

> Transitions are the glue that holds a paragraph together. These devices lead the reader from sentence to sentence, smoothing over the gaps between by indicating the relationship between the sentences. If this glue is missing, the paragraph will almost inevitably sound choppy or childish, even if every sentence in it responds to a single topic commitment. However, transitions are not substitutes for topic unity: like most glue, they are most effective when joining similar objects, or, in this case, similar ideas. For example, in a paragraph describing a chicken egg, no transition could bridge the gap created by the inclusion of a sentence concerned with naval losses in the Civil War. In other words, transitions can call attention to the topical relationships between sentences, but they cannot create those relationships.

transition words	repetition of pronouns	repetition of key words

Practicing What You've Learned

A. Identify each of the following paragraphs as ordered by time, space, or parallelism:

My dorm room is so small that it will no longer hold all my possessions. Every day when I come in the door, I am shocked by the clutter. The wall to my immediate left is completely obscured by art and movie posters that have become so numerous they often overlap, hiding even each other. Along the adjoining wall is my stereo equipment: records and tapes are stacked several feet high on two long, low tables. The big couch that runs across the back of the room is always piled so high with schoolbooks and magazines that a guest usually ends up sitting on the floor. To my right is a large sliding glass door that opens onto a balcony— or at least it used to, before it was permanently blocked by my tennis gear, golf clubs, and ten-speed bike. Even the tiny closet next to the front door is bursting with clothes, both clean and dirty. I think the time has come for me to move.

In the early part of this century, tennis was almost exclusively a pastime of the wealthy. Rich young men in long white pants and young women in long dresses gathered at country clubs to amuse themselves with the new sport. This trend continued into the fifties, when Americans suddenly found themselves with more money and time than ever before and not enough ways to spend them. As more and more people began to realize the fun and physical benefits of tennis, public courts became numerous and sporting goods manufacturers began turning out better tennis equipment and tennis clothing. In the eighties, tennis is more popular than ever and has made the significant move from being primarily a participatory sport to a spectator sport, with televised tennis matches netting the best professionals thousands of dollars. Tennis, in short, has finally arrived.

Students have diverse ways of preparing for final exams. Some stay up the night before, trying to cram into their brains what they avoided all term. Others pace themselves, spending a little time each night going over the notes they took in class that day. Still others cross their fingers and hope they absorbed enough from lectures. A dishonest few pray that their fellow students will give them the answers. In the end, though, everyone hopes the tests are easy.

B. Circle and identify the transition devices in the following paragraphs:

Making a terrarium is not as difficult as it may seem. The first step is to buy a wide-mouthed jar or bottle and fill it with a layer of sand or very fine gravel. This layer catches any excess moisture in the jar. Next, fill the jar with a rich, well-blended mixture of one part sand, one part humus, and one part sterilized soil. The plants may then be added, one by one, with the aid of long wooden tongs. When the plants are placed as you want them, add a bit more soil to cover the roots. Then mist both the plants and the soil until everything is entirely wet. To complete the last step, close the bottle and keep it out of strong sunlight for several days. After the terrarium is settled, it should take care of itself for several months.

Fans of professional baseball and football argue continually over which is America's favorite spectator sport. Though the figures on attendance for each vary with every new season, certain arguments remain the same, spelling out both the enduring appeals of each game and something about the people who love to watch. Football, for instance, is a quicker, more physical sport, and football fans enjoy the emotional involvement they feel while watching. Baseball, on the other hand, seems more mental, like chess, and attracts those fans who prefer a quieter, more complicated game. In addition, professional football teams usually play no more than fourteen games a year, providing fans with a whole week between games to work themselves up to a pitch of excitement and expectation. Baseball teams, however, play almost every day for six months, so that the typical baseball fan is not so crushed by missing a game, knowing there will be many other chances to attend. Finally, football fans seem to love the half-time pageantry, the marching bands, and the pretty cheerleaders, whereas baseball fans are more content to concentrate on the game's finer details and spend the breaks between innings filling out their own private scorecards.

C. These paragraphs lack common transition devices. Fill in each blank with the appropriate transition word or key word.

The prospect of owning a restaurant may seem to many a smart and profitable goal, but the work and frustrations involved drive many owners to bankruptcy. _____, there are the problems of getting started: finding a suitable location, raising money to fund the project, hiring qualified workers, buying or renting equipment and furniture, even planning an appetizing menu that doesn't look just like every other menu in town. _____, the supervision of a _____ can so dominate your time that you can easily find yourself worn out every night when you finally fall into bed. You should _____ remember that you are competing for business with all the other _____ in town, including the fast-food chains that have considerably more money to invest in their operations than the typical _____ owner. And _____, the prices of the produce and meat you buy are constantly rising, forcing you either to raise your own prices, _____ losing many customers, or absorb the losses until you ultimately

go broke. _____, unless you know what you're getting into, leave the
_____ business to those with time, money, and nerves of steel.

When most people think of photography as an art, they are likely to
picture vivid textures intensified by color. _____, a novice photographer
should realize that _____ photography is highly complex and much
more expensive than black-and-white. In the _____ place, _____
development chemicals cost more than black-and-white chemicals;
_____ developing and enlarging equipment is not only more expensive
_____ _____ more complicated than that used for black-and-white
photos. _____, temperature control is so _____ in _____ photography
that amateur photographers are almost always forced out of their own
darkrooms into the more _____ professional labs.

D. The sentences in each of the following exercises are out of order. By noting
the various transition devices, you should be able to arrange each group of
sentences into two coherent paragraphs.

Paragraph One: How To Cook and Eat an Artichoke

- Remove the artichoke from the water and drain before serving.
- Once the artichoke is free of dirt, place it in lightly salted boiling water.
- Before you can eat the heart, however, you must remove the cluster of
  spines that becomes visible once all the leaf ends have been eaten.
- Cover with a lid and let boil for at least thirty minutes.
- First, rinse the whole artichoke thoroughly before cooking, being
  careful to separate the leaves with your fingers to wash out any embedded dirt.
- After removing the leaves, you will reach every gourmet's delight: the
  heart of the artichoke.
- If you're still hungry after devouring the heart, repeat the entire process.
- To begin eating the artichoke, simply remove one leaf at a time,
  dipping the meaty inner end of the leaf into a small bowl of melted
  butter with a dash of lemon juice.

Paragraph Two: Henry VIII and the Problems of Succession

- After Jane, Henry took three more wives, but all these marriages were
  childless.
- Jane did produce a son, Edward VI, but he died at age fifteen.
- The problem of succession was therefore an important issue during the
  reign of Henry VIII.
- Still hoping for a son, Henry beheaded Anne and married Jane
  Seymour.
- Thus, despite his six marriages, Henry failed in his attempts to secure
  the succession.

- In sixteenth-century England it was considered essential for a son to assume the throne.
- Henry's first wife, Catherine of Aragon, had only one child, the Princess Mary.
- But Anne also produced a daughter, the future Queen Elizabeth I.
- Consequently, he divorced her and married Anne Boleyn.

Assignment

1. Write a paragraph of five sentences using enough transition devices to make the passage clearly coherent. On a second sheet of paper, recopy the paragraph in scrambled order. Exchange paragraphs with a classmate; give yourselves fifteen minutes to unscramble each other's paragraphs.
2. Find a well-developed paragraph in an essay, book, or magazine article. Circle and identify the transition devices you see.

LENGTH AND DEVELOPMENT

"How long is a good paragraph?" is a question novice writers often ask. Like a teacher's lecture or a preacher's sermon, paragraphs should be long enough to accomplish their purpose and short enough to be interesting. In truth, there is no set length, no prescribed number of lines or sentences, for any of your paragraphs. In a body paragraph, your topic sentence presents the main point, and the rest of the paragraph must give enough supporting evidence to convince the reader. While too much unnecessary or repetitious detail is boring, too little discussion will leave the reader uninformed, unconvinced, or confused.

Although paragraph length varies, beginning writers should try to avoid the one- or two-sentence paragraph frequently seen in newspapers or magazine articles. (Journalists have their own rules to follow; paragraphs are shorter in newspapers, for one reason, because large masses of print in narrow columns are hard to read quickly.) Essay writers do occasionally use the one-sentence paragraph, most often to produce some special effect, when the statement is especially dramatic or significant and needs to call attention to itself. For now, however, you may wish to practice working on paragraphs of at least five sentences.

Possibly the most serious—and most common—weakness of all essays by novice writers is *the lack of adequately developed body paragraphs*. The information in each paragraph must effectively explain, exemplify, persuade, define, or in some other way support your topic sentence. In the first place, you must include enough information in each paragraph to make your readers understand your topic sentence. Secondly, you must make the information in the paragraph clear and specific enough for the readers to understand and accept your ideas.

The next paragraph is underdeveloped. Although the topic sentence promises a discussion of Jesse James as a Robin Hood figure, the paragraph does not provide enough specific examples to explain this unusual view of the gunfighter.

Although he was an outlaw, Jesse James was considered a Robin Hood figure in my hometown in Missouri. He used to be generous to the poor, and he did many good deeds like giving away money. People in my hometown still talk about how lots of the things James did weren't all bad.

Rewritten, the paragraph might read as follows:

Although he was an outlaw, Jesse James was considered a Robin Hood figure in my hometown in Missouri. Jesse and his gang chose my hometown as a hiding place, and they set out immediately to make friends with the local people. Every Christmas for four years, the legend goes, he dumped bags of toys on the doorsteps of poor children. The parents knew the toys had been bought with money stolen from richer people, but they were grateful anyway. On three occasions, Jesse gave groceries to the dozen neediest families—he seemed to know when times were toughest—and once he even held up a stage to get money for an old man's operation. In my hometown, the old people still sing the praises of Jesse James, the outlaw who wasn't all bad.

The topic sentence promises a discussion of James's generosity and delivers just that by citing specific examples of his gifts to children, the poor, and the sick. The paragraph is, therefore, better developed.

Similarly, this paragraph offers supporting reasons but no specific examples or details to support those reasons:

Living with my ex-roommate was unbearable. First, she thought everything she owned was the best. Secondly, she possessed numerous filthy habits. Finally, she constantly exhibited immature behavior.

The writer might flesh out the paragraph this way:

Living with my ex-roommate was unbearable. First, she thought everything she owned, from clothes to cosmetics, was the best. If someone complimented my pants, she'd point out that her designer jeans looked better and would last longer because they were made of better material. If she borrowed my shampoo, she'd let me know that it didn't get her hair as clean and shiny as hers did. My hand cream wasn't as smooth; my suntan lotion wasn't as protective; not even my wire clothes hangers were as good as her padded ones! But despite her pickiness about products, she had numerous filthy habits. Her dirty dishes remained in the room for ages before she got the incentive to wash them. Piles of the "best" brand of tissues were regularly discarded from her upper bunk and strewn about the floor. Her desk and closets overflowed with heaps of dirty clothes, books, cosmetics, and whatever else she owned, and she rarely brushed her teeth (when she did brush, she left oozes of toothpaste on the sink). Finally, she constantly acted immaturely by throwing tantrums when things didn't go her way. A poor grade on an exam or paper, for example, meant ashtrays, shoes, or any other small object within her reach would hit the wall flying. Living with such a person taught me some valuable lessons about how not to win friends or keep roommates.

Having a well-developed paragraph is more than a matter of adding length, however. The information in each paragraph must effectively explain or support your topic sentence. *Vague generalities or repetitious ideas are not convincing.* After examining the two paragraphs below, decide which explains its point more effectively.

My uncle had a "green thumb." Whatever he put in the ground really grew well. Maybe it was his personality or his attitude, but his plants always grew beautifully. He certainly grew things better than anyone I know.

My uncle had a "green thumb." Whatever he put in the ground shot back up green and strong and beautiful. His tomatoes almost broke their stems and were as red as fire engines. His big roses sparkled all the time, as if dew clung to them even on the hottest afternoons. Once after supper he tossed a watermelon rind off the back porch and forgot about it; that summer his yard was full of the huge green succulent melons. Maybe it was his personality, warm and friendly, or maybe the fact that he thought of his plants as human; he prayed for them every night, just as he did for his family. Whatever it was, it worked.

The first paragraph contains, for the most part, repetitious generalities; it repeats the same idea four times (the uncle grew plants well) and fails to offer any specific details to support the point presented in the topic sentence. The second paragraph, on the other hand, does give some specific, persuasive examples—the tomatoes, roses, watermelons, prayers—which explain to the reader why the writer believes his uncle was an excellent gardener.

Here is another paragraph in which the writer offers only generalities:

Bicycles, popular for years in Europe, are becoming popular in America. Traveling by bicycle is better and easier than traveling by car. Bicycle riding is good for you, too, and it lets you get close to nature.

The paragraph is weak because none of its general statements are explained or supported with specific details. Why is travel by bicycle "better" than travel by car? "Better" in what ways? Why "easier"? "Good for you" in what ways? And what is the importance of getting "close to nature"? The writer obviously had some ideas in mind, but these ideas are not clear to the reader because they are not adequately developed in specific terms. By adding details and examples, the writer might revise the paragraph this way:

> With the price of gasoline skyrocketing every day and with parking places becoming more and more scarce, an increasing number of Americans are discovering an Old World secret: bicycling. Bicycles have long been a common sight in Europe, where gasoline has always been expensive. Now bicyclists in America are learning that bicycles not only save gasoline and costly repair, but also provide a pleasant, even exhilarating, way to exercise flabby muscles and clear clogged respiratory systems. In addition, cyclists are happily discovering a whole new way of looking at the world around them. Instead of spending their time and energy battling traffic jams and fighting for nonexistent parking spaces, they quickly sail along to their destinations, calm and relaxed, closer to the trees, flowers, and birds than any car has allowed them to be.

The reader now knows that bicycling is "better" because it improves mental and physical health and because it saves money and time.

Joseph Conrad, the famous British novelist, once remarked that a writer's purpose was to use "the power of the written word to make you hear, to make you feel . . . before all, to make you *see*. That—and no more, and it is everything." By using specific details instead of vague, general statements, you can write an interesting, convincing essay. Ask yourself as you revise your paragraphs, "Have I provided enough clear, precise details to make my readers *see* what I want them to?" In other words, a well-developed paragraph effectively presents its point with *an appropriate amount of specific supporting detail.* (Remember that the hand-written paragraph in your rough draft will look much shorter when it is typed. Therefore, if you don't know much specific information about a particular idea, perhaps you should abandon it as a major point in your essay.)

Practicing What You've Learned

A. Analyze the following paragraphs. Explain how you might improve the development of each one.

1. Professor Wilson is the best teacher I've ever had. His lectures are interesting, and he's very concerned with his students. He makes the class challenging but not too hard. On tests he doesn't expect more than one can give. I think he's a great teacher.
2. Newspaper advice columns are pretty silly. The problems are generally stupid or unrealistic, and the advice is out of touch with today's world. Too often the columnist just uses the letter to make a smart

remark about some pet peeve. The columns could be put to some good uses, but no one tries very hard.

3. Old-age homes are sad places. They are usually located in ugly old houses unfit for anyone. The people there are lonely and bored. What's more, they're often treated badly by the people who run the homes. It's a shame something better can't be done for the elderly.

4. There is a big difference between acquaintances and friends. Acquaintances are just people you know slightly, but friends give you some important qualities. For example, they can help you gain self-esteem and confidence just by being close to you. By sharing intimate things, they also help you become trustworthy. In general, being with friends makes you feel happy about being alive.

5. Last summer was the best vacation of my life. I went to Washington, D.C., and saw all the famous sights. I also enjoyed visiting Capitol Hill, where I learned a lot about government. The restaurants there are amazing, and the food is wonderful; I stuffed myself the whole time! Washington is such a pretty, complex city that I hope to go back for another visit next year.

B. Use one of the quotations below to help you generate a paragraph of your own. Feel free to use facts, personal experiences, improvised material, experiences of friends, etc., to develop your paragraph. (Hint: After selecting your quotation, be sure to narrow your subject so that your topic sentence will have a specific focus.)

1. "Few things are harder to put up with than the annoyance of a good example"—Mark Twain, writer and humorist

2. "Never look back; something might be gaining on you"—Satchel Paige, baseball player

3. "Genius is one per cent inspiration and ninety-nine per cent perspiration"—Thomas Edison, inventor

4. "There is no picking the rose without being pricked by the thorns"—Arabic proverb

5. "Nobody ever went broke underestimating the intelligence of the American public"—H. L. Mencken, writer and critic

6. "You might as well fall flat on your face as lean over too far backward"—James Thurber, writer and humorist

7. "A man who hates kids and dogs can't be all bad"—W. C. Fields, comic actor

8. "Women have served all these centuries as looking glasses possessing the magic and delicious power of reflecting the figure of man at twice its natural size"—Virginia Woolf, novelist

9. "When a person declares that he's going to college, he's announcing that he needs four more years of coddling before he can face the real world"—Al Capp, creator of the *Li'l Abner* cartoon

10. "The rich are very different from you and me"—F. Scott Fitzgerald, writer
11. "The mass of men lead lives of quiet desperation"—Henry Thoreau, writer
12. "Success is the best deodorant"—Elizabeth Taylor, actress

Assignment

A. Select two of the paragraphs from Practice A and rewrite them, adding enough specific details to make well-developed paragraphs.
B. Choose one of the quotations from Practice B and make it the basis for a paragraph composed of generalities and vague statements. Exchange this paragraph with a classmate's, and turn each other's faulty paragraphs into well-developed ones.
C. Find at least two well-developed paragraphs in an essay or book; explain why you think the two paragraphs are successfully developed.

PARAGRAPH SEQUENCE

The order in which you present your paragraphs is another decision you must make. In some essays, the subject matter itself will suggest its own order.* For instance, in an essay designed to instruct a beginning jogger, you might want to discuss the necessary equipment—good jogging shoes, loose-fitting clothing, sweatband, etc.—before moving to discussion of where to jog and how to jog. Other essays, however, may not suggest a natural order, in which case you yourself must decide which order will most effectively reach and hold the attention of your audience. Frequently, writers withhold their strongest point until last. (Lawyers often use this technique; they first present the jury with the weakest arguments, then pull out the most damning evidence—the "smoking pistol." Thus the jury members retire with the strongest argument freshest in their minds.) Study your own major points and decide which order will be the most logical, successful way of persuading your reader to accept your thesis.

TRANSITIONS BETWEEN PARAGRAPHS

As you already know, each paragraph usually signals a new major point in your discussion. These paragraphs should not appear as isolated blocks of thought, but rather as parts of a unified, step-by-step progression. To avoid a choppy essay, link each paragraph to the one before it with *transition devices*. Just as the sentences in your paragraphs are connected, so are the paragraphs themselves; therefore, you can use the same transition devices suggested on pp. 34—37.

   The first sentence of most body paragraphs frequently contains the transition device. To illustrate this point, here are some topic sentences lifted from the body paragraphs of a student essay criticizing a popular sports car, renamed the 'Gator to

*For more information on easily recognized patterns of order, see pp. 33—34.

protect the guilty and to prevent lawsuits. The transition devices are italicized.
Thesis: The 'Gator is one of the worst cars on the market.

- When you buy a *'Gator*, you buy physical inconvenience. [repetition of key word from thesis]
- *Another* reason the *'Gator* is a bad buy is the cost of insurance. [transition word, key word]
- You might overlook the *inconvenient* size and exorbitant *insurance* rates if the *'Gator* were a strong, reliable car, *but* this automobile constantly needs repair. [key words from preceding paragraphs, transition word]
- When you decide to sell this *car*, you face *still another* unpleasant surprise: the extremely low resale value. [key word, transition word]
- *But* perhaps the most serious drawback is the *'Gator's* safety record. [transition word, key word]

Sometimes, instead of using transition words or repetition of key words or their synonyms, you can use an *idea hook*. The last idea of one paragraph may lead you smoothly into your next paragraph. Instead of repeating a key word from the previous discussion, find a phrase that refers to the entire idea just expressed. If, for example, the previous paragraph discussed the highly complimentary advertising campaign for the 'Gator, the next paragraph might begin, "This view of the 'Gator is ridiculous to anyone who's pumped a week's salary into this gas guzzler." The phrase "this view" connects the idea of the first paragraph with the one that follows. Idea hooks also work well in combination with transition words: "This view, however, is ridiculous . . ."

If you do use transition words, don't allow them to make your essay sound mechanical. For example, a long series of paragraphs beginning "first . . . second . . . third . . ." quickly becomes boring. Vary the type and position of your transition devices so that your essay has a subtle but logical movement from point to point.

SUMMARY

Here is a brief restatement of what you should know about the paragraphs in the body of your essay:

1. Each body paragraph usually contains one major point of the argument announced by the thesis statement.
2. Each major point is presented in the topic sentence of a paragraph.
3. Every sentence in the paragraph should support the topic sentence (unity).
4. All sentences in the paragraph should be smoothly linked by transition devices (coherence).
5. Each paragraph should be adequately developed with supporting detail.
6. The sequence of your essay's paragraphs should be logical and effective.
7. There should be a smooth flow from paragraph to paragraph.
8. The body paragraphs should successfully persuade your reader that the opinion expressed in your thesis is valid.

Completing the Essay

To complete your rough draft, you should think of an essay as a coherent, unified whole composed of three main parts: the introduction (lead-in, thesis, and essay map), the body (paragraphs with supporting evidence), and the conclusion (final address to the reader). These three parts should flow smoothly into one another, presenting the reader with an organized, logical discussion. The following pages will suggest ways to begin and end your essay as well as how to revise and polish it.

HOW TO WRITE A GOOD LEAD-IN

The first few sentences of your essay are particularly important; first impressions, as you know, are often lasting ones. The beginning of your essay, then, must catch the readers' attention and make them want to keep reading. Recall the way you read a magazine: if you are like most people, you probably skim the magazine, reading a paragraph or two of each article that looks promising. If the first few paragraphs hold your interest, you read on. When you write your own introductory paragraph, assume that you have only a few sentences to attract your reader. Consequently, you must pay particular attention to making those first lines especially interesting and well written.

In some cases, your thesis statement alone may be controversial or striking enough to capture the readers. At other times, however, you will want to use the introductory device called a *lead-in*. The lead-in (1) catches the readers' attention, (2) announces the subject matter and tone of your essay (humorous, satiric, serious, etc.), and (3) sets up, or leads into, the presentation of your thesis and essay map.

Here are some suggestions and examples of lead-ins:

1. A paradoxical or intriguing statement

"Eat two chocolate bars and call me in the morning," says the psychiatrist to his patient. Such advice sounds like a sugar fanatic's dream, but recent studies have indeed confirmed that chocolate positively affects depression and anxiety.

2. An arresting statistic or shocking statement

One of every seven women living in Smith County will be raped this year, according to a recent report prepared by the County Rape Information and Counseling Services.

3. A question

It is twice the number of people who belong to the Southern Baptist Convention, eight times the number who serve in the U.S. armed forces, and just one million short of the number who voted for Barry Goldwater for President in 1964. What is it? It's the number of people in the U.S. who have smoked marijuana: a massive 26 million.

4. A quotation or literary allusion

"I think onstage nudity is disgusting, shameful, and damaging to all things American," says actress Shelley Winters. "But if I were twenty-two with a great body, it would be artistic, tasteful, patriotic, and a progressive religious experience."

5. A relevant story, joke, or anecdote

A group of young women were questioning Saturday afternoon shoppers about their views on the 1982 defeat of the Equal Rights Amendment. One old man in overalls answered, "ERA? Well, I like it just fine. But you know, I can't pick it up on my darned old radio after dark." That was the problem—too few people knew what the ERA really stood for.

6. A description, often used for emotional appeal

With one eye blackened, one arm in a cast, and third-degree burns on both her legs, the pretty, blond two-year-old seeks corners of rooms, refuses to speak, and shakes violently at the sound of loud noises. Tammy is not the victim of a war or a natural disaster; rather, she is the helpless victim of her parents, one of the thousands of children who suffer daily from America's hidden crime, child abuse.

7. A factual statement or a summary who-what-where-when-and-why lead-in

Texas's first execution by injection is scheduled for September 17 at the Huntsville Unit of the state's Department of Corrections, despite the protests of various human rights groups around the country.

8. An analogy or contrast

The Romans kept geese on their Capitol Hill to cackle alarm in the event of attack by night. Modern Americans, despite their technology, have hardly improved on that old system of protection. According to the latest Safety Council report, almost any door with standard locks can be opened easily with a common plastic credit card.

9. A personal experience

I realized times were changing for women when I overheard my six-year-old nephew speaking to my sister, a prominent New York lawyer. As we left her elaborate, luxurious office one evening, Tommy looked up at his mother and queried, "Mommy, can little boys grow up to be lawyers, too?"

10. A catalogue of relevant examples

A four-hundred-pound teenager quit school because no desk would hold her. A five-hundred-pound chef who could no longer stand on his feet was fired. A three-hundred-fifty-pound truck driver broke furniture in his friends' houses. All these people are now living better, happier, and thinner lives, thanks to the remarkable intestinal bypass surgery first developed in 1967.

11. Statement of a problem or a popular misconception

Some people believe that poetry is written only by aging beatniks or solemn, mournful men and women with suicidal tendencies. The Poetry in the Schools Program is out to correct that erroneous point of view.

Thinking of a good lead-in is often difficult when you sit down to begin your essay. Many writers, in fact, skip the lead-in until the first draft is written. They compose their thesis and essay map first and then write the body of the essay, saving the lead-in and conclusion for last. As you write the middle of your essay, you may discover an especially interesting piece of information you might want to save to use as part of your lead-in.

AVOIDING ERRORS IN LEAD-INS

In addition to the previous suggestions, here is some advice to help you avoid common lead-in errors:

Make Sure Your Lead-in Introduces Your Thesis. A frequent weakness in introductory paragraphs is an interesting lead-in but no smooth or clear transition to the thesis statement. To avoid a gap or awkward jump in thought in your introductory paragraph, you may need to add a connecting sentence or phrase between your lead-in and thesis. Study the paragraph below, which uses a comparison as its lead-in. The italicized transition sentence takes the reader from a general comment on all handicapped Americans to information about those in Smallville, smoothly preparing the reader for the thesis that follows.

> In the 1950's black Americans demanded and won the right to sit anywhere they pleased on public buses. Today, another large group of Americans—the handicapped confined to wheelchairs—is fighting for the simple right to board those same buses. *Here in Smallville, as well as in other cities, the lack of proper boarding facilities often denies handicapped citizens basic transportation to jobs, grocery stores, and medical centers.* In order to give persons confined to wheelchairs the same opportunities as those given to other residents, the Smallville City Council should vote the funds necessary to convert the public transportation system so that it may be used by handicapped citizens.

Make Your Lead-in Brief. Long lead-ins in short essays often give the appearance of a tail wagging the dog. Use a brief, attention-catching hook to set up your thesis; don't make your introduction the biggest part of your essay.

Don't Begin with an Apology or Complaint. Statements such as "I don't know much about coin collecting, but . . ." and "This assignment is boring, but . . ." do nothing to entice your reader.

Don't Assume Your Audience Already Knows Your Subject Matter. Identify the pertinent facts even though you know your teacher knows the assignment. ("The biggest flaw in this experiment occurred in the last step." What experiment?) If you are writing about a particular piece of literature, identify the title of the work and its author, using the writer's full name in the first reference.

Stay Clear of Overused Lead-ins. If composition teachers had a nickel for every essay that began with a dictionary definition, they could all retire to Bermuda. Leave *Webster* alone and find a livelier way to begin. Using a question for your lead-in is becoming overused, too, so use it only when it is obviously the best choice for your opener.

Assignment

Find three good lead-ins from essays, magazine articles, or newspaper feature stories. Identify the kinds of lead-ins you found and tell why you think each effectively catches the reader's attention and sets up the thesis.

HOW TO WRITE A GOOD TITLE

As in the case of lead-ins, your title may be written at any time, but many writers prefer to finish their essays before naming them. A good title is similar to a good newspaper headline, in that it attracts the readers' interest and makes them want to investigate the essay. Like the lead-in, the title also helps announce the tone of the essay. An informal or humorous essay, for instance, might have a catchy, funny title. Some titles show the writer's wit and love of wordplay; a survey of recent magazines revealed these titles: "Bittersweet News about Saccharin," "Coffee: New Grounds for Concern," and "The Scoop on the Best Ice Cream."

On the other hand, a serious, informative essay should have a more formal title that suggests its content as clearly and specifically as possible. Let's suppose, for example, that you are doing research on the meaning of color in dreams and you run across an essay listed in the library's *Readers' Guide* titled merely "Dreams." You don't know whether you should read it. To avoid such confusion in your own essay and to encourage readers' interest, always use a specific title: "Animal Imagery in Dreams," "Dream Research in Dogs," and so forth. Moreover, if your subject matter is controversial, let the reader know which side you're on (e.g., "The Advantages of Solar Power"). Never substitute a mere label, such as "Football Games" or "Euthanasia," for a meaningful title. And never, never label your essays "theme one" or "comparison and contrast theme." In all your writing, including the title, use your creativity to attract the readers' attention and to invite their interest in your ideas.

If you're unsure about how to present your title, here are two basic rules:

1. Your own title should *not* be underlined or put in quotation marks. It should be written at the top of page one of your essay or on an appropriate cover sheet with no special marks of punctuation.

2. Only the first word and the important words of your title should be capitalized. Generally we do not capitalize words such as "an," "and," "a," or "the," or prepositions, unless they appear as the first word of the title.

HOW TO WRITE A GOOD CONCLUDING PARAGRAPH

Like a good story, a good essay should not stop in the middle. It should have a satisfying conclusion, one that gives the reader a sense of completion on the subject. Don't allow your essay to drop off or fade out at the end—instead, use the concluding paragraph to emphasize the validity of your argument. Remember that the concluding paragraph is your last chance to convince the reader. (As one cynical but realistic student pointed out, the conclusion is the last part of your essay the teacher reads before putting a grade on your paper.) Therefore, make your conclusion count.

Because a concluding paragraph must grow out of the specific points covered in a particular essay, it is not useful to present examples of conclusions in this text. Nevertheless, below are a few ways you might end your essay:

- a restatement of thesis and major points (for long essays only)
- an evaluation of the importance of the essay's ideas
- a discussion of the essay's broader implications
- a call to action
- a prophecy based on the essay's argument
- a story, joke, quotation, or witticism that sums up the point of the essay

AVOIDING ERRORS IN CONCLUSIONS

Try to omit the following common errors in your concluding paragraphs:

Avoid a Mechanical Ending. One of the most frequent weaknesses in student essays is the conclusion that rigidly restates the thesis and its main points. A short essay of 500–750 words rarely requires a summary conclusion—in fact, such an ending often insults the readers' intelligence by implying that their attention spans are extremely short. Only after reading very long essays do most readers need a recap of the writer's ideas.

Don't Introduce New Points. Treat the major points of your essay in separate body paragraphs.

Don't Tack On a Conclusion. There should be a smooth flow from your last body paragraph into your concluding statements.

Don't Change Your Stance. Sometimes writers who have been critical of something throughout their essays will soften their stance or offer apologies in their last paragraph. For instance, someone complaining about the poor quality of a particular college course might abruptly conclude with statements that declare the class wasn't so bad after all, maybe he or she should have worked harder, maybe he or she really did learn something after all, etc. Such reneging may seem polite, but in actuality it undercuts the thesis and confuses the reader who has taken the writer's criticisms seriously. Instead of contradicting themselves, writers should stand their ground, forget about puffy clichés or "niceties," and find an empathetic way to conclude that is consistent with their thesis.

Avoid Trite Expressions. Don't begin your conclusions by declaring, "in conclusion," "in summary," or "as you can see, this essay proves my thesis that. . . ."

End your essay so that the reader clearly senses completion; don't merely announce that you're finished.

Assignment

Find three good concluding paragraphs. Identify each kind of conclusion and tell why you think it is an effective ending for the essay or article.

Effective Sentences

A welfare worker once broke up a staff meeting when he reported on one of his clients: "Mrs. Smith hasn't had any clothes for a year and has been visited regularly by the clergy." And students at the University of Delaware may have been similarly surprised when they learned from their Student Directory that the Office of Women's Affairs was "available for confidential advice, including sexual harassment."

Certainly the social worker didn't mean to imply anything obscene about local religious leaders, nor did the writers of the Student Directory mean to suggest that sexual harassment was a service of the Office of Women's Affairs. But the implications (and humor) are nevertheless present—solely because of the faulty way the sentences are constructed.

To improve your own writing, you must express your thoughts in clear, coherent sentences that produce precisely the reader response you want. Effective sentences are similar to the threads in a piece of knitting or weaving: each thread helps form the larger design; if any one thread becomes tangled or lost, the pattern becomes muddled. In an essay, the same is true: if any sentence is fuzzy or obscure, the reader may lose the thread of your argument and in some cases never bother to regain it. Therefore, to persuade your reader, you must concentrate on writing informative, emphatic sentences that consistently clarify the purpose of your essay.

Many problems in sentence clarity involve errors in grammar, usage, and word choice; the most common of these errors are discussed in Chapter 6 and Part Three of this text. In this chapter, however, you'll find some general suggestions for writing *clear, lively,* and *emphatic* sentences.

DEVELOPING A CLEAR STYLE

When you revise the sentences in your rough draft, try to follow the next four rules:

Always Have Something Definite To Say

Fuzzy sentences are often the result of fuzzy thinking. When you examine your sentences, ask yourself, "Do I know what I'm talking about here? Or are my sentences vague or confusing because I'm really not sure what my point is or where it's going?" Look at this list of content-less sentences taken from student essays; how could you reword and put more information into each one?

If you were to view a karate class, you would become familiar with the aspects that make it up.

The meaning of the poem isn't very clear the first time you read it, but after several readings, the poet's meaning comes through.

One important factor that is the basis for determining a true friend is the ability that person has for being a real human being.

Don't pad your paragraphs with sentences that run in circles, leading nowhere; rethink your ideas and revise your writing so that every sentence—like each brick in a wall—contributes to the construction of a solid argument. In other words, commit yourself to a position and make each sentence contain information pertinent to your discussion; leave the job of padding to mattress manufacturers.

Sometimes, however, you may have a definite idea in mind but still continue to write "empty sentences"—statements that alone do not contain enough information to make a specific point in your discussion. Frequently, an "empty sentence" may be revised by combining it with the sentence that follows, as shown in the examples below. The "empty" or overly general sentences are underlined.

Poor: There are many kinds of beautiful tropical fish. The kind most popular with aquarium owners is the angelfish.

Better: Of the many kinds of beautiful tropical fish, none is more popular with aquarium owners than the angelfish.

Poor: D. W. Griffith made movie history by introducing many new cinematic techniques. Some of these techniques were contrast editing, close-ups, fade-outs, and the freeze-frame shot.

Better: D. W. Griffith made movie history by introducing such new cinematic techniques as contrast editing, close-ups, fade-outs, and the freeze-frame shot.

Poor: Yankee Stadium was built because of Babe Ruth. It was often referred to as "the house that Ruth built" because the great slugger drew such enormous crowds that the Yankees were forced to build a bigger ball park.

Better: Yankee Stadium was often referred to as "the house that Ruth built" because their great slugger Babe Ruth drew such enormous crowds, the Yankees were forced to build a bigger ball park.

For more help on combining sentences, see pp. 78-79.

Make Your Sentences Specific

In addition to containing a specific (and complete) thought, each of your sentences should provide the readers with enough *specific details* for them to "see" the picture you are creating. Sentences full of vague or bland words produce blurry, boring prose and drowsy readers. Remember your reaction the last time you asked a friend about a recent vacation? If the response you received was something like, "Oh, it was real nice—a lot of fun," you probably yawned and proceeded quickly to a new topic. But if your friend had begun an exciting account of a recent wilderness rafting trip, with detailed stories about narrow escapes from freezing white water, treacherous rocks, and uncharted whirlpools, you'd probably have stopped and listened. The same principle works in your writing—colorful, specific details are the only sure way to attract and hold the reader's interest. Therefore, write boldly; make each sentence contribute something new and interesting to the overall discussion.

The examples below first show sentences far too bland to lure or sustain anyone's interest. Rewritten, these sentences contain specific details that make them much more intriguing.

Vague: She went home in a bad mood. [What kind of a bad mood? How did she act or look?]

Specific: She stomped home, hands jammed in her pockets, angrily kicking rocks, dogs, small children, and anything else that crossed her path.

Vague: It was a big, old, beautiful house. [How big was it? How old? Beautiful in what ways? Do you have a distinct picture of this house in your mind?]

Specific: Built during the Confederacy, the mansion boasted nine elegant bedrooms, white porch pillars, and a double door constructed of solid Louisiana oak.

Vague: He was an attractive man. [Attractive in what ways—his appearance, personality, or both? Again, do you "see" this man?]

Specific: He had Paul Newman's eyes, Robert Redford's smile, Sylvester Stallone's body, and Howard Hughes's money.

Make Your Sentences Simple

Because our society is becoming increasingly specialized and highly technical, we tend to equate complexity with excellence and simplicity with simplemindedness. This assumption is unfortunate, because it often leads to a preference for unnecessarily complicated and even contorted writing. In a recent survey, for example, a student chose a sample of bureaucratic hogwash over several well-written paragraphs, explaining his choice by saying that it must have been better since he didn't understand it.

Our best writers have always worked hard to present their ideas simply and specifically, so that their readers could easily understand them. Mark Twain, for instance, once praised a young author this way: "I notice that you use plain simple language, short words, and brief sentences. This is the way to write English. It is the modern way and the best way. Stick to it." And when a critic asked Hemingway to define his theory of writing, he replied, "[I] put down what I see and what I feel in the best and simplest way I can tell it."

In your own writing, therefore, work for a simple, direct style. Avoid sentences that are overpacked (too many ideas or too much information at once) as in the following example on racquetball:

John told Phil that to achieve more control over the ball, he should practice flicking or snapping his wrist, because this action is faster in the close shots and placing a shot requires only a slight change of the wrist's angle instead of an acute movement of the whole arm, which gives a player less reaction time.

Don't run the risk of losing your reader in a sentence that says too much to comprehend in one bite; simply divide the ideas into two or more sentences, as in the following:

John told Phil that to achieve more control over the ball, he should practice flicking or snapping his wrist, because this action is faster in the close shots. Placing a shot requires only a slight change of the wrist's angle instead of an acute movement of the whole arm, which gives a player less reaction time.

Also try to avoid the use of complicating "deadwood" constructions in your sentences. Having a clear, simple style does not mean limiting your writing to choppy, childish Dick-and-Jane sentences; it only means that all unnecessary, distracting words, phrases, and clauses should be deleted. Below are some sentences containing common deadwood constructions and ways they may be pruned:

Poor: *The reason why* the painter wasn't happy despite his first-prize award was because the judges had hung his painting upside down.
Better: The painter was unhappy despite his first-prize award because the judges had hung his painting upside down.

Poor: The land settlement *was an example where* the Indians did not receive fair treatment.
Better: The land settlement was unfair to the Indians.

Poor: He *is one who* makes his teacher wish she had chosen the calmer life of a secret agent or bank robber.

Better: He makes his teacher wish she had chosen the calmer life of a secret agent or bank robber.

Poor: Because *of the fact that* his surfboard business failed after only a month, my brother decided to leave Minnesota.

Better: Because his surfboard business failed after only a month, my brother decided to leave Minnesota.

Other notorious deadwood constructions include:

regardless of the fact that	(use "although")
due to the fact that	(use "because")
the reason is that	(omit)
as to whether or not to	(omit "as to" and "or not")
at this point in time	(use "now" or "today")
it is believed that	(use a specific subject and "believes")
concerning the matter of	(use "about")
by means of	(use "by")
these are the kinds of . . . that	(use "these" plus a specific subject)

"There Are," "It Is." These introductory phrases are often space wasters. When possible, omit them or replace them with specific subjects, as shown in the following:

Wordy: *There are* thirty thousand students attending this university.

Revised: Thirty thousand students attend this university.

Wordy: *There are* many reasons why I do not eat liver.

Revised: I do not eat liver for many reasons.

Wordy: *It is* hard for some people to learn to enjoy proofreading.

Revised: Some people never learn to enjoy proofreading.

"Who" and "Which" Clauses. Some "who" and "which" clauses are unnecessary and may be turned into modifiers placed before the noun:

Wordy: The getaway car, *which was* stolen, turned the corner.

Revised: The stolen getaway car turned the corner.

Wordy: The police chief, *who was* overly critical, ordered his force to slim down.

Revised: The overly critical police chief ordered his force to slim down.

When adjective clauses are necessary, the words "who" and "which" may sometimes be omitted:

Wordy: Betty Sue, *who was* a small-town girl, stared in awe at the Empire State Building.

Revised: Betty Sue, a small-town girl, stared in awe at the Empire State Building.

"To Be." Most "to be's" are inessential and ought not to be. Delete them every time you can.

Wordy: She seems *to be* angry.
Revised: She seems angry.

Wordy: The freeze-fracture technique proved *to be* unsuccessful.
Revised: The freeze-fracture technique proved unsuccessful.

Wordy: Material *to be* presented on the cover of the essay includes your name, address, and social security number.
Revised: The cover of the report should include your name, address, and social security number.

"Of" and Infinitive Phrases. Many "of" and infinitive ("to" plus verb) phrases may be omitted or revised by using possessives, adjectives, and verbs, as shown below:

Wordy: At the *time of registration* students are required *to make* payment *of their library fees.*
Revised: At registration students must pay their library fees.

Wordy: The *eyes of the director of personnel* drifted to the want ads.
Revised: The personnel director's eyes drifted to the want ads.

Including deadwood phrases makes your prose puffy; streamline your sentences to present a simple, direct style.

Make Your Sentences Concise

Almost all writing suffers from wordiness—the tendency to use more words than necessary. When useless words weigh down your prose, the meaning is often lost, confused, or hidden. Flabby prose calls for a reducing plan; put those obese sentences on a diet by cutting out unnecessary words, just as you avoid fatty foods to keep yourself trim. Mushy prose is ponderous and boring; crisp, to-the-point writing, on the other hand, is both accessible and pleasing. Beware, however, a temptation to overdiet; you don't want your prose to become so thin or brief that your meaning disappears completely. Therefore, cut out only the *unessential* words and phrases.

Wordy prose is frequently the result of using one or more of the following: (a) circumlocutions; (b) redundancies; (c) pretentiousness; (d) deadwood constructions (already discussed on pp. 58–60).

Avoid Circumlocution

To rid your prose of *circumlocutions* (roundabout ways of saying something simple), reduce all unnecessarily long or cumbersome phrases to one or two words. Here are a few examples of this construction and how to correct it:

Wordy: She *made her decision* after *giving consideration to* his report.
Concise: She *decided* after *considering* his report.

Wordy: Each candidate should be evaluated *on an individual basis*.
Concise: Each candidate should be evaluated *individually*.

Wordy: I am hopeful that we can *come to some agreement*.
Concise: I hope that we can *agree*.

Wordy: Rover usually *shows a great deal of obedience*.
Concise: Rover *is usually obedient*.

Wordy: Television does not portray violence *in a realistic fashion*.
Concise: Television does not portray violence *realistically*.

Wordy: The New York blackout produced a *crisis-type situation*.
Concise: The New York blackout produced a *crisis*.

To retain your reader's interest and improve the flow of your prose, trim all the fat from your sentences.

Avoid Redundancy

Many flabby sentences contain *redundancies* (words that repeat the same idea or whose meanings overlap). Consider the following examples:

His speech on flying saucers aroused my deepest feelings and emotions. [How are "feelings" different from "emotions"?]

In this day and time, people expect to live at least seventy years. ["Day" and "time" present a similar idea.]

He repeated the winning bingo number over again. ["Repeated" means "to say again," so there is no need for "over again."]

Weight lifting improves the physical development of my body. ["Physical means "relating to the body."]

Some other common redundancies include:

reverted back   new innovation
reflected back   red in color
retreated back   burned down up
fell down   pair of twins/two twins
climb up   resulting effect (or just "result")
a true fact   group consensus

Avoid Pretentiousness

Another enemy of clear, concise prose is *pretentiousness*. Pompous, inflated language surrounds us, and because it often sounds learned or official, we may be tempted to use it when we want to impress others with our writing. But as George Orwell, author of *1984*, noted, an inflated style is like "a cuttlefish squirting out ink." If you want your prose easily understood, write as clearly and plainly as possible.

To illustrate how confusing pretentious writing can be, here is a copy of a government memo announcing a blackout order, issued in 1942 during World War II:

> Such preparations shall be made as will completely obscure all Federal buildings and non-Federal buildings occupied by the Federal government during an air raid for any period of time from visibility by reason of internal or external illumination.

President Franklin Roosevelt rewrote the order as it appears below in plain English, clarifying its message and reducing the number of words by half:

> Tell them that in buildings where they have to keep the work going to put something across the windows.

By translating the obscure original memo into easily understandable language, Roosevelt demonstrated that a natural prose style can get necessary information to the reader more quickly and efficiently than bureaucratic jargon.

In other—shorter—words, to attract and hold your readers' attention, to communicate clearly and quickly, make your sentences as meaningful, simple, specific, and concise as possible.

PRACTICING WHAT YOU'VE LEARNED

A. Some of the following sentences are vague, overly general, or "empty." Rewrite them using more specific words and combining sentences when necessary.

1. There are nine planets. They are Earth, Mercury, Venus, Mars, Jupiter, Saturn, Uranus, Neptune, and Pluto.
2. Zilker Park is a good place for children.
3. Persons under twenty-five are especially hard hit by the cost of insurance. The under-twenty-five group is charged more than any other group of drivers.
4. The Godfather's car was really fancy.

5. The blue whale is a big animal. Some of its arteries are large enough for a small child to crawl through.
6. The Grand Canyon at twilight is a pretty sight.
7. There are several health benefits to yogurt. The most important is that yogurt contains a small number of calories.
8. My father advised me on many things. These included everything from how to dress for a date to which college I should attend.
9. Dave has one main reason for wearing boots. That is so everyone will think he is a cowboy.
10. Frank's apartment was a mess.

B. In the sentences below, omit or substitute concise words for the underlined phrases.

1. Raymond is a man who thinks smiling is a sign of weakness.
2. The reason that no one came to the party is due to the fact that Sue forgot to mail the invitations.
3. It is believed by most scientists that the universe was formed by a huge explosion billions of years ago.
4. In a fast manner, Amy passed by the window of the drive-in funeral parlor.
5. It is a fact that no living person can be portrayed on American paper currency.
6. Freddy Finch, who was the first person on our block to own a buffalo, was found trampled to death in his yard yesterday.
7. There are some city planners who apparently like concrete better than trees.
8. In order to advance in the business world, you must be able to organize and write about your ideas.
9. Artie failed his driver's test at this point in time.
10. It is often the case that a ring of mist will appear around the moon the night before a rainy day.

C. Rewrite the sentences below so that each one is less wordy.

1. In order to enhance my opportunities for advancement, I arrived at the decision to seek the hand of my employer's daughter in matrimony.
2. In this modern world of today, we often criticize and disapprove of advertising that is thought to be damaging to women by representing them in an unfair way.
3. When the prosecution tried to introduce the stolen fountain pen, this was objected to by the defense attorney.
4. What the poet is trying to get across to the reader in the fourth stanza is her expression of disgust with the telephone company.

5. There existed among us a feeling that we soon had to come to a decision and make a choice concerning which candidate to support.
6. In opposition to the opinion of many Americans, the conclusion reached by many writers in regard to the matter of money is that it is not necessarily a crucial factor in obtaining a measure of happiness.
7. To prevent early termination from this employment, it is advisable that you constantly appear occupied with something or other.
8. My education has allowed me to be knowledgeable about a variety of subjects and encourages me to make a special effort of being observant of all that goes on.
9. Of all the drinks I feel favorable about, I feel the most favorable toward orange juice due to the fact that its qualities are those that are the most healthful and the flavor is one of good taste.
10. The reason why capital punishment should not be allowed to exist is because it is not a method that is humane and also due to the fact that it does not serve as a deterrent.

Assignment

Write a paragraph of at least five sentences as clearly and concisely as you can. Then rewrite this paragraph, filling it with as many vague words, circumlocutions, redundancies, and deadwood constructions as possible. Exchange this rewritten paragraph for a similarly faulty one written by a classmate; give yourselves fifteen minutes to "translate" each other's sentences into effective prose.

DEVELOPING A LIVELY STYLE

Good writing demands clarity and conciseness—but that's not all. Good prose must also be lively, forceful, and interesting. It should excite, intrigue, and charm; each line should seduce the reader into the next. Consider, for example, one of the duller textbooks you've read lately. It probably was written clearly, but it may have failed to inform because of its insufferably bland tone; by the time you finished your assignment, most likely your brain was asleep.

You can prevent your readers from succumbing to a similar case of the blahs by developing a vigorous prose style that continually surprises and pleases them. As one writer has pointed out, all subjects—with the possible exceptions of sex and money—are dull until somebody makes them interesting. As you revise your rough draft, remember: bored readers are not born but made. Therefore, below are ten practical suggestions to help you transform ho-hum prose into lively sentences and paragraphs:

Use Specific, Descriptive Verbs. Avoid bland verbs that must be supplemented by nouns and modifiers.

Poor: His fist *broke* the window *into many pieces*.
Better: His fist *shattered* the window.

Poor: Dr. Love *repeatedly spoke to* his congregation *about* donating money to his "love mission."
Better: Dr. Love *hounded* his congregation into donating money to his "love mission."

Poor: When Mickey *hit* his record-breaking home run, the crowd *yelled very loudly*.
Better: When Mickey *smashed* his record-breaking home run, the crowd *roared*.

In general, try to avoid such colorless verbs as "to be," "to have," "to get," "to do," and "to make." (For more advice on using specific, colorful words, see also pp. 88–95 in Chapter 6.)

Poor: The airplane *made a slow circle around* the field.
Better: The airplane *slowly circled* the field.

Poor: By the time she was forty, Linda had *made* her way to the top of the corporation.
Better: By the time she was forty, Linda had *battled* her way to the top of the corporation.

Poor: Jim was expelled because he *had a fight* with Bob.
Better: Jim was expelled because he *fought* with Bob.

Use Active Rather than Passive Verbs Whenever Possible. When the subject of the sentence performs the action, the verb is *active*; when the subject of the sentence is acted upon, the verb is *passive*. You can often recognize sentences with passive verbs because they contain the word *by*, telling who performed the action.

Passive: The Indians *were considered* uncivilized by the early settlers.
Active: The early settlers *considered* the Indians uncivilized.

Passive: A high moral standard *was set* by the President.
Active: The President *set* a high moral standard.

Passive: Your letter of application *was read* by me with great amusement.
Active: I *read* your letter of application with great amusement.

In addition to being wordy and weak, passive sentences often disguise the performer of the action in question. You might have heard a politician, for example, say something similar to this: "It was decided this year to give all congressmen an increase in salary." The question of *who* decided to raise salaries remains foggy—perhaps purposefully so. But in your own prose, you should strive for clarity and directness; therefore, use active verbs as often as you can except when you wish to stress the person or thing that receives the action, as shown below:

The baby was born September 30, 1980.
The elderly man was struck by a drunk driver.

Use Specific, Precise Modifiers That Make the Reader See, Hear, or Feel What You Are Describing. Adjectives such as "good," "bad," "many," "more," "great," "a lot," "important," and "interesting" are too vague to paint the reader a clear picture. Similarly, the adverbs "very," "really," "too," and "quite" are overused and add little to sentence clarity. The following are examples of weak sentences and their revisions:

Imprecise: The potion changed the scientist into a *very old* man.
Better: The potion changed the scientist into an *eighty-year-old* man.

Imprecise: Marcia is an *interesting* person.
Better: Marcia is *witty, intelligent,* and *talented*.

Imprecise: A license is *really important* to anyone who wants to drive a car, hunt ducks, or get married.
Better: A license *is required* of anyone who wants to drive a car, hunt ducks, or get married.

In addition to using precise modifiers, try placing adjectives before the nouns to avoid cumbersome, wordy phrases. (For more advice on using precise words, see pp. 88–90 in Chapter 6.)

Poor: The girl *who was overweight* took up jogging and soon was outrunning everybody.
Better: The *overweight* girl took up jogging and soon was outrunning everybody.

Poor: One factor *that tends to be annoying* is his habit of going to sleep while I'm talking.
Better: One *annoying* factor is his habit of going to sleep while I'm talking.

Poor: A characteristic that tourists have *that distinguishes them* is the ever-present camera.
Better: A *distinctive* characteristic of tourists is the ever-present camera.

Attention to Word Order Is Crucial for Clarity. Always place a modifier near the word it modifies. The position of a modifier can completely change the meaning of your sentence; for example, each sentence below presents a different idea because of the placement of the modifier "only."

A. Naomi can communicate *only* in sign language. [The phrase "only in sign language" implies that Naomi cannot communicate in any way except sign language, that it is her sole means of communication.]

B. *Only* Naomi can communicate in sign language. ["Only Naomi" implies that Naomi is the sole person in the group who can communicate in sign language.]

To avoid confusion, therefore, place your modifiers close to the words or phrases they modify.

A modifier that seems to modify the wrong part of a sentence is called "misplaced." Not only can misplaced modifiers change or distort the meaning of your sentence, they can also provide unintentional humor as well, as illustrated by the following excerpt from the 1929 Marx Brothers' movie *Coconuts*:

Woman: There's a man waiting outside to see you with a black
         mustache.
Groucho: Tell him I've already got one.

Of course, the woman didn't mean to imply that the man outside was waiting with (that is, accompanied by) a mustache; she meant to say, "There's a man with a black mustache who is waiting outside. . . ." Here are some other examples of misplaced modifiers:

Misplaced: Because she is thoroughly housebroken, Sarah can take her dog almost anywhere she goes. [Did the writer mean that Sarah—or the dog—was housebroken?]

Revised: Because she is thoroughly housebroken, Sarah's dog can accompany her almost anywhere she goes.

Misplaced: Now that it's flu season, learn how to protect yourself from your family doctor. [Did the writer mean that you should protect yourself from your doctor—or from the flu?]

Revised: Now that it's flu season, learn from your family doctor how to protect yourself.

Misplaced: Stupid and dishonest, the playwright did not give his leading character many admirable traits. [Did the writer mean that the playwright—or the character—is stupid and dishonest?]

Revised: The playwright did not give his stupid, dishonest leading character many admirable traits.

Misplaced: Paul Smith became a father for the third time today, completing his work for a Masters of Arts degree in drama at Harvard. [Did the writer mean that having a baby completed Smith's degree work at Harvard?]

Revised: Paul Smith, now completing his work for a Masters of Arts degree in drama at Harvard, became a father for the third time today.

In each of the preceding examples the writer forgot to place the modifying phrase so that it modifies the correct subject. In most cases, a sentence with a misplaced modifier can be corrected easily by moving the word or phrase closer to the word that should be modified.

In some sentences, however, the object of the modifying phrase is missing entirely. Such a phrase is called a "dangling modifier." Most of these errors may be corrected by adding the missing subject. Here are some examples followed by their revisions:

Dangling: Waving farewell, the plane began to roll down the runway. [Did the writer mean that the plane was waving farewell?]
Revised: Waving farewell, we watched as the plane began to roll down the runway.

Dangling: While telling a joke to my roommate, a cockroach walked across my soufflé. [Did the writer mean that the cockroach was telling the joke?]
Revised: While telling a joke to my roommate, I saw a cockroach walking across my soufflé.

Dangling: Having tucked the children into bed, the cat was put out for the night. [Did the writer mean that the cat tucked the children into bed?]
Revised: Having tucked the children into bed, Mother and Father put the cat out for the night.

Dangling: After eating all their vegetables, the plates were washed and dried. [Did the writer mean that the plates ate their vegetables?]
Revised: After eating all their vegetables, the children washed and dried the plates.

Misplaced and dangling modifiers frequently occur when you think faster than you write; a careful reading of your rough draft will help you weed out any confused or unintentionally humorous sentences. (For additional examples of misplaced and dangling modifiers, see p. 221 in Part Three.)

Emphasize People When Possible. Try to focus on persons rather than abstractions whenever you can. Next to our fascinating selves, we most enjoy hearing about other people. Although all the sentences in the first paragraph following are correct, the second one, revised by a class of composition students at Brown University, is clearer and more personal because the jargon has been eliminated and the focus changed from the tuition rules to the students.

Tuition regulations currently in effect provide that payment of the annual tuition entitles an undergraduate-degree candidate to full-time enrollment, which is defined as registration for three, four, or five courses per semester. This means that at no time may an undergraduate student's official registration for courses drop below three without a dean's permission for part-time status and that at no time may the official course registration exceed five. (Brown University Course Announcement 1980–81)

If students pay their tuition, they may enroll in three, four, or five courses per semester. Fewer than three or more than five can be taken only with a dean's permission.

Vary Your Sentence Style. The only torture worse than listening to someone's nails scraping across a blackboard is being forced to read a paragraph full of identically constructed sentences. To illustrate this point, below are a few sentences composed in the all-too-common subject + predicate pattern:

Soccer is the most popular sport in the world. Soccer exists in almost every country. Soccer players are sometimes more famous than movie stars. Soccer teams compete every few years for the World Soccer Cup. Soccer fans often riot if their team loses. Some fans even commit suicide. Soccer is the only game in the world that makes people so crazy.

Excruciatingly painful, yes? Each of us has a tendency to repeat a particular sentence pattern (though the choppy subject + predicate is by far the most popular); you can often detect your own by reading your prose aloud. To avoid overdosing your readers with the same pattern, vary the length, arrangement, and complexity of your sentences. Of course, this doesn't mean that you should contort your sentences merely for the sake of illustrating variety; just read your rough draft aloud, listening carefully to the rhythm of your prose so you can revise any monotonous passages or disharmonious sounds. (Try, also, to avoid the hiccup syndrome, in which you begin a sentence with the same word that ends the preceding sentence: The first president to install a telephone on his desk was Herbert *Hoover*. *Hoover* refused to use the telephone booth outside his office.)

Avoid Overuse of Any One Kind of Construction in the Same Sentence. Don't, for example, pile up too many negatives, "who" or "which" clauses, prepositional or infinitive phrases in one sentence.

He *couldn't* tell whether she *didn't* want him to go or *not*.

I gave the money to my brother, *who* returned it to the bank president, *who* said the decision to prosecute was up to the sheriff, *who* was out of town.

I went *to* the store *for* a dozen eggs *for* my mother *to* cook *for* me *for* my lunch.

Don't Change Your Point of View between or within Sentences. If, for example, you begin your essay discussing students as "they," don't switch midway—or mid sentence—to "we" or "you."

> Poor: Students pay tuition, which should entitle *them* to some voice in the university's administration. Therefore, *we* deserve one student on the Board of Regents.
>
> Better: Students pay tuition, which should entitle *them* to some voice in the university's administration. Therefore, *they* deserve one student on the Board of Regents.

> Poor: *I* liked camping in the primitive area of the park. *You* could feel both the joy of solitude and the excitement of being solely responsible for *your* own welfare.
>
> Better: *I* liked camping in the primitive area of the park. *I* could feel both the joy of solitude and the excitement of being solely responsible for my *own* welfare.

Perhaps this is a good place to dispel the myth that the pronoun "I" should never be used in an essay; on the contrary, many of our best essays have been written in the first person. Some of your former teachers may have discouraged the use of "I" for these two reasons: (1) overuse of "I" makes your essay sound like the work of an egomaniac; (2) writing in the first person often results in too many empty phrases such as "I think that" and "I believe that." Nevertheless, if the situation demands a personal point of view, feel free—if you're comfortable doing so—to use the first person, but use it in moderation; make sure that every sentence doesn't begin with "I" plus a verb.

Avoid Mixed Constructions and Faulty Predication. Sometimes you may begin with a sentence pattern in mind and then shift, mid sentence, to another pattern— a change that often results in a generally confusing sentence. In many of these cases, you will find that the subject of your sentence simply doesn't fit with the predicate. Look at the following examples and note their corrections:

> Faulty: The song is one of the risks run by moonshiners. [The song itself isn't a risk—it tells about one of the risks.]
>
> Better: The song tells about one of the risks run by moonshiners.

> Faulty: The reason I'm quitting my fire-swallowing act is because of my heartburn. ["The reason . . . is because" is both wordy and ungrammatical. If you have a reason, you don't need a "reason because."]
>
> Better: I'm quitting my fire-swallowing act because of my heartburn.

> Faulty: Success is when you can buy whatever you want without looking at

the price. [A thing is never a "when" or a "where"; rewrite all "is when" or "is where" constructions.]

Better: You're a success if you can buy whatever you want without looking at the price.

Many mixed constructions occur because the writer is in too much of a hurry; check your rough draft carefully to see if you have included sentences in which you started one pattern and switched to another. (For more help on faulty predications and mixed constructions, see pp. 224–225 in Part Three.)

Don't Try To Apply All These Rules to the First Draft of Your Essay. Trying to do so will probably result in panic and/or writer's block. Work first on your essay's content and general organization; then, in a later draft, rewrite your sentences so that each one is informative and persuasive. Your reader reads only the words on the page, not those in your mind — so it's up to you to make sure the sentences in your essay approximate the thoughts in your head as closely and vividly as possible.

Remember: All good writers revise their sentences.

Practicing What You've Learned

A. Replace the underlined words below to make the sentences more vivid and forceful. Add specific details where necessary; don't worry about slightly changing the content of the sentence.

1. To watch Joe Bob eat his pork chops was <u>interesting</u>.
2. When I fell into the reptile pit at the zoo, I was <u>very afraid</u>.
3. My mother-in-law is <u>nice</u> and does many <u>good things</u> for me.
4. The rain was <u>really cold</u> as it <u>went down</u> our necks.
5. There are several ways to cook badger, but in every case the meat tastes <u>funny</u>.
6. Displaying the teeth marks on his leg, the postal carrier <u>asked</u> the City Council to pass a leash law.
7. The game show contestant <u>appeared pleased</u> that he had won the vacation to Borneo.
8. Kim <u>made a noise</u> when Alfred slammed the car door on her hand.
9. After she learned of her loss on the stock market, Jennifer began acting <u>really crazy</u>.
10. When I saw Rupert's car after the accident, I felt <u>just terrible</u>.

B. Rewrite the following sentences, correcting any confusion or weakness in sentence construction.

1. The doll was dressed by Fred to look like Dolly Parton.
2. One should be careful approaching a rabid dog because you might get bitten.
3. Having just been trampled by a herd of migrating antelope, the doctor thought I should stay in bed for a few days.
4. The reason for abolishing the pornography law is on the grounds of freedom of speech.
5. I can't help but wonder whether or not he isn't unwelcome.
6. After moving to Colorado, the mountains were beautiful.
7. It was revealed by her lawyers today that FiFi LaPeu left her entire fortune to her poodle, Itty-Bitty.
8. Writing greeting cards is not an easy way for me to make a living because you become bored so quickly thinking up those silly jingles.
9. Ernest was warned by his astrologer to avoid redheads on Thursday.
10. Although lacking only one course in Prehistoric History, the college still refused to give JoJo his diploma.
11. The story of Rip Van Winkle is one of the dangers endured by those who oversleep.
12. Finishing this exercise, each sentence was correct.

Assignment

Fill in the blanks with colorful words. Make the paragraph as interesting, exciting, or humorous as you can. Avoid clichés—make your responses original and creative.

As midnight approached, Janet and Brad _____ toward the _____ castle to escape the _____ storm. Their _____ car had _____, _____, and finally _____ on the road nearby. The night was _____ and Brad _____ at the shadows with _____ and _____. As they _____ up the _____ steps to the _____ door, the _____ wind was filled with _____ and _____ sounds. Janet _____ on the door, and moments later, it opened to reveal the _____ scientist, clutching a _____. Brad and Janet _____ at each other and then _____ (complete this sentence, ending the paragraph and the story).

DEVELOPING AN EMPHATIC STYLE

Some words and phrases in your sentences are more important than others and, therefore, need more emphasis. Three ways to vary emphasis are by (1) word order, (2) coordination, and (3) subordination.

Word Order

The arrangement of words in a sentence can determine which ideas receive the most emphasis. To stress a word or phrase, place it at the end of the sentence. The second most emphatic position is the beginning of the sentence. Accordingly, a word or phrase receives least emphasis when buried in the middle of the sentence. Compare the examples below, in which the word "murder" receives varying degrees of emphasis:

Least emphatic: Colonel Mustard knew *murder* was his only plan.
More emphatic: *Murder* was Colonel Mustard's only plan.
Most emphatic: Colonel Mustard had only one plan: *murder*.

Another use of word order to vary emphasis is *inversion*, taking a word out of its natural or usual position in a sentence and inserting it in an unexpected place.

Usual order: The *forgetful* man consults his address book to find his way home from work.
Inverted order: *Forgetful* is the man who consults his address book to find his way home from work.

Not all your sentences will contain words that need special emphasis; good writing generally contains a mix of some sentences in natural order and others rearranged for special effects.

Coordination

When you have two closely related ideas and want to stress them equally, coordinate them.[1] In coordination, you join two clauses with a coordinating conjunction (the most common ones are "and," "or," "but," and "so"). Use coordination to show a relationship between ideas and to add variety to your sentence structures. Be careful, however, to avoid linking nonrelated ideas, such as the two that appeared in the welfare worker's report quoted earlier in this chapter: "Mrs. Smith hasn't had any clothes for a year and has been visited regularly by the clergy." Study the following examples:

Choppy: You can send the package by mail. The package will arrive quicker by bus. [The two related ideas here are presented without coordination.]
Coordinated: You can send the package by mail, but it will arrive quicker by bus. [A relationship between the ideas is established.]

[1]To remember that the term "coordination" refers to equally weighted ideas, think of other words with the prefix "co," such as "copilots" or "coauthors."

Unrelated: The bank called to say my account was overdrawn, and tomorrow is my day off from work. [These two unrelated ideas should not be coordinated.]

You should also avoid using coordinating conjunctions to string too many ideas together like linked sausages:

Poor: I went to the park and I watched David play volleyball and I swam in the pool and then I went home.

Better: After I watched David play volleyball in the park, I swam in the pool and then went home.

Subordination

Some sentences contain one main statement and one or more less-emphasized elements; the less important ideas are subordinate to, or are dependent upon, the sentence's main idea.[2] Subordinating conjunctions introducing dependent clauses show a variety of relationships between the clauses and the main part of the sentence. Here are four examples of subordinating conjunctions and their uses:

1. To show time
   Without subordination: Superman stopped changing his clothes. He realized the phone booth was made of glass.
   With subordination: Superman stopped changing his clothes *when* he realized the phone booth was made of glass.

2. To show cause
   Without subordination: John did not pass the Army's entrance exam. John did not want to be a soldier.
   With subordination: John did not pass the Army's entrance exam *because* he did not want to be a soldier.

3. To show condition
   Without subordination: I ought to stop biting my nails. Then they will grow long and beautiful.
   With subordination: *If* I stop biting my nails, they will grow long and beautiful.

4. To show place
   Without subordination: Bulldozers are smashing the old movie theater. That's the place I first saw Roy Rogers and Dale Evans ride into the sunset.

[2]To remember that the term "subordination" refers to sentences containing dependent elements, think of words such as "a subordinate" (someone who works for someone else) or a post office "substation" (a branch of the post office less important than the main branch).

With subordination: Bulldozers are smashing the old movie theater *where* I first saw Roy Rogers and Dale Evans ride into the sunset.

Subordination is especially useful in ridding your prose of choppy Dick-and-Jane sentences and those "empty sentences" discussed on pp. 56–57. Below are some examples of choppy, weak sentences and their revisions, which contain subordinate clauses:

Poor: Lew makes bagels on Tuesday. Lines in front of his store are a block long.

Better: When Lew makes bagels on Tuesday, lines in front of his store are a block long.

Poor: Sue's husband was last seen at the Pussycat Lounge. She returned there the next night.

Better: Sue returned the next night to the Pussycat Lounge, where her husband was last seen.

A correctly subordinated sentence is one of the marks of a sophisticated writer, because it presents adequate information in one smooth flow instead of in monotonous drips. Subordination, like coordination, also adds variety to your sentence construction.

Generally, when you subordinate one idea, you emphasize another, so to avoid the tail-wagging-the-dog problem, put your important idea in the main clause. Also, don't let your most important idea become buried under an avalanche of subordinate clauses, as in the sentence that follows:

When he was told by his boss, *who* had always treated him fairly, that he was being fired from a job *that* he had held for twenty years at a factory *where* he enjoyed working *because* the pay was good, Henry felt angry and frustrated.

Practice combining choppy sentences by studying the sentence combining exercise below. In this exercise a description of a popular movie or book has been chopped into simple sentences and then combined into one complex sentence.

1. *Bananas* (1971)
   The protagonist is a product tester.
   He is bored.
   His boredom is with his everyday routine.
   He goes to a small Latin American country.
   He becomes a dictator.
   He becomes a dictator during a political upheaval.

A product tester, bored with his everyday routine, goes to a small Latin

American country, where he becomes a dictator during a political upheaval.

2. *Friday the 13th* (1980)
   A summer camp reopens.
   It had been closed for twenty years.
   It had been closed because of three murders.
   The camp attracts a killer.
   The killer is vindictive.
   The killer knifes teenagers.
   The teenagers are unsuspecting.

   The reopening of a summer camp, closed twenty years earlier after three murders, attracts a vindictive killer who knifes unsuspecting teenagers.

3. *The Great Gatsby* (1925)
   A young man moves to the East.
   He is from the Midwest.
   He lives next door to a mysterious man.
   The mysterious man is rich.
   The mysterious man loves a married woman.
   The mysterious man takes the blame for an auto accident.
   The auto accident was the married woman's fault.
   The mysterious man is ultimately murdered.
   The young man tells the story of the rich man's death.

   After moving to the East from the Midwest, a young man tells the story of his next-door neighbor, a mysterious, rich man who is ultimately murdered after taking the blame for an auto accident caused by the married woman he loves.

Please note that the simple sentences in the exercises above may be combined effectively in a number of ways. For instance, the description of *Bananas* might be rewritten this way: "Fed up with his boring everyday routine, a product tester becomes a dictator during a political upheaval in a small Latin American country." How might you rewrite the other two sample sentences?

Practicing What You've Learned

A. Revise the sentences below so that the underlined words receive the most emphasis.

1. W. C. Fields once filled a child actor's baby bottle with <u>gin</u> to show his dislike for the little boy.
2. According to recent polls, <u>television</u> is where most Americans get their news.
3. Of all the world's problems, it is <u>hunger</u> that is most urgent.

4. Claude read the *Playboy* "Advisor" to prepare for his Ph.D. examination in family planning.
5. <u>Snoring</u> is one habit I will not tolerate from a roommate.

B. Rewrite the pairs of choppy sentences below by using coordination or subordination.

1. Elbert wanted to win the skateboard championship. He broke his leg practicing.
2. The earthquake shook the city. Louise was performing primal-scream therapy.
3. Bubba started hoarding pennies as a child. Today he opened his own bank.
4. Parrots and other birds often give the impression of being able to talk. They can imitate the sound of the human voice so well.
5. Plants are sometimes kicked, cursed, or ignored. They eventually wither and die.
6. Frances hit her professor with her shoe. He decided to reevaluate her essay.
7. The postman quit because the mailbag was too heavy. He also quit because he could not remember all the zip codes.
8. She inherited a million dollars. She remained a simple, unspoiled girl.
9. A dolphin's brain is bigger than a person's. Humans are still smarter.
10. The most common given name of women over sixty-two is Mary. The most common given name of men over sixty-two is John.

C. Complete the simple sentences below into one complex sentence. See if you can guess the name of the books and movies described in the sentences (answers appear on p. 79).

1. A boy runs away from home.
   His companion is a runaway slave.
   He lives on a raft.
   The raft is on the Mississippi River.
   He has many adventures.
   The boy learns many lessons.
   Some lessons are about human kindness.
   Some lessons are about friendship.
2. A young man returns from prison.
   He returns to his family
   His family lives in the Dust Bowl.
   The family decides to move.
   The family moves to California.

The family expects to find jobs in California.
The family finds intolerance.
They also find dishonest employers.
3. A scientist is obsessed.
He is mad.
He wants to re-create life.
He creates a monster in his laboratory.
The monster is gruesome.
The monster rebels against the scientist.
The monster kills his creator.
The villagers revolt.
The villagers storm the castle.
4. A man is a gambler.
He goes to a prison farm.
He cons his way into a mental institution.
He rebels against the head nurse.
The head nurse is straightlaced.
She is domineering.
The man helps a group of patients become better.
These patients become well enough to leave the mental institution.
The man himself is forced to have an unnecessary lobotomy.
The lobotomy comes after the man has revealed the nurse as she really is.
She is a monster.

Assignment

A. Make up your own sentence combining exercise by finding one-sentence descriptions of popular or recent movies, books, or television episodes. Divide the complex sentences into simple sentences and exchange papers with a classmate. Give yourselves ten minutes to combine sentences and guess the titles or shows.
B. The paragraphs below are poorly written because of their choppy, wordy, and monotonous sentences. Rewrite the passages so that they are clear, lively, and emphatic.

There is a new invention on the market. It is called a "dieter's conscience." It is a small box to be installed in one's refrigerator. When the door of the refrigerator is opened by you, a tape recorder begins to start. A really loud voice yells, "You eating again? No wonder you're getting fat." Then the very loud voice says, "Close the door; it's getting warm." Then the voice laughs a lot in an insane and crazy fashion. The idea is one that is designed to mock people into a habit of stopping eating.

In this modern world of today, man has come up with another new invention. This invention is called the "Talking Tombstone." It is made by the "Gone-But-Not-Forgotten" Company, which is located in Burbank, California. This company makes a tombstone that has a device in it that makes the tombstone appear to be talking aloud in a realistic fashion when people go close by it. The reason is that the device is really a recording machine that is turned on due to the simple fact of the heat of the bodies of the people who go by. The closer the people get, the louder the sound the tombstone makes. It is this device that individual persons who want to leave messages after death may utilize. A hypochondriac, to cite one example, might leave a recording of a message that says over and over again in a really loud voice, "See, I told you I was sick!" It may be assumed by one and all that this new invention will be a serious aspect of the whole death situation in the foreseeable future.

Answers to sentence combining exercise:

1. *Huckleberry Finn*
2. *The Grapes of Wrath*
3. *Frankenstein*
4. *One Flew over the Cuckoo's Nest*

Chapter

6

Word Choice

The English language contains over a half million words—quite a selection for you as a writer to choose from. But such a wide choice may make you feel like a starving person confronting a six-page, fancy French menu: which choice is best? how do I choose? is the choice so important?

Word choice can make an enormous difference in the quality of your writing for at least one obvious reason: if you substitute an incorrect or vague word for the right one, you take the risk of being totally misunderstood. Ages ago Confucius made the same point: "If language is incorrect, then what is said is not meant. If what is said is not meant, then what ought to be done remains undone." It isn't enough that *you* know what you mean; you must transfer your ideas onto paper in the proper words so that others understand your exact meaning.

To help you avoid possible paralysis from indecision over word choice, this chapter offers some practical suggestions on selecting words that are not only accurate and appropriate but also memorable and persuasive.

SELECTING THE CORRECT WORDS

Accuracy: Confused Words

Unless I get a bank loan soon, I will be forced to lead an <u>immortal</u> life.

How dare you brand my son <u>illiterate!</u> This is a dirty lie, as I was married a week before he was born!

Dobermans make good pets if you train them with enough <u>patients.</u>

The gypsy wore a turban, lots of gold jewelry, and a red scarf tied around her <u>waste</u>.

He dreamed of eating <u>desert</u> after <u>desert</u>.

The preceding sentences share a common problem: each one contains an error in word choice. In each sentence, the underlined word is incorrect, causing the sentence to be nonsensical or silly. To avoid such problems in word choice, make sure you check words for *accuracy*. Use only those words whose precise meaning, usage, and spelling you know; look in your dictionary to double-check any words whose definitions (or spellings) are fuzzy to you. As Mark Twain noted, the difference between the right word and the wrong one is the difference between lightning and the lightning bug.

Here is a list of words that are often confused in writing. Use your dictionary to determine the meanings or usage of any word unfamiliar to you.

affect/effect	lead/led
to/too/two	there/their/they're
its/it's	your/you're
complement/compliment	who's/whose
capitol/capital	stationary/stationery
lay/lie	principal/principle
accept/except	precede/proceed
good/well	cite/sight/site
choose/chose	number/amount
council/counsel	illusion/allusion
where/wear	are/or/our

Accuracy: Idiomatic Phrases

Occasionally you may have an essay returned to you with words marked "awkward" or "idiom." In English, as in all languages, we have word groupings that seem governed by no particular logic except the ever-popular "that's-the-way-we-say-it" rule. Many of these idiomatic expressions involve prepositions beginning writers sometimes confuse or misuse. Below are some common idiomatic errors and their corrected forms:

regardless ~~to~~ of	different ~~than~~ ~~to~~ from
insight ~~of~~ into	must ~~of~~ have known
similar ~~with~~ to	superior ~~than~~ to
comply ~~to~~ with	prior ~~than~~ to
~~to~~ in my opinion	contrast ~~against~~ to
aptitude ~~toward~~ for	capable ~~to~~ of
meet ~~to~~ her standards	relate ~~with~~ to

To avoid idiomatic errors, consult your dictionary and read your essay aloud; often your ears will catch mistakes in usage that your eyes have overlooked.[1]

Levels of Language

In addition to choosing the correct word, you should also select words whose status is suited to your purpose. For convenience here, language has been classified into three categories or levels of usage: (1) colloquial, (2) informal, (3) formal.

Colloquial Language Is the Kind of Speech You Use Most Often in Conversation with Your Friends, Classmates, and Family. It may not always be grammatically correct ("it's me"); it may include fragments of speech, contractions, some slang, words identified as nonstandard by the dictionary (such as "gripe" or "lousy"), and shortened or abbreviated words ("grad school," "photos," "T.V."). Colloquial speech is everyday language, and while you may use it in some writing (personal letters, journals, memos, and so forth), you should avoid becoming colloquial in college essays or in professional letters, reports, or papers, because such language implies too personal a relationship between writer and reader.

Informal Language Is Called For in Most College and Professional Assignments. The tone is more formal than in colloquial writing or speech; no slang or nonstandard words are permissible. Informal writing consistently uses correct grammar; fragments are used for special effect or not at all. Authorities disagree on the use of contractions in informal writing: some say avoid them entirely; others say they're permissible; still others advocate using them only to avoid stilted phrases ("let's go," for example, is preferable to "let us go"). Most, if not all, of your essays in English classes will be written in informal language.

Formal Language Is Found in Important Documents and in Serious, Often Ceremonial, Speeches. Characteristics include an elevated—but not pretentious—tone, no contractions, and correct grammar. Formal writing often uses inverted word order and balanced sentence structure. John F. Kennedy's 1960 Inaugural Address, for example, was written in a formal style ("Ask not what your country can do for you; ask what you can do for your country"). Most people rarely, if ever, need to write formally; if you are called upon to do so, however, be careful to avoid formal diction that sounds pretentious, pompous, or phony.

---

[1]You may not immediately recognize what's wrong with words your teacher has labeled "awk" or "idiom," as these marks often cover many sins. If you're uncertain about an error, don't hesitate to ask your teacher for clarification; after all, if you don't know what's wrong with your sentence, you can't very well avoid making the same mistake again. To illustrate this point, here's a true story: A bright young woman was having trouble with prepositional phrases in her essays, and although her professor repeatedly marked her incorrect expressions with the marginal note "idiom," she never improved. Finally, one day near the end of the term, she approached her teacher in tears and wailed, "Professor Jones, I know I'm not a very good writer, but must you write 'idiot,' 'idiot,' 'idiot' all over my papers?" The moral of this story is simple: it's easy to misunderstand a correction or misread your teacher's writing; since you can't improve until you know what's wrong, always ask when you're in doubt.

Tone

Tone is a general word that describes writers' attitudes toward their subject matter and audience. There are as many different kinds of tones as there are emotions. Depending on how the writer feels, an essay may sound humorous, ironic, indignant, or solemn, to name but a few of the possible choices. In addition to presenting a specific attitude, a good writer gains credibility by maintaining a tone that is generally calm, reasonable, and sincere.

While it is impractical to analyze all the various kinds of tones one finds in essays, it is nevertheless beneficial to discuss some of those that repeatedly give students trouble. Listed below are some tones that should be used carefully or avoided altogether:

Invective

Invective is unrestrained anger, usually expressed in the form of violent accusation or denunciation. Let's suppose, for example, you hear a friend argue that "anyone who votes for Joe Smith is a Fascist pig"; whether you support Smith or not, you are probably offended by your friend's abusive tone. Raging emotion, after all, does not sway the opinions of intelligent people; they need to hear the facts presented in a calm, clear discussion. Therefore, in your own writing, aim for a reasonable tone. You want your readers to think, "Now here is someone with a good understanding of the situation, who has evaluated it with a calm, analytical mind." Keeping a controlled tone doesn't mean you shouldn't feel strongly about your subject—on the contrary, you certainly should—but you should realize that a hysterical or outraged tone defeats your purpose by causing you to sound irrational and therefore untrustworthy. For this reason, you should also avoid using profanity in your essays; the shock value of a "hell" or "damn" isn't worth what you lose in credibility (and besides, is anyone other than your Aunt Fanny really shocked by profanity these days?). The most effective way to get your point across is to persuade, not offend, your reader.

Sarcasm

In most of your writing you'll discover that a little sarcasm—bitter, derisive remarks—goes a long way. Like invective, too much sarcasm can damage the reasonable tone your essay should present. Instead of saying, "You can recognize the supporters of the new tax law by the points on the tops of their heads," give your readers some reasons why you believe the tax bill is flawed. Sarcasm often backfires by causing the writer to sound like a childish name-caller rather than a judicious commentator.

Irony

Irony is a figure of speech whereby the writer or speaker says the opposite of what is meant; for the irony to be successful, however, the audience must understand the writer's true intent. For example, if you have slopped to school in a rainstorm and your drenched teacher enters the classroom saying, "Ah, nothing like this beautiful sunny weather," you know that your teacher is being ironic. Perhaps one of the most famous cases of irony occurred in 1938, when Sigmund Freud, the famous Viennese psychiatrist, was arrested by the Nazis. After being harassed by the Gestapo, he was released on the condition that he sign a statement swearing he had been treated well by the secret police. Freud signed it, but he added a few words after his signature: "I can heartily recommend the Gestapo to anyone." Looking back, we easily recognize Freud's jab at his captors; the Gestapo, however, apparently overlooked the irony and let him go.

While irony is often an effective device, it can also cause great confusion, especially when it is written rather than spoken. Unless your readers thoroughly understand your position in the first place, they may become confused by what appears to be a sudden contradiction. Irony that is too subtle, too private, or simply out of context merely complicates the issue. Therefore, you must make certain that your reader has no trouble realizing when your tongue is firmly embedded in your cheek. And unless you are assigned to write an ironic essay (in the same vein as Swift's "A Modest Proposal"), don't overuse irony. Like any rhetorical device, its effectiveness is reduced with overkill.

Flippancy or Cuteness

If you sound too flip or bored in your essay ("I hate this assignment, but since it's two A.M., I might as well begin . . ."), your readers will not take you seriously and, consequently, will disregard whatever you have to say. Writers suffering from cuteness will also antagonize their readers. For example, let's assume you're assigned the topic "Which Person Has Done the Most to Arouse the Laboring Class in Twentieth-Century England?" and you begin your essay with a discussion of the man who invented the alarm clock. While that joke might be funny in an appropriate situation, it's not likely to impress your professor, who's looking for serious commentary. How much cuteness is too much is often a matter of taste, but if you have any doubts about the quality of your humor, leave it out. Also, omit personal messages or comic asides to your teacher (such as "Ha, ha, just kidding, teach!" or "I knew you'd love this part"). Humor is often effective, but remember that the point of any essay is to persuade an audience to accept your thesis, not merely to entertain. In other words, if you use humor, make sure it is appropriate and that it works to help you make your point.

Sentimentality

Sentimentality is the excessive show of cheap emotions—"cheap" because they are not deeply felt but evoked by clichés and stock tear-jerking situations. In the nineteenth century, for example, a typical melodrama played on the sentimentality of the audience by presenting a black-hatted, cold-hearted, mustache-twirling villain tying a golden-haired, pure-hearted "Little Nell" to the railroad tracks after driving her ancient, sickly mother out into a snowdrift. Today, politicians (among others) often appeal to our sentimentality by conjuring up vague images they feel will move us emotionally rather than rationally to take their side: "My friends," says Senator Stereotype, "this fine nation of ours was founded by men like myself, dedicated to the principles of family, flag, and freedom. Vote for me, and let's get back to those precious basics that make life in America so grand." Such gush is hardly convincing; good writers and speakers use logic and reason to persuade their audience. For example, don't allow yourself to become carried away with emotion as did this student: "My dog, Cuddles, is the sweetest, most precious little puppy in the world because she loves me for what I am and because she will always be my best friend." In addition to sending the reader into sugar shock, this passage fails to present any sound reasons why anyone should appreciate Cuddles. In other words, be sincere in your writing, but don't lose so much control of your emotions that you become mushy or maudlin.

Preachiness

Even if you are so convinced of the rightness of your position that a burning bush couldn't change your mind, try not to sound smug about it. No one likes to be lectured by someone perched atop the mountain of morality. Instead of preaching, adopt a tone that says, "I believe my position is correct, and I am glad to have this opportunity to explain why." Then give your reasons and meet objections in a positive but not holier-than-thou manner.

Pomposity

The "voice" of your essay should sound as natural as possible; don't strain to sound scholarly, scientific, or sophisticated. If you write "My summer sojourn through the western states of this grand country was immensely pleasurable" instead of "My vacation last summer in the Rockies was fun," you sound merely phony, not dignified and learned. Select only words you know and can use easily. Never write anything you wouldn't say in an ordinary conversation. (For more information on correcting pretentious writing, see pp. 61−62 and 91−93.)

To achieve the appropriate tone, be as sincere, forthright, and reasonable as you can. Let the tone of your essay establish a basis of mutual respect between you and your reader.

Connotation and Denotation

A word's *denotation* refers to its literal meaning, the meaning defined by the dictionary; a word's *connotation* refers to the emotional associations surrounding its meaning. For example, "home" and "residence" both may be defined as the place where one lives, but "home" carries connotations of warmth, security, and family that "residence" lacks. Similarly, "old" and "antique" have identical denotative meanings, but "antique" has the more positive connotation because it suggests something that also has value. Reporters and journalists do the same job, but the latter name somehow seems to indicate someone more sophisticated and professional. Because many words with similar denotative meanings do carry different connotations, good writers must be careful with their word choice. *Select only words whose connotations fit your purpose.* If, for example, you want to describe your grandmother in a positive way as someone who stands up for herself, you might refer to her as "assertive" or "feisty"; if you want to present her negatively, you might call her "aggressive" or "pushy."

In addition to selecting words with the appropriate connotations for your purpose, be careful to avoid offending your audience with particular connotations. For instance, if you were trying to persuade a group of politically conservative doctors to accept your stand on Medicare, you would not want to refer to your opposition as "right-wingers" or "reactionaries," extremist terms that have negative connotations. Remember, you want to inform and persuade your audience, not antagonize them.

You should also be alert to the use of words with emotionally charged connotations, especially in advertising and propaganda of various kinds. Car manufacturers, for example, often use names of swift, bold, or graceful animals (Jaguar,Cougar, Impala) to sway prospective buyers; cosmetic manufacturers in recent years have taken advantage of the trend toward lighter makeup by associating words such as "nature," "natural," "organic," and "healthy glow" with their products. Politicians, too, are heavy users of connotation; they often drop in emotionally positive, but practically meaningless, words and phrases such as "defender of the American Way" and "friend of the common man" to describe themselves, while describing their opponents with such negative, emotionally charged labels as "radical" and "elitist." Of course, intelligent readers, like intelligent voters and consumers, want more than emotion-laden words; they want facts and logical argument. Therefore, as a good writer, you should use connotation as only one of many persuasive devices to enhance your presentation of evidence; never depend solely on an emotional appeal to convince your audience that your position—or thesis—is correct.

Practicing What You've Learned

A. The underlined words below are used incorrectly; substitute the accurate word in each case.

1. The finances of the chicken ranch were in <u>fowl</u> shape.
2. The professor is famous for his <u>photogenic</u> memory.
3. <u>Its to</u> bad you don't like <u>they're</u> new Popsicle sculpture since <u>their</u> giving it to you for Christmas.

4. The only <u>affect</u> the team's loss had on our coach was to make him <u>lay</u> down on the sidelines and kick his feet.
5. "I am impressed by the <u>continuity</u> of his physical presence"—Howard Cosell
6. After Marvin Marvelous caught a large <u>amount</u> of touchdown passes last year, the coach <u>complemented</u> him by making an <u>illusion</u> to "Crazy Legs" Hirsch.
7. Lloyd had to <u>chose between</u> his own <u>principals</u>, the solution offered by the City <u>Counsel</u>, and the settlement proposed in the State <u>Capital</u>.
8. Seymour <u>is persistent on</u> wanting to take <u>coarses</u> in medicine, even though he can't stand the sight of white coats.
9. Sara June felt she deserved an "A" in math, <u>irregardless</u> of her score of 59 on the final examination.
10. Aunt Hattie was amazed at how <u>good</u> little Hortense could ice skate considering how <u>bad</u> she walks.

B. The sentences below contain words and phrases that interfere with the sincere, reasonable tone good writers try to create. Rewrite each sentence, replacing sarcasm, sentimentality, cuteness, invective, and pretentiousness with more appropriate language.

1. The last dying rays of day were quickly ebbing in the West as if to signal the noble feline creature to begin its lonely vigil.
2. Only a jerk would support the President's Mideast peace plan.
3. After giving the question prolonged and careful scrutiny, I must indeed admit that I would be neglectful of my duties as a good citizen of this great country were I to stand idly by, unprotesting, while the mad scientists at NASA spent my hard-earned funds on such a stupid program as attempting to land a person on, of all places, the moon.
4. I'm holding my breath until football season because, I mean, who can sleep thinking of the thrill of watching grown men out there bashing each other's brains out over a worthless piece of pigskin.
5. Alas, when I look at those teensie little white mice with their cute, itty-bitty red eyes, I can hardly stand to feed them to those big, bad alligators.
6. It might be well to remind her that tomorrow is the date on which she is to unencumber herself of her domicile.
7. Dirty, punk student-bums with no respect for the Red, White, and Blue should be taken out and shot.
8. I was desirous of acquiring knowledge about members of our lower income brackets, so I esconced my frail but not inconsiderably determined person at a local establishment offering patronage to indigents and other undesirables for nocturnal repose.

9. Any snake who criticizes my girl friend is obviously not aware of her ability to compose epistolary notices of an affectionate nature.
10. If the bill to legalize marijuana is passed, we can safely assume that the whole country will soon be going to pot (heh, heh!).

C. In each group of words listed below, identify the words with the most pleasing and most negative connotations.

1. discriminating/picky/choosy/finicky/hard-to-please
2. obese/fat/plump/pudgy/paunchy
3. politician/statesman/political leader/political hack
4. odor/fragrance/smell/stench/aroma
5. famous/notorious/well-known/infamous

D. Replace the underlined words in the sentences below with words arousing more positive feelings:

1. She was an <u>old maid</u>.
2. Textbook writers admit to having a few <u>bizarre</u> habits.
3. Carol was a <u>mediocre</u> student.
4. The mayor's <u>fanaticism</u> about the project impressed everyone.
5. Senator Foghorn was a man of strong <u>biases</u>.
6. His clothes made Mary think he was a <u>hick</u>.
7. The High Priest explained his tribe's <u>superstitions</u>.
8. Despite her twenty-three years, Charlotte had managed to stay <u>naive</u>.
9. Many of the Board members were amazed to see how Algernon <u>dominated</u> the meeting.
10. The fashion model was an <u>undernourished</u> woman with long, <u>skinny</u> legs and an expression of <u>arrogance</u>.

SELECTING THE BEST WORDS

In addition to selecting the correct word and appropriate tone, good writers also choose words that firmly implant their ideas in the minds of their readers. The best prose not only makes cogent points but also states these points memorably. To help you select the best words to express your ideas, the following is a list of do's and don't's covering the most common diction (word choice) problems in students' writing today:

Do Make Your Words as Precise as Possible. Always choose vigorous, active verbs and colorful, specific nouns and modifiers. "The big tree was hit by lightning," for example, is not as informative or interesting as "Lightning splintered the neighbors' thirty-foot oak." *Don't* use words whose meanings are unclear:

VAGUE VERBS

Unclear: She was *involved with* a sailor. [How?]
Clear: She was engaged to a sailor.

Unclear: Tom can *relate to* Mary. [In what way?]
Clear: Tom can discuss his family problems easily with Mary.

Unclear: He won't *deal with* his ex-wife. [In what ways?]
Clear: He refuses to speak to his ex-wife.

Unclear: Clyde *participated in* a major crime. [How?]
Clear: Clyde drove the getaway car in the bank holdup.

VAGUE NOUNS

Unclear: She causes *trouble* wherever she goes. [What kind?]
Clear: She causes car accidents wherever she goes.

Unclear: The burglar took several valuable *things* from our house.[2] [What items?]

Clear: The burglar took a color T.V., a stereo, and a microwave oven from our house.

Unclear: Sometimes I feel I've made a *mess* of my life. [How?]
Clear: Sometimes I feel I should have studied harder in college and become an engineer, as I had planned to do.

Unclear: My brother never found his *place in the world*. [In what ways?]
Clear: My brother never found a job he wanted to do, a city he wanted to live in, or a woman he wanted to marry.

VAGUE MODIFIERS

Unclear: His *bad* explanation left me *very* confused. [Why "bad"? How confused?]

Clear: His disorganized explanation left me too confused to begin the project.

Unclear: After hiking six miles, I was *pretty tired*. [How tired?]
Clear: After hiking six miles, I was exhausted.

Unclear: The boxer hit the punching bag *really* hard. [How hard?]
Clear: The boxer hit the punching bag so hard it split open.

---

[2]One specific piece of advice: banish the word "thing" from your writing. In nine out of ten cases, it is a lazy substitute for some other word. Unless you mean "an inanimate object," replace "thing" with the specific word it stands for.

Unclear: *Casablanca* is a *good* movie *with something for everyone.* [Why "good" and for everyone?]

Clear: *Casablanca* is a witty, sentimental movie that successfully combines an adventure story and a romance.

Do Make Your Word Choices as Fresh and Original as Possible. Instead of saying, "My hometown is very quiet," you might say, "My hometown's definition of an orgy is a light burning after midnight." In other words, if you can make your readers admire and remember your prose, you have a better chance of persuading them to accept your ideas.

Conversely, to avoid ho-hum prose, *don't* fill your sentences with clichés and platitudes—overworked phrases that cause your writing to sound lifeless and trite. Although we use clichés in everyday conversation, good writers avoid them in writing because (1) they are often vague or imprecise (just how pretty is "pretty as a picture"?), (2) they are used so frequently that they rob your prose style of personality and uniqueness ("it was raining cats and dogs"—does that phrase help your reader "see" the particular rainstorm you're trying to describe?).

Novice writers often include trite expressions because they do not recognize them as clichés; therefore, below is a partial list (there are literally thousands more) of phrases to avoid. Instead of using a cliché, try substituting an original phrase to describe what you see or feel. Never try to disguise a cliché by putting it in quotation marks—a baboon in dark glasses and a wig is still a baboon.

busy as a bee	hot as fire
cross that bridge when I come to it	cold as ice
happy as a lark	mad as a wet hen
jump to a conclusion	quick as a wink
blind as a bat	in a nutshell
squeal like a stuck pig	better late than never
got what he deserved	fate worse than death
to be left in the cold	few and far between
poor as a church mouse	true blue
acted like a rat	the Grim Reaper
painted the town red	in hot water
didn't sleep a wink	all hell broke loose
all work and no play	blessing in disguise
eat, drink, and be merry	needle in a haystack
sweat of one's brow	bed of roses
crack of dawn	soft as silk
a crying shame	hard as nails
white as a sheet	white as snow
depths of despair	almighty dollar
dead of night	naked truth
shadow of a doubt	blessed event
	clinging vine

hear a pin drop	budding genius
nip in the bud	first and foremost
hit below the belt	it stands to reason
found a silver lining	after all is said and done
smell a rat	to make a long story short

It would be impossible, of course, to memorize all the clichés and trite expressions in our language, but do check your prose for recognizably overworked phrases so that your words will not be predictable and, consequently, dull. If you aren't sure if a phrase is a cliché—but you've heard it used frequently—your prose will probably be stronger if you substitute an original phrase for the suspected one.

Don't Use Trendy Expressions or Slang in Your Essays. Slang generally consists of commonly used words made up by special groups to communicate among themselves. Slang has many origins, from sports to space travel; for example, surfing gave us the expression "to wipe out" (to fail), the military lent "snafu" (from the first letters of "situation normal—all fouled up"), the astronauts provided "A-OK" (all systems working).

While slang often gives our speech color and vigor, it is unacceptable in most writing assignments for several reasons. First, slang is often part of a private language understood only by members of a particular professional, social, or age group. Secondly, slang often presents a vague picture or one that changes meanings from person to person or from context to context. More than likely, each person has a unique definition for a particular slang expression, and while these definitions may overlap, they are not precisely the same. Consequently, your reader could interpret your words one way while you mean them in another, a dilemma that might result in total miscommunication. Too often beginning writers rely on vague, popular clichés ("His behavior really grossed me out") instead of thinking of specific words to express specific ideas. Moreover, slang becomes dated quickly, and almost nothing sounds worse than yesterday's "in" expressions. (In his movie *Annie Hall*, Woody Allen pointed out the silliness of some of our psychological slang; when he was told to "mellow out," he replied, "When I get mellow, I ripen and then I rot.") Try to write so that your prose will be as fresh and pleasing ten years from now as today. Don't allow slang to give your writing a flippant tone that detracts from a serious discussion. Therefore, to communicate clearly with your reader, avoid including slang in your essays. Putting slang in quotation marks isn't the solution—omit the slang and use precise words instead.

Do Select Simple, Direct Words Your Readers Can Easily Understand. *Don't* use pompous or pseudosophisticated language in place of plain speech. Wherever possible, avoid *jargon*—that is, words and phrases that are unnecessarily technical, pretentious, or abstract.

Technical jargon—terms specific to one area of study or specialization—should be omitted because it is often inaccessible to anyone outside a particular field. By now most of us are familiar with bureaucratese, journalese, and psychobabble, in addition to gobbledygook from business, politics, advertising, and education. If, for example, you worry that "a self-actualized person such as yourself cannot transcend either your hostile environment or your passive-aggressive behavior to make a commitment to a viable lifestyle and meaningful interpersonal relationships," then you are indulging in psychological or sociological jargon; if you "review existing mechanisms of consumer input, thruput, and output via the consumer communications channel module," you are speaking business jargon. While most professions do have their own terms, you should limit your use of specialized language to writing aimed solely at your professional colleagues; always try to avoid technical jargon in prose directed at a general audience.

Today the term "jargon" also refers to prose containing an abundance of abstract, pretentious, multisyllable words. The use of this kind of jargon often betrays a writer's attempt to sound sophisticated and intellectual; actually, it only confuses meaning and delays communication. Here, for instance, is an excerpt of incomprehensible jargon from a college president who obviously prefers twenty-five-cent words to simple, straightforward nickel ones: "We will divert the force of this fiscal stress into leverage energy and pry important budgetary considerations and control out of our fiscal and administrative procedures." Or look at the thirty-nine-word definition of "exit" written by an Occupational Safety and Health Administration bureaucrat: "That portion of a means of egress which is separated from all spaces of the building or structure by construction or equipment as required in this subpart to provide a protected way of travel to the exit discharge." Such language is not only pretentious and confusing but almost comic in its wordiness.

Jargon is so pervasive these days that even some English teachers are succumbing to its use. A group of high school teachers, for instance, was asked to indicate a preference for one of the following sentences:

> His expression of ideas that are in disagreement with those of others will often result in his rejection by them and his isolation from the life around him.

> If he expresses ideas that others disagree with, he will often be rejected by them and isolated from the life around him.

Surprisingly, only nineteen percent chose the more direct second sentence. The others saw the wordy, pompous first statement as "mature" and "educated," revealing that some teachers themselves may be both the victims and perpetrators of doublespeak.

To avoid such verbal litter in your own writing, always select the simplest, plainest, most precise words you know. In addition, try to use single active verbs ("He obviously *dislikes* cats" is stronger than "His *dislike* of cats *is* obvious") and avoid adding "-ize" and "-wise" to form verbs and adverbs (as in "finalize" or "health-wise"). Remember that good writing is clear and direct, never wordy, cloudy, or ostentatious. (For more hints on developing a clear style, see pp. 55–62.)

Do Call Things by Their Proper Names. *Don't* sugarcoat your terms by substituting euphemisms—words that sound nice or pretty applied to subjects some people find distasteful. For example, you've probably heard someone say, "she passed away" instead of "she died," or "he was under the influence of alcohol" instead of "he was drunk," or "she was a lady of the night" instead of "she was a prostitute." Often euphemisms are used to soften the names of jobs: "sanitary engineer" for garbage collector, "field representative" for salesperson, "information processor" for typist, and so forth.

Some euphemisms are dated and now seem plain silly; in Victorian times, for example, the word "leg" was considered unmentionable in polite company, so people spoke of "piano limbs" and asked for the "first joint" of a chicken rather than the drumstick. The phrases "white meat" and "dark meat" were euphemisms some people used to avoid asking for a piece of chicken breast or thigh.

Today, euphemisms still abound. Though our generation is perhaps more direct about sex and death, many current euphemisms gloss over unpleasant or unpopular business, military, and political practices. When he was president of Uganda, for example, Idi Amin called his feared and despised secret police "the State Research Unit"; our own Central Intelligence Agency once called its assassination teams "Health Alteration Committees" and was recently conducting brainwashing experiments under the cover of an organization known as the "Society for the Investigation of Human Ecology." Ex-president Richard Nixon was faulted by the Watergate investigators for speaking of withholding information as "containment" and of refusing to testify as "stonewalling." A recent Secretary of Health, Education, and Welfare once tried to camouflage cuts in social services by calling them "advance downward adjustments." In the same vein we learn that government programs no longer simply fail; they are "rendered inoperative." And in some jails a difficult prisoner, who once would have been sent to solitary confinement, is now placed in the "meditation room" or in the "adjustment center." The military, too, has added its share of euphemisms to the language; these range from the comic transformation of the lowly shovel into a "combat emplacement evacuator" to the deadly serious use of the words "liberation" and "pacification" to mean the invasion and destruction of other countries.

Because euphemisms can be used unscrupulously to manipulate people by sugarcoating the truth, you should always avoid them in your own prose and be suspicious of them in the writing of others. As Aldous Huxley, author of *Brave New World*, noted, "An education for freedom is, among other things, an education in the proper uses of language."

In addition to weakening the credibility of one's ideas, euphemisms can make prose unnecessarily abstract, wordy, pretentious, or even silly. For a clear and natural prose style, use terms that are straightforward and simple. In other words, call a spade a spade, not "an implement for use in horticultural environments."

Do Enliven Your Writing with Figurative Language, When Appropriate.
Figurative language produces pictures or images in a reader's mind, often by
comparing something unfamiliar to something familiar. The two most common
figurative devices are the simile and the metaphor. A *simile* is a comparison
between two people, places, feelings, or things, using the word "like" or "as"; a
more forceful comparison, omitting the word "like" or "as," is a *metaphor*. Below
are two examples:

> Simile: George eats his meals like a hog.
> Metaphor: George is a hog at mealtime.

In both sentences George, whose eating habits are unfamiliar to the reader, is
likened to a hog, whose sloppy manners are generally well known. By comparing
George to a hog, the writer gives the reader a clear picture of George at the table.
Figurative language can not only help you present your ideas in clear, concrete,
economical ways, but can also make your prose more memorable—especially if
the image or picture you present is a fresh, arresting one. Below are some examples
of striking images designed to catch the reader's attention and to clarify the writer's
point:

- An hour away from her is like a month in the country.
- The atmosphere of the meeting room was as tense as a World Series game
  tied up in the ninth inning.
- If love makes the world go round, jealousy is the monkey wrench thrown
  into the gears.
- The banker looked at my loan application like an English teacher looks at a
  misspelled word.
- Dreams are the mind's rewriting of reality.
- The factory squatted on the bank of the river like a huge black toad.

Figurative language can spice up your prose; but like any spice, it can be
misused, thus spoiling your soup. Therefore, *don't* overuse figurative language;
not every point needs a metaphor or simile for clarity or emphasis. Too many
images are confusing. Moreover, *don't* use stale images. (Clichés—discussed on
pp. 90–91—are often tired metaphors or similes: snake in the grass, hot as fire,
quiet as a mouse, etc.) If you can't catch your readers' attention with a fresh
picture, don't bore them with a stale one.

And finally, don't mix images—this too often results in a confusing or
unintentionally comic scene. For example, a former mayor of Denver once
responded to a question about city fiscal requirements this way: "I think the proper
approach is to go through this Garden of Gethsemane that we're in now, give birth
to a budget that will come out of it, and then start putting our ducks in order with
an appeal and the backup we would need to get something done at the state level."
Or take ex-president Gerald Ford's description of the difficulties involved in
building his presidential library: "Two years ago, we were literally back on our own
goal line and we had a long row to hoe. Now we are on the doorstep of success."

Perhaps a newspaper columnist wins the prize for confusion with this triple-decker: "The Assemblymen also were miffed at their Senate counterparts because they have refused to bite the bullet that now seems to have grown to the size of a millstone to the Assemblymen whose necks are on the line."

In summary, use figurative language sparingly and consistently to present a vivid picture to your reader.

Do Vary Your Word Choice so That Your Prose Does Not Sound Wordy, Repetitious, or Monotonous. Consider the following sentence:

> According to child psychologists, depriving a child of artistic stimulation in the earliest stages of childhood can cause the child brain damage.

Reworded, the sentence below eliminates the tiresome, unnecessary repetition of the word "child":

> According to child psychologists, depriving infants of artistic stimulation can cause brain damage.

By omitting or changing repeated words, you can add variety and crispness to your prose. Of course, don't ever change your words or sentence structure to achieve variety at the expense of clarity or precision; at all times your goal is making your prose clear to your readers.

Do Remember That Wordiness Is a Major Problem for All Writers, Even the Professionals. State your thoughts directly and specifically in as few words as are necessary to communicate your meaning clearly. In addition to the advice given here on avoiding wordy, vague jargon, euphemisms, clichés, and so forth, you should review the sections on simplicity and conciseness in Chapter 5.

The most important key to effective word choice is *revision*. As you write your first draft, don't fret about selecting the best words to communicate your ideas; in later drafts one of your main tasks will be replacing the inaccurate or imprecise words with better ones (Dorothy Parker, famous for her witty essays, once lamented, "I can't write five words but that I change seven"). All good writers rewrite, so revise your prose to make each word count.

Practicing What You've Learned

A. Rewrite the sentences following, eliminating all the clichés, euphemisms, and mixed metaphors you find.

1. When my mother didn't return from the little girl's room, we were fit to be tied.

2. The icy tone in Sally's voice made Ted burn with anger.
3. Using tear gas, clubs, and attack dogs on the protestors, the police persuaded them to abandon their march.
4. The City Councilman was stewing in his juices when he learned that his son had been arrested for fooling around with the ballot box.
5. On election day, all of us over the ripe age of eighteen should exercise our most sacred democratic privilege.
6. After milking dry the goose that laid the golden eggs, Jack discovered he had cut off his nose to spite his face.
7. Although he once regarded her as sweet and innocent as a newborn babe, he realized then and there that she was a wolf in sheep's clothing.
8. Just as Harry thought his business was sinking for the third time, the bank loan came through to save the day.
9. The director of the funeral parlor showed us to the eternal sleep chamber where the loved one rested.
10. The general called for the liquidation of the civilian populace.

B. Rewrite the following sentences, replacing the jargon, slang, and vague language with clear, precise words and phrases.

1. Mabel's essay on the importance of the educational factor in securing employment affected us. I mean, we could really relate to it.
2. The objective inherent in the functioning of this committee is the establishment of a viable base from which it can consider the initially motivating factors of its conception.
3. An accumulation of material possessions is not sufficient insurance that an individual will experience mental tranquility.
4. Our local gladiators in shoulder pads again emerged victorious last night.
5. Another significant aspect we as a global community must instruct ourselves to consider is the dearth of edible foodstuffs.
6. The students were instructed to return to their pupil stations so that the teacher could hand back papers with corrective feedback.
7. My institute of higher learning announced today that its academic evaluation program had been "delayed and in all probability indefinitely postponed due to circumstances relating to financial insolvency."
8. To get your head together, try getting behind Ping-Pong as a consciousness-raising experience; it was a real trip for me.
9. The motivational tendencies of infants who continually insert digital extremities into oral cavities is as yet unexplained.
10. The utilization of abstract verbalization renders informational content inaccessible.

Assignment

A. Write two of the following paragraphs and then exchange them with a classmate. Translate the faulty prose into crisp, clear sentences.

- a paragraph of clichés, slang, and jargon on the importance of a college education
- a paragraph of clichés and jargon extolling the virtues of some product or process
- a paragraph of jargon and euphemisms by a politician explaining why he/she supports (or opposes) a leash law for dogs
- a paragraph of slang, clichés, and jargon advising your roommate on some problem in his/her social life
- a paragraph of clichés and jargon persuading your best friend to lend you ten dollars so you can perfect your new invention

Chapter

Revising Your Drafts

"There is no good writing, only rewriting"—James Thurber .

"When I say writing, O, believe me, it is rewriting that I have chiefly in mind"—Robert Louis Stevenson

The absolute necessity of rewriting cannot be overemphasized. All good writers rewrite large portions of their prose. The French novelist Colette, for instance, wrote everything over and over. In fact, she often spent an entire morning working on a single page. Hemingway, to cite another example, rewrote the ending to *A Farewell to Arms* thirty-nine times. While no one expects you to make thirty-nine drafts of each essay, the point is clear: revision is an essential part of good writing. It is part of your commitment to your reader. Therefore, plan to spend at least a third of your overall writing time revising and polishing your essay.

Try not to think of revision as an activity to do only when you've completed your essay and are preparing to turn it in. Revision is a process that occurs while you are writing and between rough drafts as well as at the end of your last rough draft. Here are some suggestions that may help you revise during each stage of your writing:

WRITING THE FIRST DRAFT

1. Once you have a focused topic, a working thesis, and perhaps an essay map or rough outline to guide you, begin your first draft. One of the most important points to remember now is that no part of your rough draft is sacred or permanent. No matter what you have written, you can always change it.

2. Always write on one side of your paper only, in case you want to cut and tape together portions of your first and/or subsequent drafts rather than recopying the entire essay over and over. Leave big margins on all sides of your rough drafts so you can add information or jot down minor corrections. If you are typing, double space for the same reason.

3. As you write, you may find yourself deciding to delete a sentence or an entire passage here and there. If so, mark a single "X" or line through the material; don't scratch it out completely—you might decide later you want to reinsert the material or use it elsewhere.

4. If you cannot think of a word you want, put down a word close to the one you want, circle it, and go on. Keep writing; don't agonize over every word. Similarly, put a check in the margin by sentences that don't quite hit the mark. The important point now is to keep going.

5. If you experience Writer's Block, read the suggestions on p. 102 of this chapter.

REVISING THE FIRST DRAFT

1. Two thousand years ago, the Roman author Horace advised a young writer, "Put all your manuscript away and keep it for nine years. You can always destroy what you have not published; there is no art to unsay what you have once let go of." Of course, you won't often have the time to follow this wise advice, but it is still a good idea, after you've written the first draft, to go away for several hours—overnight, if possible. All writers become tired, and if you push yourself too hard, the fatigue will show in your prose. You're also much more aware of the weak spots in your essay when you have had some distance from your prose than when it's still hot from the pen.

2. When you return to your draft, read it over for *purpose* and *organization* only. Trying to look at all the parts of your paper from word choice to mechanics will only overload and frustrate you. First, ask yourself if your essay has fulfilled the purpose of your assignment. For example, if you were asked to analyze a book's character, did you or did you merely summarize plot? If you were asked to address a particular audience, did you do so or did you begin writing to someone else (or to yourself)? Once you're satisfied with your commitment to your essay's purpose, look closely at your essay's organization. Is your thesis sufficiently narrowed and expressed in clear, specific terms? Do the major points in your body paragraphs support your thesis? Are your body paragraphs presented in a logical order with smooth transitions from one to the next? (If you discover that after you've written your rough draft, your body paragraphs do not support the thesis, don't despair. See if the thesis can be rewritten to fit the essay; you may have had a slightly different thesis in mind all along, or a better one may have evolved as you organized your thoughts in writing.) Last, does your essay begin and end appropriately and emphatically? If you are like most writers, you will almost certainly need to prepare a second draft to untangle some of the organizational snags.

REVISING THE SECOND DRAFT

Once you are happy with the organization of the paper, evaluate it in terms of *content* and *development*. Check the ideas and the evidence you've used to support your thesis; are your comments clear, logical, sincere, persuasive? Are your ideas developed in enough specific detail to convince the reader to accept each of your major points and, ultimately, your thesis? Remember that hazy development is frequently the major problem for beginning writers, so look closely to see if, first, you have provided enough information and, second, if that information has been expressed in enough detail. (See pages 41 to 44 for help with development.)

In your third draft or revision, work on adding details to those paragraphs that seem sparse or unconvincing; delete material that's off the subject or that's only padding.

REVISING THE THIRD DRAFT

Revision at this point should focus on *clarity, conciseness,* and *vividness*.

1. Read each sentence carefully. Is each one as clear and precise as possible? Are there any that run on for too long or any that contain misplaced words or phrases that might cause confusion? Are your words and their connotations accurate and appropriate?

2. Almost every writer has a wordiness problem. Scrutinize your writing for ways to cut excess words. Search out and destroy deadwood phrases, circumlocutions, "to be" and other space-wasting verb-and-noun combinations (review pp. 58–61 for some specific phrases to guard against). Combine choppy or repetitive sentences wherever possible. (To help you judge if you need to combine sentences, you might try this experiment. Select a body paragraph and count the number of words it contains. Then count the number of sentences; divide the number of words by the number of sentences to discover the average number of words per sentence. If your score is less than 15–18, you may need to combine some sentences.)

3. After pruning your essay to the essentials, work on making your writing as vivid and pleasing as possible. Replace bland or passive verbs with active, vigorous ones; change blah surface descriptions into more fascinating ones by adding specific details. Delete unnecessary jargon or "officialese," and substitute original, arresting words for clichés and predictable phrases. (Try to put yourself in the reader's place by thinking of the Johnny Carson show. Carson: "The lake was so beautiful today." Audience: "How beautiful was it?" Help the reader, your audience, see how "it" was by selecting the best words to describe it.)

THE FINAL TOUCHES

1. Review your essay for errors in spelling, grammar, and punctuation. If these are major problems for you, keep a list of the mistakes you make in each essay. Read your rough draft for one of these errors at a time: once for fragments,

once for comma splices, once for spelling errors, and so on. In addition, while you are looking for grammar and punctuation errors, you may find it helpful to read your essay one sentence at a time—starting at the *end* of the essay and working toward the beginning. This way you are less likely to begin thinking about the content of your essay and wander off the job of looking for errors in mechanics.

2. Go over the checklist below. Revise (yes, again!) any part of your essay that seems weak.

3. Try to type your final draft. Not only will your essay look better, but you will also be able to catch more errors yourself before you hand in the paper. Misspelled words and underdeveloped paragraphs, for example, are much more obvious to a writer once the essay is typed. Avoid typing paper that smears easily or that is too slick to mark with a ball-point pen—leave onion skin to onions.

4. Proofread your final draft at least twice, preferably several hours after you have typed it.

5. Make a copy of your final draft—or at least save your rough drafts—in case your essay is accidentally lost. If you are asked to rewrite parts of your essay, referring to the early drafts may suggest some worthwhile options.

A CHECKLIST FOR YOUR ESSAY

If you have written an effective essay, you should be able to answer "yes" to the following questions:

1. Do I feel I have something important to say to my reader?

2. Am I sincerely committed to communicating with my reader and not just with myself?

3. Have I considered my audience? (See Chapter 1.)

4. Do my title and lead-in attract the reader's attention and help set up my thesis? (See Chapter 4.)

5. Does my thesis statement assert one specific idea? (See Chapter 2.)

6. Does my thesis and/or essay map give the reader an indication of what points the essay will cover? (See Chapter 2.)

7. Do each of my body paragraphs contain a main point in the essay's argument, and is that point expressed in a clear topic sentence? (See Chapter 3.)

8. Does each body paragraph have unity, coherence, and adequate development? (See Chapter 3.)

9. Does each body paragraph have sufficient specific details to prove or explain my essay's main points? (See Chapter 3.)

10. Are all the paragraphs in my essay smoothly linked in an effective order? (See Chapter 3.)

11. Does my concluding paragraph provide a suitable ending for the essay? (See Chapter 4.)

12. Are all my sentences clear, precise, and emphatic? (See Chapter 5.)

13. Are my words accurate, necessary, and meaningful? (See Chapter 6.)

14. Is the grammar, punctuation, and spelling correct throughout my essay? (See Part Three.)

15. Have I revised and proofread my essay as extensively as possible?

SOME LAST ADVICE: HOW TO PLAY WITH YOUR MENTAL BLOCKS

Every writer, sooner or later, suffers from some form of Writer's Block, the inability to think of and/or organize ideas. Symptoms may include sweaty palms, pencil chewing, and a pronounced tendency to sit in corners and weep. While not every "cure" works for everyone, below are a few suggestions to help minimize your misery:

Try To Give Yourself as Much Time As Possible To Write Your Essay. Don't try to write the entire paper in one sitting. By doing so, you may place yourself under too much pressure. Writer's Block often accompanies the "up against the wall" feeling that strikes at two A.M. the morning your essay is due at nine. Rome wasn't constructed in a day, and neither are most good essays.

If Writer's Block Does Hit, Remember That It Is a Temporary Bogdown, Not a Permanent One. Other writers have had them—and survived to write again. Try leaving your papers and taking a walk outdoors or at least into another room. Think about your readers—what should they know or feel at this point in your essay? As you walk, try to complete the sentence "What I am trying to say is. . . ." Keep repeating this phrase and your responses aloud until you find the answer you want.

Since Most of You Have Had More Experience Talking than Writing, Try Verbalizing Your Ideas. Sometimes it's helpful to discuss your ideas with a friend or classmate. Their questions and comments (not to mention their sympathy for your temporary block) will often trigger the thoughts you need to begin writing again. Or you might want to talk into a tape recorder so you can hear what you want to say.

Sometimes While You're Blocked at One Point, a Bright Idea for Another Part of Your Essay Will Pop into Your Head. If possible, skip the section that's got you stuck and start working on the new part. (At least jot down the new idea somewhere so it won't be lost when you need it later.)

Here's The Single Most Important Piece of Advice To Remember: Relax. No one—not even the very best professional writer—produces perfect prose every time pen hits paper. If you're blocked, you may be trying too hard; if your expectations of your first draft are too high, you may not be able to write at all for fear of failure. You just might be holding yourself back by being a perfectionist at this point. You can always revise and polish your prose in another draft—the first important step is jotting down your ideas. Remember that once the first word or phrase appears on your blank page, a major battle has been won.

Practicing What You've Learned

Applying what you know about effective essay writing, identify the strengths and weaknesses of the following two student themes. Use the checklist on pp. 101–102 to help you evaluate parts of the essays. What changes would you recommend to improve the quality of these essays?

DORM LIFE

Dorm life is not at all what I had expected it to be. I had anticipated meeting friendly people, quiet hours for studying, eating decent food, and having wild parties on weekends. My dreams, I soon found out, were simply illusions, erroneous perceptions of reality.

My roommate, Kathy, and I live in Holland Hall on the third floor. The people on our dorm floor are about as unfriendly as they can possibly be. I wonder whether or not they're just shy and afraid or if they are simply snobs. Some girls, for example, ignore my roommate and me when we say "hello." Occasionally, they stare straight ahead and act like we aren't even there. Other girls respond, but it's as if they do it out of a sense of duty rather than being just friendly. The guys seem nice, but some are just as afraid or snobby as the girls.

I remember signing up for "quiet hours" when I put in my application for a dorm room last December. Unfortunately, I was assigned to a floor that doesn't have any quiet hours at all. I am a person who requires peace and quiet when studying or reading. The girls in all the rooms around us love to stay up until early in the morning and yell and turn up their stereos full blast. They turn their stereos on at about eight o'clock at night and turn them off early in the morning. There is always at least one girl who has a record playing at maximum volume. Now, I am very appreciative of music, but listening to "acid rock" until three in the morning isn't really my idea of what music is. The girls right across from us usually play Neil Diamond or Simon and Garfunkel and I enjoy that. On the other hand, though, the girls on either side of our room love to listen to Z. Z. Top or Bachman-Turner Overdrive into the wee hours of the morning. It is these girls who run up and down the hall, yell at each other, laugh obnoxiously, and try to attract attention. All this continuous racket makes it nearly impossible to study, read, or get any sleep. Kathy and I usually end up going to the library or student cafeteria to study. As far as sleep goes, it doesn't matter what time we go to bed, but rather it depends on how noisy it is, and how late the stereos are on. Sometimes the noise gets so loud and rambles on for so long that even when it stops, my ears are ringing and my stomach keeps churning. It is on nights like this that I never go to sleep. I wish the people here were a little more considerate of the people around them.

Parties, on weekends, are supposedly the most important part of dorm life. Parties provide the opportunity to meet others and have a good time. Holland Hall has had two parties that are even worth mentioning. One of them was a Fifties dance held in the courtyard approximately three weeks ago. Unfortunately, all the other dormitories, the fraternities, and the sororities heard about it, and by eight o'clock at night there were masses of people. It was so packed that it was hard to move around. The other party, much to my dismay, turned out to be a luau party. I do not really care for roast pig, and my stomach turned from the scent of it when I entered the room. Our floor never has parties. Everyone leaves their doors open, turns up the stereo, and yells back and forth. I suppose that there will be more dorm parties once everyone becomes adjusted to this life and begins to socialize.

Dorm food is what I anticipated it would be, terrible, and I was right, it is awful. Breakfast is probably the hardest meal to digest. The bacon and sausage are cold, slightly uncooked, and very greasy. Sometimes, it's as though I am eating pure grease. The eggs look and taste like nothing I ever had before. They look like plastic and they are never hot. I had eggs once and I vowed I would never have another one as long as I lived in Holland Hall. The most enjoyable part of breakfast is the orange juice. It's always cold and it seems to be fresh. No one can say dorm food is totally boring because the cooks break up the monotony of the same food by serving "mystery meat" at least once every two weeks. This puts a little excitement in the student's day because everyone cracks jokes and wonders just what's in this "mystery meat." I think a lot of students are afraid to ask, fearful of the answer, and simply make snide remarks and shovel it in.

All in all, I believe dorm life isn't too great, even though there are some good times. Even though I complain about dorm food, the people, the parties, and everything else, I am glad I am here. I am happy because I have learned a lot about other people, responsibilities, consideration, and I've even learned a lot about myself.

MAYBE YOU SHOULDN'T GO AWAY TO COLLEGE

Going away to college is not for everyone. There are good reasons why a student might choose to live at home and attend a local school. Money, finding stability while changes are occurring, and accepting responsibility are three to consider.

Money is likely to be most important. Not only is tuition more expensive, but extra money is needed for room and board. Whether room and board is a dorm or an apartment, the expense is great.

Most students never stop to consider that the money that could be saved from room and board may be better spent in future years on graduate school, which is likely to be more important in their careers.

Going to school is a time of many changes anyway, without adding the pressure of a new city or even a new state. Finding stability will be hard enough, without going from home to a dorm. Starting college could be an emotional time for some, and the security of their home and family might make everything easier.

When students decide to go away to school, sometimes because their friends are going away, or maybe because the school is their parents' alma mater, something that all need to decide is whether or not they can accept the responsibility of a completely new way of life.

Everyone feels as if they are ready for total independence when they decide to go away to college, but is breaking away when they are just beginning to set their futures a good idea?

Going away to school may be the right road for some, but those who feel that they are not ready might start looking to a future that is just around the corner.

Assignment

Select one of the preceding student essays and rewrite it, making any changes in organization, sentence construction, word choice, or anything else you feel is necessary. Feel free to elaborate on, eliminate, change, or add to the essay's content in order to improve paragraph development or the essay as a whole.

THE BASICS OF THE SHORT ESSAY: PART ONE SUMMARY

Here are eight fundamental rules to keep in mind while writing the rough drafts of your essay:

1. Be confident that you have something important and interesting to say.
2. Become determined to communicate effectively with your audience.
3. Be informative, reasonable, and enthusiastic about your subject.
4. Organize your essay logically and persuasively.
5. Compose sentences that are clear, lively, and emphatic.
6. Select accurate, specific, forceful words.
7. Revise your prose.
8. Revise your prose.

MODES AND STRATEGIES

Communication may be divided into four types (or "modes" as they are often called): exposition, argumentation, description, and narration. While each one will be explained in greater detail in this section of the text, the four modes may be defined briefly as follows:

exposition:	the writer intends to explain or inform
argumentation:	the writer intends to convince or persuade
description:	the writer intends to create in words a picture of a person, place, object, or feeling
narration:	the writer intends to tell a story or recount an event

While we commonly refer to exposition, argumentation, description, and narration as the basic types of prose, in reality it is difficult to find any one mode in a pure form. In fact, almost all essays are combinations of two or more modes; it would be virtually impossible, for instance, to write a story—narration—without including description, or to argue without also giving some information. Nevertheless, by determining a writer's *main* purpose, we can usually identify an essay or prose piece as primarily exposition, argumentation, description, or narration. In other words, an article may include a brief description of a new mousetrap, but if the writer's main intention is to explain how the trap works, then we may designate the essay as exposition. In almost all cases, the primary mode of any essay will be readily apparent to the reader.

In Part Two of this text, you will study each of the four modes in detail and learn some of the patterns of development, called *strategies,* that will enable you to write the kind of prose most frequently demanded in college and professional work. Mastering the most common prose patterns in their simplest forms now will help you successfully assess and organize any kind of complex writing assignment you may face in the future.

8

Exposition

Exposition refers to prose whose primary purpose is giving information. Some familiar examples of expository writing include encyclopedias, dictionaries, news magazines, and textbooks. In addition, much of your own college work may be classified as exposition: book reports, political analyses, lesson plans, laboratory and business reports, and most essay exams, to cite only a few of the possibilities.

But while all expository writing does present information, a good expository essay is more than a collection of facts, figures, and details. First, each essay should contain a thesis statement announcing the writer's purpose and position. Then the essay should be organized so that the body paragraphs explain and support that thesis. In an expository essay the writer says, in effect, here are the facts *as I see them*; therefore, the writer's main purpose is not only to inform the readers but also to convince them that this essay explains the subject matter in the clearest, most truthful way.

THE STRATEGIES OF EXPOSITION

There are a variety of ways to organize an expository essay, depending upon your purpose. The most common strategies, or patterns, of organization include development by *example, process analysis, comparison and contrast, definition, classification,* and *causal analysis.* However, an essay is rarely developed completely by a single strategy (an essay developed by comparison and contrast, for instance, may also contain examples; a classification essay may contain definitions, and so forth); therefore, as in the case of the four modes, we identify the kind of expository essay by its *primary* strategy of development. To help you understand every expository strategy thoroughly before going on to the next, each is presented here separately. Each discussion section follows a similar pattern, which includes the definition of the strategy, some familiar examples, tips on developing your essay, warnings about common problems, a list of essay topics, and two sample essays—one written by a student and the other by a professional writer.

STRATEGY ONE: DEVELOPMENT BY EXAMPLE

Perhaps you've heard a friend complain lately about a roommate. "Tina is an inconsiderate boor, impossible to live with," she cries. Your natural response might be to question your friend's rather broad accusation: "What makes her so terrible? What does she do that's so bad?" Your friend might then respond with specific examples of Tina's insensitivity: she never washes her dishes, she ties up the telephone for hours, and she plays her stereo until three every morning. By citing several examples, your friend clarifies and supports her general criticism of Tina, thus persuading you to accept her point of view.

Examples in an essay work precisely the same way as in the hypothetical story above: they *support, clarify, interest,* and *persuade.*

In your writing assignments, you might want to assert that dorm food is cruel and inhuman punishment, that recycling is a profitable hobby, or that the cost of housing is rising dramatically. But without some carefully chosen examples to show the truth of your statements, these remain unsupported generalities or mere opinions. Your task, then, is to provide enough specific examples to support your general statements, to make them both clear and convincing. Below is a statement offering the reader only hazy generalities:

> Our locally supported T.V. channel presents a variety of excellent educational shows. The shows are informative on lots of different subjects for both children and adults. The information they offer makes channel 19 well worth the public funds that support it.

Rewritten below, the same paragraph explains its point clearly through the use of specific examples:

> Our locally supported T.V. channel presents a variety of excellent educational shows. For example, young children can learn their alphabet and numbers from *Sesame Street*; imaginative older children can be encouraged to create by watching *Kids' Writes*, a show on which four hosts read and act out stories written and sent in by youngsters from eight to fourteen. Adults may enjoy learning about antiques and collectibles from a program called *The Collector*; each week the show features an in-depth look at buying, selling, trading, and displaying collectible items, from Depression glass to teddy bears or Shaker furniture. Those folks wishing to become handy around the home can use information on repairs from plumbing to wiring on *This Old House*, while the nonmusical can learn the difference between skat singing and arias on such programs as *Jazz!* and *Opera Today*. And the money-minded can profit from the tips dropped by stockbrokers who appear on *Wall Street Week*. The information offered makes these and other educational shows on channel 19 well worth the public funds that support the station.

Although the preceding example is based on real shows, you may also use personal experiences, hypothetical situations, anecdotes, parables, analogies, or any combination thereof, to explain or support the points in your essays.

You may also find that in some cases, one long, detailed example (called an *extended example*) is more useful than several brief examples. If you were writing a paragraph urging the traffic department to install a stop sign at a particularly dangerous corner, you probably should cite numerous examples of accidents there. On the other hand, if you were praising a certain kind of local architecture, you might select one representative house and discuss it in detail. In the paragraph below, for instance, the writer might have supported his main point by citing a number of cases in which lives had been saved by Citizens' Band radios; he chose instead to offer one detailed example, in the form of a personal experience:

Although some people think of a Citizens' Band radio as an expensive toy or merely a gadget to outwit the local highway patrol, a C.B. radio can be, and frequently is, a life-saving device. Last year, for example, I used my C.B. to summon help for my seriously ill grandfather, who might have died had the radio not been working. We had gone out into the country to see a rarely visited relative; late that night, coming back, we took the wrong ranch road and became completely lost. About that time, my grandfather began to gasp and complain of terrible pain in his left arm and chest. I quickly recognized the symptoms of a heart attack and sprang to my car's radio. Within moments I had raised several nearby ranchers, who figured out where we were from the description I gave of the landmarks around us. Help arrived shortly thereafter, and my grandfather was taken to the nearest hospital, where he recovered. Thanks to the C.B. radio, a tragedy was averted.

The story of the grandfather's rescue illustrates the writer's claim that C.B. radios can save lives; without such an example, the writer's statement would be only an unsupported generalization.

In addition to making general statements specific and thus more convincing, good examples can explain and clarify unfamiliar, abstract, or difficult concepts for the reader. For instance, Newton's law of gravity might be more easily understood once it is explained through the simple, familiar example of an apple falling from a tree.

Moreover, clear examples can add to your prose vivid details that hold the reader's attention while you explain your points. A general statement decrying child abuse, for instance, may not be as effective as a single extended example detailing the brutal treatment of one particular child.

The use of good example is not, however, limited only to essays primarily developed by example. In actuality, you will probably use examples in every essay you write. You couldn't, for instance, write an essay classifying kinds of T.V. comedy shows without including examples to help identify your categories. Similarly, you couldn't write essays defining the characteristics of a good teacher or a comparison between two kinds of cars without ample use of specific examples. To illustrate the importance of examples in all patterns of essay development, here are two excerpts from student essays reprinted in other parts of this text. The first excerpt comes from an essay classifying the Indian eras at Mesa Verde National Park. In his discussion of a particular time period, the writer uses a dwelling called Balcony House as an example to illustrate his claims about the Indians' new skills in building construction.

> The third period lasted until A.D. 1300 and saw the innovation of pueblos, or groups of dwellings, instead of single-family units. Nearly eight hundred dwellings show the large number of people who inhabited the complex, tunneled houses, shops, storage rooms, courtyards, and community centers whose masonry walls, often elaborately decorated, were three and four stories high. At the spacious Balcony House pueblo, for example, an adobe court lies beneath another vaulted roof; on three sides stand two-story houses with balconies that lead from one room to the next. In back of the court is a spring, and along the front side is a low wall that kept the children from falling down the seven-hundred-foot cliff to the canyon floor below. Balcony House also contains two *kivas*, circular subterranean ceremonial chambers that show the importance of fellowship and religion to the Indians of this era.

Another student presents a hypothetical example to help her argue for adoptees' rights to their birth records. By asking the reader to consider the case of a young man who needs medical assistance available only from blood relatives, she hopes to show a valid reason why birth records should be open.

> In addition to wanting to know about his heritage, an adoptee can have important medical reasons for knowing about his parents. Consider the hypothetical case of a young man who is in an accident or who develops a serious illness. He may need medical information, donor organs, blood transfusions or bone marrow transplants from biological relatives—whose names he cannot obtain in time to save himself. The adoptee's welfare is sacrificed because of the laws of confidentiality.

Learning to support, explain, or clarify your assertions by clear, thoughtful examples will help you develop virtually every piece of writing you are assigned, both in school and on the job. Development by example is the most widely used of all the expository strategies and by far the most important.

Developing Your Essay

An essay developed by example is one of the easiest to organize. In most cases, your first paragraph will present your thesis; each body paragraph will contain a topic sentence and as many effectively arranged examples as necessary to explain or support each major point; your last paragraph will conclude your essay in some appropriate way. Although the general organization is fairly simple, you should double-check the examples in your rough draft by asking these questions:

Are All My Examples Relevant? Each specific example should support, clarify, or explain the general statement it illustrates; each example should provide the reader with additional insight into the subject under discussion. Keep the purpose of your paragraphs in mind: don't wander off into an analysis of the causes of crime if you are only supposed to show examples of it in your neighborhood.

Are There Enough Examples To Make Each Point Clear and Persuasive? Put yourself in your reader's place: would you be convinced with three brief examples? Five? One extended example? Use your own judgment, but be careful to support or explain your major points adequately. It's better to risk overexplaining than to leave your reader confused or unconvinced.

Are My Examples Well Chosen? To convince your reader to accept your opinions, you must present persuasive examples that indicate an unbiased selection. For instance, your essay on the weakened state of marriage wouldn't be very convincing if, to support your thesis, you only used interviews with recently divorced people. Similarly, generalizations about the performance of a Democratic president wouldn't be as persuasive if you only gave the opinions of Republican senators. Nor would you convince a reader who hated cold weather that Minnesota is the ideal place to live by only describing its beautiful, temperate summers. In other words, to make your supporting examples persuasive, select from a good cross section that will suggest a fair and thorough survey.

Problems To Avoid

The Most Common Weakness in Essays Developed by Example Is a Lack of Specific Detail. Too often novice writers present a sufficient number of relevant, well-chosen examples, but the illustrations themselves are too general, vague, or brief to be helpful. Examples should be clear, specific, and adequately detailed so that the reader receives the full persuasive impact of each one. For instance, in an essay claiming that college football has become too violent, don't merely say: "Too many players got hurt last year." Such a statement only hints; it lacks enough development to be fully effective. Go into more detail by giving the readers examples of jammed fingers, wrenched backs, bruised legs, broken kneecaps, and busted dreams. Present these examples in specific, vivid language; once your readers begin to "see" that field covered with blood and broken bodies, you'll have less trouble convincing them that your point of view is accurate.

The Second Biggest Problem in Example Essays Is the Lack of Coherence. The reader should never sense an interruption in the flow of thought from one example to the next in paragraphs containing more than one example. Each body paragraph of this kind should be more than a topic sentence and a choppy list of examples. You should first arrange the examples in an order that best explains the major point presented by your topic sentence; then carefully check to make sure each example is smoothly connected in thought to the statements preceding and following it. You can avoid a listing effect by using transition devices where necessary to insure easy movement from example to example and from point to point. A few common transition words often found in essays of example include "for instance," "for example," "to illustrate," "in particular," and "in addition." (For a list of other transition words and additional help on writing coherent paragraphs, review pp. 32–37.)

Essay Topics

Use the statements below to lead you to your essay topic. Be sure to narrow these suggestions as you focus your thesis.

1. Success involves sacrifice.
2. Modern technology often produces more inconvenience than convenience.
3. Job hunting today is a difficult process.
4. Science fiction writers often accurately predict the future.
5. Movies today are/are not aimed at audiences who want entertainment, not thought.
6. The appeal of today's rock groups is theatrical, not musical.
7. My hometown was a terrible/wonderful place to grow up.
8. Many required courses are/are not relevant to a student's education.
9. My high school did/did not adequately prepare me for college.
10. Grades are/are not a fair way of determining progress in a course.
11. The most popular political attitude among students today is "I'm apathetic, and I don't care."
12. Fad diets can cause harmful results.

Sample Student Essay

Study the use of specific examples in the brief student essay that follows. See if you can identify the transition devices that help move the reader from point to point and from example to example.

RIVER RAFTING TEACHES WORTHWHILE LESSONS

Introduction: a description	Sun-warmed water slaps you in the face, the blazing sun beats down on your shoulders, and canyon walls speed by as you race down rolling waves of water. No
Thesis	experience can equal that of river rafting. Along with

being fun and exciting, rafting has many educational advantages as well, especially for those involved in school-sponsored rafting trips. River trips teach students how to prevent some of the environmental destruction that concerns the park officials and, in addition, river trips also teach students to work together in a way few other experiences can.

Essay map

Topic sentence one: trip teaches respect for environment

Two examples of respect:
1. cleaning up trash
2. forgoing suds in river

Topic sentence two: the trip teaches cooperation

Two examples of noncooperation:
1. difficulties in paddling raft
2. a near accident

The most important lesson a rafting trip teaches students is respect for the environment. When students are exposed to the outdoors, they can better learn to appreciate its beauty and feel the need to preserve it. For example, I went on a rafting trip three summers ago with the biology department at my high school. Our trip lasted seven days down the Green River through the isolated Desolation Canyon in Utah. After the first day of rafting, I found myself surrounded by steep canyon walls and saw virtually no evidence of human life. The starkly beautiful, unspoiled atmosphere soon became a major influence on us during the trip. By the second day I saw classmates, whom I had previously seen fill an entire room with candy wrappers and empty soda cans, voluntarily inspecting our campsite for trash. And when twenty-four high school students sacrifice washing their hair for the sake of a sudsless and thus healthier river, some new, better attitudes about the environment have definitely been established.

In addition to the respect for nature a rafting trip encourages, it also teaches the importance of group cooperation. Since school-associated trips put students in command of the raft, the students find that in order to stay in control each member must be reliable, able to do his or her own part, and alert to the actions of others. These skills are quickly learned when students see the consequences of noncooperation. Usually this occurs the first day, when the left side of the raft paddles in one direction, and the right the other way, and half the crew ends up seasick from going in circles. An even better illustration is another experience I had on my river trip. Because an upcoming rapid was usually not too rough, our instructor said a few of us could jump out and swim in it. Instead of deciding as a group who should go, though, five eager swimmers bailed out. This left me, an angry instructor, and another student to steer the raft. As it turned out, the rapid was fairly rough, and we soon found ourselves heading straight for a huge hole (a hole is formed from swirling funnel-like currents and can pull a raft under). The combined effort of the three of us was not enough to get the raft completely clear of the hole, and the raft tipped up vertically on its side, spilling us into the river. Luckily, no one was hurt, and the raft did not topple over, but the near loss of our food rations for the next five days, not to mention the raft itself, was enough to make us all more willing to work as a group in the future.

Conclusion: importance of lessons

Despite the obvious benefits rafting offers, the number of river permits issued to school groups continues to decline because of financial cutbacks. It is a shame that those in charge of these cutbacks do not realize that in addition to having fun and learning about themselves, students are learning valuable lessons through rafting trips—lessons that may help preserve the rivers for future rafters.

Professional Essay

Things: The Throw-Away Society

Alvin Toffler

Alvin Toffler is a well-known commentator, editor, and author. He has been a Washington correspondent for various newspapers and magazines, an associate editor of *Fortune*, a visiting university professor, and a consultant for numerous foundations and companies. He has edited three books and written four, including the popular *Future Shock* (1970), from which this selection is taken, and *The Third Wave* (1980).

"Barbie," a twelve-inch plastic teen-ager, is the best-known and best-selling 1 doll in history. Since its introduction in 1959, the Barbie doll population of the world has grown to 12,000,000—more than the human population of Los Angeles or London or Paris. Little girls adore Barbie because she is highly realistic and eminently dress-upable. Mattel, Inc., maker of Barbie, also sells a complete wardrobe for her, including clothes for ordinary daytime wear, clothes for formal party wear, clothes for swimming and skiing.

From *Future Shock* by Alvin Toffler. Copyright © 1970 by Alvin Toffler. Reprinted by permission of Random House, Inc.

Recently Mattel announced a new improved Barbie doll. The new version 2 has a slimmer figure, "real" eyelashes, and a twist-and-turn waist that makes her more humanoid than ever. Moreover, Mattel announced that, for the first time, any young lady wishing to purchase a new Barbie would receive a trade-in allowance for her old one.

What Mattel did not announce was that by trading in her old doll for a 3 technologically improved model, the little girl of today, citizen of tomorrow's super-industrial world, would learn a fundamental lesson about the new society: that man's relationships with *things* are increasingly temporary.

The ocean of man-made physical objects that surrounds us is set within a 4 larger ocean of natural objects. But increasingly, it is the technologically produced environment that matters for the individual. The texture of plastic or concrete, the iridescent glisten of an automobile under a streetlight, the staggering vision of a cityscape seen from the window of a jet—these are the intimate realities of his existence. Man-made things enter into and color his consciousness. Their number is expanding with explosive force, both absolutely and relative to the natural environment. This will be even more true in super-industrial society than it is today.

Anti-materialists tend to deride the importance of "things." Yet things are 5 highly significant, not merely because of their functional utility, but also because of their psychological impact. We develop relationships with things. Things affect our sense of continuity or discontinuity. They play a role in the structure of situations, and the foreshortening of our relationships with things accelerates the pace of life.

Moreover, our attitudes toward things reflect basic value judgments. Nothing 6 could be more dramatic than the difference between the new breed of little girls who cheerfully turn in their Barbies for the new improved model and those who, like their mothers and grandmothers before them, clutch lingeringly and lovingly to the same doll until it disintegrates from sheer age. In this difference lies the contrast between past and future, between societies based on permanence, and the new, fast-forming society based on transience.

That man-thing relationships are growing more and more temporary may be 7 illustrated by examining the culture surrounding the little girl who trades in her doll. This child soon learns that Barbie dolls are by no means the only physical objects that pass into and out of her young life at a rapid clip. Diapers, bibs, paper napkins, Kleenex, towels, non-returnable soda bottles—all are used up quickly in her home and ruthlessly eliminated. Corn muffins come in baking tins that are thrown away after one use. Spinach is encased in plastic sacks that can be dropped into a pan of boiling water for heating, and then thrown away. TV dinners are cooked and often served on throw-away trays. Her home is a large processing machine through which objects flow, entering and leaving, at a faster and faster rate of speed. From birth on, she is inextricably embedded in a throw-away culture.

The idea of using a product once or for a brief period and then replacing it 8 runs counter to the grain of societies or individuals steeped in a heritage of poverty. Not long ago Uriel Rone, a market researcher for the French advertising agency Publicis, told me: "The French housewife is not used to disposable products. She likes to keep things, even old things, rather than throw them away. We represented one company that wanted to introduce a kind of plastic throw-away curtain. We did a marketing study for them and found the resistance too strong." This resistance, however, is dying all over the developed world.

Thus a writer, Edward Maze, has pointed out that many Americans visiting 9 Sweden in the early 1950's were astounded by its cleanliness. "We were almost awed by the fact that there were no beer and soft drink bottles by the roadsides, as, much to our shame, there were in America. But by the 1960's, lo and behold, bottles were suddenly blooming along Swedish highways . . . What happened? Sweden had become a buy, use and throw-away society, following the American pattern." In Japan today throw-away tissues are so universal that cloth hand-kerchiefs are regarded as old fashioned, not to say unsanitary. In England for sixpence one may buy a "Dentamatic throw-away toothbrush" which comes already coated with toothpaste for its one-time use. And even in France, dispos-able cigarette lighters are commonplace. From cardboard milk containers to the rockets that power space vehicles, products created for short-term or one-time use are becoming more numerous and crucial to our way of life.

The recent introduction of paper and quasi-paper clothing carried the trend 10 toward disposability a step further. Fashionable boutiques and working-class clothing stores have sprouted whole departments devoted to gaily colored and imaginatively designed paper apparel. Fashion magazines display breathtakingly sumptuous gowns, coats, pajamas, even wedding dresses made of paper. The bride pictured in one of these wears a long white train of lacelike paper that, the caption writer notes, will make "great kitchen curtains" after the ceremony.

Paper clothes are particularly suitable for children. Writes one fashion expert: 11 "Little girls will soon be able to spill ice cream, draw pictures and make cutouts on their clothes while their mothers smile benignly at their creativity." And for adults who want to express their own creativity, there is even a "paint-yourself-dress" complete with brushes. Price: $2.00.

Price, of course, is a critical factor behind the paper explosion. Thus a 12 department store features simple A-line dresses made of what it calls "devil-may-care cellulose fiber and nylon." At $1.29 each, it is almost cheaper for the consumer to buy and discard a new one than to send an ordinary dress to the cleaners. Soon it will be. But more than economics is involved, for the extension of the throw-away culture has important psychological consequences.

We develop a throw-away mentality to match our throw-away products. This 13 mentality produces, among other things, a set of radically altered values with respect to property. But the spread of disposability through the society also implies decreased durations in man-thing relationships. Instead of being linked with a single object over a relatively long span of time, we are linked for brief periods with the succession of objects that supplant it.

Questions on Content, Style, and Structure

1. Toffler introduces his essay with a discussion of the popular Barbie doll. Why?
2. What, according to Toffler's essay, is different today about our attitude toward man-made things?
3. What is Toffler's attitude toward our throw-away culture? Is his attitude specifically stated somewhere in the essay, or is it implied?
4. Why are our relationships to "things" psychologically important? What, according to Toffler, happens to our sense of continuity and the pace of life in a throw-away society?
5. Toffler says our new attitudes toward things "reflect basic value judgments." How does he use contrasting examples in paragraph 6 to illustrate some people's belief that newer is always better?
6. What other examples does Toffler offer to illustrate our throw-away culture? Does he use enough persuasive examples?
7. What kinds of societies or individuals don't subscribe to a throw-away mentality? What country is offered as an example? Is this country entirely free of throw-away products?
8. How does Toffler support his claim that other countries, following in America's footsteps, have become throw-away societies?
9. In paragraphs 10 through 12 Toffler uses a number of examples developed with specific details to help the reader understand the concept of disposable paper clothing. Point out some of these useful details.
10. How does Toffler conclude his essay? Is his choice appropriate? Why/ why not?

Vocabulary[1]

eminently (1)	lingeringly (6)
iridescent (4)	transcience (6)
deride (5)	inextricably (7)
continuity (5)	embedded (7)
foreshortening (5)	supplant (13)

[1]Numbers in parentheses following vocabulary words refer to paragraphs in the essay.

STRATEGY TWO: DEVELOPMENT BY PROCESS ANALYSIS

Process analysis identifies and explains what steps must be taken to complete an operation or procedure. There are two kinds of process analysis essays: directional and informative.

A *directional process* tells the reader how to do or make something; in other words, it gives directions. You are more familiar with directional process than you might think; when you open a telephone book, for example, you see the pages in the front explaining how to make a long-distance call. When you tell friends how to find your house, you're asking them to follow a directional process. The most widely read books in American libraries fall into the how-to-do-it (or how-to-fix-it) category: how to wire a house, how to repair a car, how to play winning poker, how to become a millionaire overnight, and so forth. And almost every home contains at least one cookbook full of recipes providing step-by-step directions for preparing various dishes. (Even Part One of this text is, in detailed fashion, a directional process telling how to write a short essay, with steps beginning with the selection of a topic and concluding with advice on revision.)

An *informative process* tells the reader how something is or was made or done, or how something works. Informative process differs from directional process in that it is not designed primarily to tell people how to do it; instead, it describes the steps by which someone other than the reader does or makes something (or how something was made or done in the past). For example, an informative process essay might describe how a television show is produced, how scientists re-created DNA in the lab, how you chose your major in college, how the Huns sacked Rome, or how an engine propels a tank. In other words, this type of essay gives information on processes that are not intended to be—or cannot be—duplicated by the individual reader.

Developing Your Essay

Of all the expository essays, students usually agree that the process paper is the easiest to organize, mainly because it is presented in simple, chronological steps. To prepare a well-written process essay, however, you should remember the following advice:

Select an Appropriate Subject. First, make sure you know your subject thoroughly; one fuzzy step could wreck your entire process. Secondly, choose a process that is simple and short enough to describe in detail. In a 500–800-word essay, for instance, it's better to describe how to fold a paper boat for a child's toy than to try telling how to construct a life-size replica of Noah's Ark. On the other hand, don't choose a process so simpleminded, mundane, or mechanical that it insults your readers' intelligence. (Ten years ago at a major state university it was popular to assign a process essay on "How To Sharpen a Pencil"; with the assignment of such stirring, creative topics, it's a wonder that English department produced any majors at all that year.)

Describe Any Necessary Equipment and Define Special Terms. In some process essays, you will need to indicate what equipment, ingredients, or tools are required. Such information is often provided in a paragraph following the thesis, before the process itself is described; in other cases, explanation of proper equipment is presented as the need arises in each step of the process. As the writer, you must decide which method is best for your subject. The same is true for any terms that need defining. Don't lose your reader by using terms only you, the specialist, can comprehend. Always remember that you're trying to tell people about a process they don't understand.

State Your Steps in a Logical, Chronological Order. Obviously, if someone wanted to know how to bake bread, you wouldn't begin with "Put the prepared dough in the oven." Start at the beginning and carefully follow through, step by step, until the process is completed. Don't omit any steps or directions, no matter how seemingly insignificant. Without complete instructions, for example, the would-be baker might end up with a gob of dough rather than a loaf of bread— simply because the directions didn't say to preheat the oven.

Explain Each Step Clearly, Sufficiently, and Accurately. If you've ever tried to assemble a child's toy or a piece of furniture, you probably already know how frustrating—and infuriating—it is to work from vague, inadequate directions. Save your readers from tears and tantrums by describing each step in your process as clearly as possible. Use enough specific details to distinguish one step from another. As the readers finish each step, they should know how the subject matter is supposed to look, feel, smell, or taste, or sound at that stage of the process. You might also explain why each step is necessary ("Cutting back the young avocado stem is necessary to prevent a spindly plant." "Senator Snort then had to win over the chairman of the Arms Committee to be sure his bill would go to the Senate floor for a vote"). In some cases, especially in directional processes, it's helpful to give warnings ("When you begin tightrope walking, the condition of your shoes is critical; be careful the soles are not slick") or descriptions of errors and how to rectify them ("If you pass a white church, you've gone a block too far; turn right at the church and circle back on Candle Lane." "If the sauce appears gray and thick, add one teaspoon more of cornstarch until the gravy is white and bubbly").

Organize Your Steps Effectively. If you have a few big steps in your process, you probably will devote a paragraph to each one. On the other hand, if you have several small steps, you should organize them into a few manageable units. For example, in an essay on "How to Prepare Fresh Fish" the list of small steps on the left has been grouped into three larger units, each of which becomes a body paragraph:

1. scaling	I. Cleaning
2. beheading	A. scaling
3. gutting	B. beheading
4. washing	C. gutting
5. seasoning	II. Cooking
6. breading	A. washing
7. frying	B. seasoning
8. draining	C. breading
9. portioning	D. frying
10. garnishing	III. Serving
	A. draining
	B. portioning
	C. garnishing

In addition, don't forget to use enough transition devices between steps to avoid the effect of a mechanical list. Some frequently used linking words in process essays include the following:

next	first, second, third, etc.
then	at this point
now	following
to begin	when
finally	at last
before	afterward

Vary your transition words sufficiently so that your steps are not linked by a monotonous repetition of "and then" or "next."

Problems To Avoid

Don't Forget To Include a Thesis. You already know, of course, that every essay needs a thesis, but the advice bears repeating here because for some reason some writers often omit the statement in their process essays. Your thesis might be (a) your reason for presenting this process—why you feel it's important or necessary for the readers to know ("Because rescue squads often arrive too late, every adult should know how to give artificial respiration to accident victims") or (b) an assertion about the nature of the process itself ("Needlepoint is a simple, restful, fun hobby for both men and women"). Here are some other subjects and sample theses:

- Donating blood is not the painful process one might suspect.

- The discovery of radium was the result of much trial and error in the laboratory of Madame Curie.
- Learning to pitch horseshoes is harder than it looks.
- Every driver should know how to change a tire in case a blowout occurs late at night or away from civilization.
- The American Revolution began following a series of unfair British laws.

Presenting a thesis and referring to it in each step gives your essay unity and coherence, as well as insuring against a monotonous list of steps.

Pay Special Attention to Your Conclusion. Don't allow your essay to grind to an abrupt halt after the final step. You might conclude the essay by telling the significance of the completed process or by explaining other uses it may have. Or, if it is appropriate, finish your essay with an amusing story or comment. However you conclude, leave the reader with a feeling of satisfaction, with a sense of having completed an interesting procedure. (For more information on writing good conclusions, see pp. 52—54.)

Essay Topics

Below are suggested topics for both directional and informative process essays. Some of the topics may also be used in humorous essays such as "How To Flunk a Test," "How To Remain a Bench Warmer," or "How To Say Nothing in Eight Hundred Words."

1. how to stop smoking (or break some other habit)
2. how to select a college course or major
3. how to begin a collection or hobby
4. how a historical event occurred (such as how eighteen-year-olds won the vote or how the Japanese succeeded in a sneak attack on Pearl Harbor)
5. how to develop a photograph
6. how to cure a cold or hangover
7. how to lose or gain weight
8. how you arrived at a major decision
9. how to select a car (new or used), house, apartment, roommate
10. how to vacation on five dollars a day
11. how a famous invention occurred
12. how to get rid of roaches or other pests (human or otherwise)
13. how to succeed or fail in a job interview
14. how to repair some small item
15. how to plan the perfect party, wedding, funeral, birthday, etc.

Sample Student Essay

The essay below is a directional process telling the reader how to rent, plant, and cultivate a successful campus vegetable garden. To make the instructions easier to follow, the writer uses many specific details and sufficient transition devices.

GROWING A CAMPUS GARDEN

Introduction: establishing the writer's authority

For a vegetarian like myself, growing a garden is a money-saving treat. At home I'd always had a garden, but when I came to the University I thought I was doomed to canned peas for four years. By accident, however, I learned that any student can rent a garden plot from the University, and soon I was enjoying fresh vegetables again. For those of you who also wish to

Thesis

savor fresh vegetables, cultivating a campus garden is hard work but well worth the effort.

Step one: obtaining the plot

The easiest part of campus gardening is obtaining the plot. All you do is watch the campus newspaper during registration week; a notice will appear in the "Agriculture News" column announcing the availability and location of campus plots. Before you are issued your plot, however, you must pay a six-dollar fee to the Campus Finances Office, which then re-

A note on equipment

serves a space in your name. Don't worry about tools and fertilizer; they are provided by the University at the garden site.

Step two: preparing the plot

Once you arrive at the plot, you will discover that there's more to do than just putting seeds in the ground and watering. You must first till the ground—that is, you break up the soil with a hoe or shovel—to a depth of about four inches. Tilling is punishing work: your back aches and your hands blister. Still, you have that wonderful feeling of tearing something up. Next, rake out the rocks. You may feel at this point that no matter how many times you rake, you have exactly as many stones to contend with as the first time—but don't give up! After tilling and raking the soil, your next step is to sprinkle fertilizer around the plot according to the directions on the bottle or sack. (Each brand of fertil-

A warning

izer has its own directions; follow them closely, because too much fertilizer can burn your plants' roots.) By this time you may be wondering if being a farmer is really for you, but you are almost finished preparing the soil. The last step before planting the seeds is to plow the plot with the hand plow available at the plot site. To plow correctly, you should struggle through the soil making straight rows about two feet apart. This is all the work you want to do the first day unless you are exceptionally ambitious.

Step three: buying the seeds

Meanwhile, before your next visit to the plot, you need to buy seeds at any garden center or hardware store. If you are planting in the spring, you will probably want to cultivate green beans, tomatoes, squash, okra, cucumbers, and mustard greens. In the fall, the following vegetables are grown: mustard greens, broccoli, turnip greens, carrots, green beans, and potatoes. If you are growing tomatoes or green onions, buy these

Special considerations

as small plants, because their growing season is longer. Don't even consider asparagus because it takes two years to grow.

Step four: planting the seeds

When you are ready to plant, you must do more than scatter the seeds in the dirt. Be careful to plant the seeds at least half an inch in the ground so that when you water them they won't slide down into the ditches.

Additional warnings

Also, if you are planting squash, give them about five feet of growing space on all sides. Because I planted tomatoes and green beans too close to a squash plant in my garden, the squash is blocking their sun.

Step five: weeding the garden

After about a week, seedlings will begin to sprout, but so will many weeds. For a first-time gardener, it is probably best to ignore the weeds until you can easily distinguish vegetable plants from them. Weeding is important, because the weeds rob the nutrients needed for the other plants. Be sure to tear out each weed by its roots, so it won't grow back again. After this initial weeding, a weekly weeding is sufficient.

Step six: maintaining the garden

Now all you need to do is maintain the garden. This means watering it every day, weeding once a week, and fertilizing twice a month. In addition, you should follow the special instructions for any particular plant that are listed on the back of the seed packet; green beans, for example, require a string or wire above them to climb on. A circular fence around tomato plants will give them support and increase the number of tomatoes three times. If you have planted and cultivated your garden correctly, you should see vegetables appearing in about five weeks. After that,

| | each day becomes an adventure for the gardener, as you inspect your plot like a delighted child looking for Easter eggs. |

Conclusion:
additional advice,
ending on a
humorous note

But don't be too disappointed if your first garden isn't as successful as you wished; you can always try again with additional help from the many gardening books available at any library or bookstore. If you're really insecure about growing a garden, you can even take a University course, Agricultural Crops 201, for which you receive two credits for growing vegetables in a campus plot. But watch out: if the crops fail, so do you!

Professional Essay

To Bid the World Farewell

Jessica Mitford

Jessica Mitford has written many articles and books, including *Daughters and Rebels*, *The Trial of Doctor Spock*, and *Kind and Unusual Punishment*, a critical study of the American penal system. This essay is an excerpt from her best-selling book *The American Way of Death*.

Embalming is indeed a most extraordinary procedure, and one must wonder 1
at the docility of Americans who each year pay hundreds of millions of dollars for
its perpetuation, blissfully ignorant of what it is all about, what is done, how it is
done. Not one in ten thousand has any idea of what actually takes place. Books on
the subject are extremely hard to come by. They are not to be found in most
libraries or bookshops.

In an era when huge television audiences watch surgical operations in the 2
comfort of their living rooms, when, thanks to the animated cartoon, the geogra-
phy of the digestive system has become familiar territory even to the nursery school
set, in a land where the satisfaction of curiosity about almost all matters is a
national pastime, the secrecy surrounding embalming can, surely, hardly be
attributed to the inherent gruesomeness of the subject. Custom in this regard has
within this century suffered a complete reversal. In the early days of American
embalming, when it was performed in the home of the deceased, it was almost
mandatory for some relative to stay by the embalmer's side and witness the
procedure. Today, family members who might wish to be in attendance would
certainly be dissuaded by the funeral director. All others, except apprentices, are
excluded by law from the preparation room.

From *The American Way of Death*. Copyright © 1963, 1978 by Jessica Mitford. Reprinted by permission of Simon & Schuster, a division of Gulf & Western Corporation.

A close look at what does actually take place may explain in large measure the 3
undertaker's intractable reticence concerning a procedure that has become his
major *raison d'être*. Is it possible he fears that public information about embalming
might lead patrons to wonder if they really want this service? If the funeral men are
loath to discuss the subject outside the trade, the reader may, understandably, be
equally loath to go on reading at this point. For those who have the stomach for it,
let us part the formaldehyde curtain. . . .

The body is first laid out in the undertaker's morgue—or rather, Mr. Jones is 4
reposing in the preparation room—to be readied to bid the world farewell.

The preparation room in any of the better funeral establishments has the tiled 5
and sterile look of a surgery, and indeed the embalmer-restorative artist who does
his chores there is beginning to adopt the term "dermasurgeon" (appropriately
corrupted by some mortician-writers as "demisurgeon") to describe his calling. His
equipment, consisting of scalpels, scissors, augers, forceps, clamps, needles,
pumps, tubes, bowls and basins, is crudely imitative of the surgeon's as is his
technique, acquired in a nine- or twelve-month post-high-school course in an
embalming school. He is supplied by an advanced chemical industry with a
bewildering array of fluids, sprays, pastes, oils, powders, creams, to fix or soften
tissue, shrink or distend it as needed, dry it here, restore the moisture there. There
are cosmetics, waxes and paints to fill and cover features, even plaster of Paris to
replace entire limbs. There are ingenious aids to prop and stabilize the cadaver: a
Vari-Pose Head Rest, the Edwards Arm and Hand Positioner, the Repose Block (to
support the shoulders during the embalming), and the Throop Foot Positioner,
which resembles an old-fashioned stocks.

Mr. John H. Eckels, president of the Eckels College of Mortuary Science, 6
thus describes the first part of the embalming procedure: "In the hands of a skilled
practitioner, this work may be done in a comparatively short time and without
mutilating the body other than by slight incision—so slight that it scarcely would
cause serious inconvenience if made upon a living person. It is necessary to
remove the blood, and doing this not only helps in the disinfecting, but removes
the principal cause of disfigurements due to discoloration."

Another textbook discusses the all-important time element: "The earlier this 7
is done, the better, for every hour that elapses between death and embalming will
add to the problems and complications encountered. . . ." Just how soon should
one get going on the embalming? The author tells us, "On the basis of such scanty
information made available to this profession through its rudimentary and haphazard system of technical research, we must conclude that the best results are to
be obtained if the subject is embalmed before life is completely extinct—that is,
before cellular death has occurred. In the average case, this would mean within an
hour after somatic death." For those who feel that there is something a little
rudimentary, not to say haphazard, about this advice, a comforting thought is
offered by another writer. Speaking of fears entertained in early days of premature
burial, he points out, "One of the effects of embalming by chemical injection,
however, has been to dispel fears of live burial." How true; once the blood is
removed, chances of live burial are indeed remote.

To return to Mr. Jones, the blood is drained out through the veins and 8
replaced by embalming fluid pumped in through the arteries. As noted in *The
Principles and Practices of Embalming*, "every operator has a favorite injection and
drainage point—a fact which becomes a handicap only if he fails or refuses to
forsake his favorites when conditions demand it." Typical favorites are the carotid
artery, femoral artery, jugular vein, subclavian vein. There are various choices of
embalming fluid. If Flextone is used, it will produce a "mild flexible rigidity. The
skin retains a velvety softness, the tissues are rubbery and pliable. Ideal for women
and children." It may be blended with B. and G. Products Company's Lyf-Lyk
tint, which is guaranteed to reproduce "nature's own skin texture . . . the velvety
appearance of living tissue." Suntone comes in three separate tints: Suntan;
Special Cosmetic Tint, a pink shade "especially indicated for young female
subjects"; and Regular Cosmetic Tint, moderately pink.

About three to six gallons of a dyed and perfumed solution of formaldehyde, 9
glycerin, borax, phenol, alcohol and water is soon circulating through Mr. Jones,
whose mouth has been sewn together with a "needle directed upward between the
upper lid and gum and brought out through the left nostril," with the corners
raised slightly "for a more pleasant expression." If he should be bucktoothed, his
teeth are cleaned with Bon Ami and coated with colorless nail polish. His eyes,
meanwhile, are closed with flesh-tinted eye caps and eye cement.

The next step is to have at Mr. Jones with a thing called a trocar. This is a 10
long, hollow needle attached to a tube. It is jabbed into the abdomen, poked
around the entrails and chest cavity, the contents of which are pumped out and
replaced with "cavity fluid." This done, and the hole in the abdomen sewn up,
Mr. Jones's face is heavily creamed (to protect the skin from burns which may be
caused by leakage of the chemicals), and he is covered with a sheet and left
unmolested for a while. But not for long—there is more, much more, in store for
him. He has been embalmed, but not yet restored, and the best time to start the
restorative work is eight to ten hours after embalming, when the tissues have
become firm and dry.

The object of all this attention to the corpse, it must be remembered, is to 11
make it presentable for viewing in an attitude of healthy repose. "Our customs
require the presentation of our dead in the semblance of normality . . . unmarred
by the ravages of illness, disease or mutilation," says Mr. J. Sheridan Mayer in his
Restorative Art. This is rather a large order since few people die in the full bloom of
health, unravaged by illness and unmarked by some disfigurement. The funeral
industry is equal to the challenge: "In some cases the gruesome appearance of a
mutilated or disease-ridden subject may be quite discouraging. The task of restora-
tion may seem impossible and shake the confidence of the embalmer. This is the
time for intestinal fortitude and determination. Once the formative work is begun
and affected tissues are cleaned or removed, all doubts of success vanish. It is
surprising and gratifying to discover the results which may be obtained."

The embalmer, having allowed an appropriate interval to elapse, returns to 12
the attack, but now he brings into play the skill and equipment of sculptor and

cosmetician. Is a hand missing? Casting one in plaster of Paris is a simple matter. "For replacement purposes, only a cast of the back of the hand is necessary; this is within the ability of the average operator and is quite adequate." If a lip or two, a nose or an ear should be missing, the embalmer has at hand a variety of restorative waxes with which to model replacements. Pores and skin texture are simulated by stippling with a little brush, and over this cosmetics are laid on. Head off? Decapitation cases are rather routinely handled. Ragged edges are trimmed, and head joined to torso with a series of splints, wires and sutures. It is a good idea to have a little something at the neck—a scarf or high collar—when time for viewing comes. Swollen mouth? Cut out tissue as needed from inside the lips. If too much is removed, the surface contour can easily be restored by padding with cotton. Swollen necks and cheeks are reduced by removing tissue through vertical incisions made down each side of the neck. "When the deceased is casketed, the pillow will hide the suture incisions . . . as an extra precaution against leakage, the suture may be painted with liquid sealer."

The opposite condition is more likely to be present itself—that of emaciation.   13 His hypodermic syringe now loaded with massage cream, the embalmer seeks out and fills the hollowed and sunken areas by injection. In this procedure the backs of the hands and fingers and the under-chin area should not be neglected.

Positioning the lips is a problem that recurrently challenges the ingenuity of   14 the embalmer. Closed too tightly, they tend to give a stern, even disapproving expression. Ideally, embalmers feel, the lips should give the impression of being ever so slightly parted, the upper lip protruding slightly for a more youthful appearance. This takes some engineering, however, as the lips tend to drift apart. Lip drift can sometimes be remedied by pushing one or two straight pins through the inner margin of the lower lip and then inserting them between the two front teeth. If Mr. Jones happens to have no teeth, the pins can just as easily be anchored in his Armstrong Face Former and Denture Replacer. Another method to maintain lip closure is to dislocate the lower jaw, which is then held in its new position by a wire run through holes which have been drilled through the upper and lower jaws at the midline. As the French are fond of saying, *il faut souffrir pour être belle.*[2]

If Mr. Jones has died of jaundice, the embalming fluid will very likely turn   15 him green. Does this deter the embalmer? Not if he has intestinal fortitude. Masking pastes and cosmetics are heavily laid on, burial garments and casket interiors are color-correlated with particular care, and Jones is displayed beneath rose-colored lights. Friends will say, "How *well* he looks." Death by carbon monoxide, on the other hand, can be rather a good thing from the embalmer's viewpoint: "One advantage is the fact that this type of discoloration is an exaggerated form of a natural pink coloration." This is nice because the healthy glow is already present and needs but little attention.

---

[2]"One must suffer in order to be beautiful."

The patching and filling completed, Mr. Jones is now shaved, washed and 16
dressed. Cream-based cosmetic, available in pink, flesh, suntan, brunette and
blond, is applied to his hands and face, his hair is shampooed and combed (and, in
the case of Mrs. Jones, set), his hands manicured. For the horny-handed son of toil
special care must be taken; cream should be applied to remove ingrained grime,
and the nails cleaned. "If he were not in the habit of having them manicured in
life, trimming and shaping is advised for better appearance—never questioned by
kin."

Jones is now ready for casketing (this is the present participle of the verb "to 17
casket"). In this operation his right shoulder should be depressed slightly "to turn
the body a bit to the right and soften the appearance of lying flat on the back."
Positioning the hands is a matter of importance, and special rubber positioning
blocks may be used. The hands should be cupped slightly for a more lifelike,
relaxed appearance. Proper placement of the body requires a delicate sense of
balance. It should lie as high as possible in the casket, yet not so high that the lid,
when lowered, will hit the nose. On the other hand, we are cautioned, placing the
body too low "creates the impression that the body is in a box."

Jones is next wheeled into the appointed slumber room where a few last 18
touches may be added—his favorite pipe placed in his hand or, if he was a great
reader, a book propped into position. (In the case of little Master Jones a Teddy
bear may be clutched.) Here he will hold open house for a few days, visiting hours
10 A.M. to 9 P.M.

Questions on Content, Style, and Structure

1. By studying the first three paragraphs, summarize both Mitford's reason
   for explaining the embalming process and her attitude toward undertakers who wish to keep their patrons uninformed about this procedure.
2. Identify this process as either directional or informative.
3. Does this process flow smoothly from step to step? Identify the transition
   devices connecting the paragraphs.
4. Does Mitford use enough specific details to help you visualize each step
   as it occurs? Point out examples of details that create vivid descriptions by
   appealing to your sense of sight, smell, or touch.
5. How does the technique of using the hypothetical "Mr. Jones" make the
   explanation of the process more effective? Why didn't Mitford simply
   refer to "the corpse" or "a body" throughout her essay?
6. What is Mitford's general attitude toward this procedure? The overall
   tone of the essay? Study Mitford's choice of words and then identify the
   tone in each of the following passages:

   "The next step is to have at Mr. Jones with a thing called a
   trocar." (10)[3]

[3]Numbers in parentheses following questions and vocabulary terms refer to paragraphs
in the essay.

"The embalmer, having allowed an appropriate interval to elapse, returns to the attack. . . ." (12)

"Friends will say, 'How *well* he looks.'" (15)

"On the other hand, we are cautioned, placing the body too low 'creates the impression that the body is in a box.'" (17)

"Here he will hold open house for a few days, visiting hours 10 A.M. to 9 P.M. (18)

What other words and passages reveal Mitford's attitude and tone?

7. Why does Mitford repeatedly quote various undertakers and textbooks on the embalming and restorative process (" 'needle directed upward between the upper lip and gum and brought out through the left nostril'")? Why is the quote in paragraph 7 that begins, " 'On the basis of such scanty information made available to this profession through its rudimentary and haphazard system of technical research'" particularly effective in emphasizing Mitford's attitude toward the funeral industry?
8. What does Mitford gain by quoting euphemisms used by the funeral business, such as "dermasurgeon," "Repose Block," and "slumber room"? What are the connotations of the words "poked," "jabbed," and "left unmolested" in paragraph 10? What effect is Mitford trying to produce with the series of questions (such as "Head off?") in paragraph 12?
9. Evaluate Mitford's last sentence. Does it successfully sum up the author's attitude and conclude the essay?
10. By supplying information about the embalming process, did Mitford change your attitude toward this procedure or toward the funeral industry? Should we subject our dead to this process? Are there advantages Mitford fails to mention? How would you prepare an essay to defend your position?

Vocabulary

To understand this essay completely, you should know the meanings of the following words:

docility (1)
perpetuation (1)
inherent (2)
mandatory (2)
intractable (3)
reticence (3)
raison d'être (3)
ingenious (5)
cadaver (5)

somatic (7)
rudimentary (7)
dispel (7)
pliable (8)
semblance (11)
ravages (11)
stippling (12)
emaciation (13)

STRATEGY THREE: DEVELOPMENT BY COMPARISON AND CONTRAST

Every day you exercise the mental process of comparison and contrast. When you get up in the morning, for instance, you may compare two choices of clothing—a short-sleeved shirt versus a long-sleeved one—and then make your decision after hearing the weather forecast. Or you may compare and choose between Sugar-Coated Plastic Pops and Organic Mullet Kernels for breakfast, between the health advantages of walking to campus and the speed afforded by your car or bicycle. Once on campus, preparing to register, you may first compare both professors and courses; similarly, you probably compared the school you attend now to others before you made your choice. In short, you frequently use the process of comparison and contrast to come to a decision or make a judgment about two or more objects, persons, ideas, or feelings.

When you write a comparison and contrast essay, your judgment about the two elements[4] in question becomes your thesis statement; the body of the paper then shows why you arrived at that judgment. For example, if your thesis states that Mom's Kum-On-Back Hamburger Haven is preferable to McPhony's Mystery Burger Stand, your body paragraphs might compare the two restaurants in terms of food, service, and atmosphere, revealing the superiority of Mom's on all three counts.

Developing Your Essay

There are two principal patterns of organization for comparison and contrast essays. For most short papers you should choose one of the patterns and stick with it throughout the essay. Later, if you are assigned a long essay, you may want to mix the patterns for variety, but do so only if you can maintain clarity and logical organization.

Pattern One: Point by Point

This method of organization calls for body paragraphs that compare and contrast the two subjects first on point one, then on point two, then point three, and so on. Study the example outlined below:

Thesis: Mom's Hamburger Haven is a much better restaurant than McPhony's because of its superior food, service, and atmosphere.
Point 1: Food
          A. Mom's
          B. McPhony's

[4]It is, of course, possible to compare or contrast more than two elements. But until you feel confident about the organizational patterns for this kind of essay, you should probably stay with the simpler format.

Point 2: Service
      A. Mom's
      B. McPhony's
Point 3: Atmosphere
      A. Mom's
      B. McPhony's
Conclusion

If you select this pattern of organization, you must make a smooth transition from subject "A" to subject "B" in each discussion to avoid a choppy seesaw effect. Be consistent: present the same subject first in each discussion of a major point; above, for instance, Mom's is always introduced before McPhony's.

Pattern Two: The Block

This method of organization presents body paragraphs in which the writer first discusses subject "A" on points one, two, three, etc., then discusses subject "B" on the same points. The model below illustrates this block pattern:

Thesis: Mom's Hamburger Haven is a better restaurant than McPhony's because of its superior food, service and atmosphere.
    A. Mom's
       1. Food
       2. Service
       3. Atmosphere
    B. McPhony's
       1. Food
       2. Service
       3. Atmosphere
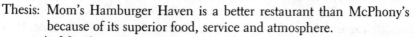
Conclusion

If you use the block pattern, you should discuss the three points—food, service, atmosphere—in the same order for each subject. In addition, you must include in your discussion of subject "B" specific references to the points you made earlier about subject "A" (see outline above). In other words, because your statements about Mom's superior food may be several pages away by the time your comments on McPhony's food appear, the readers may not remember precisely what you said. Gently, unobtrusively, remind them with a specific reference to the earlier discussion. For instance, you might begin your paragraph on McPhony's service like this: "Unlike the friendly, attentive help at Mom's, service at McPhony's features grouchy persons who wait on you as if they consider your presence an intrusion on their privacy." The discussion of atmosphere might begin, "McPhony's atmosphere is as cold, sterile, and plastic as its decor, in contrast to the warm, homey feeling that pervades Mom's." Without such connecting phrases, what should be one unified essay will look more like two distinct mini-essays, forcing readers to do the job of comparing and contrasting for you.

Problems To Avoid

The Single Most Serious Error in Comparison and Contrast Essays Is the Writer's Failure To Take a Clear Stand. Too often, the writer presents a noncommittal thesis such as "There are many similarities and differences between Mom's and McPhony's" or "Mom's and McPhony's have many advantages and disadvantages." To such vague theses, the reader can only respond, "So what?" There are a lot of similarities and differences (or advantages and disadvantages) between countless numbers of people, places, or things—but what's the point? To avoid the "so what" problem, take a side, choose a position, declare a judgment. Comparing or contrasting two subjects for no apparent reason is a worthless endeavor; tell the reader the purpose of your essay in as specific terms as possible. Instead of merely announcing, "There are many similarities in the styles of Ernest Hemingway and Stephen Crane," write, "The many similarities in style—syntax, diction, and irony—clearly suggest that Ernest Hemingway was greatly influenced by Stephen Crane." In other words, make a point in your thesis and then support it through comparison and contrast.

Avoid a Choppy Essay. Whether you organize your essay by the point-by-point method or the block pattern, you need to use enough transition devices to ensure a smooth flow from one subject to another and from one point to the next. Without transitions, your essay may assume the distracting movement of a Ping-Pong game, as you switch back and forth between discussions of your two subjects. Listed below are some appropriate words to link your points:

COMPARISON	CONTRAST
also	however
similarly	on the contrary
too	on the other hand
both	in contrast
like	although
not only . . . but also	unlike
have in common	though
share the same	instead of
in the same manner	but

(For a review of other transition devices, see pp. 34–37.)

Essay Topics

Following are some topics that may be compared and contrasted. Remember to narrow your subject, formulate a strong thesis, and follow one of the two organizational patterns discussed on pp. 132–133.

1. an expectation and its reality
2. a first impression and a later point of view
3. two views on a current controversial issue (campus, local, national, or international)
4. two conflicting theories you are studying in another college course
5. a memory of a person or place and a more recent encounter with that person or place
6. two books or a book and its movie
7. two jobs or employers
8. two places that are special for you
9. two T.V. shows of the same genre (cops and robbers, situation comedies, soap operas, variety shows)
10. an opinion you held before coming to college that has changed now that you are in college
11. two musical groups or an early and recent album by the same artist
12. two sports or athletes or pieces of sports equipment
13. the perfect parent/friend/roommate and the not-so-perfect parent/friend/roommate

Sample Student Essay

Note that this writer takes a definite stand—that local food co-ops are superior to chain stores—and then contrasts two local stores, Lane Grocer and the Fort Collins Co-op, to argue her thesis. She selected the point-by-point pattern to organize her essay, contrasting prices, atmosphere, and benefits to local producers. See if you can identify her transition devices as well as some of her uses of detail that make the essay more interesting and convincing.

BRINGING BACK THE JOY OF MARKET DAY

Now that the old family-run corner grocery is almost extinct, many people are banding together to form their own neighborhood stores as food cooperatives.

Thesis   Locally owned by their members, food co-ops such as the one here in Fort Collins are welcome alternatives to the impersonal chain-store markets such as Lane Grocer. In exchange for volunteering a few hours each

Essay map   month, co-op members share savings and a friendly experience while they shop; local producers gain loyal, local support from the members as well as better prices for their goods in return for providing the freshest, purest food possible.

Point one: prices   Perhaps the most crucial distinction between the two kinds of stores is that while supermarkets are set up

Examples of Lane
Grocer's prices
contrasted to

to generate profit for their corporations, co-ops are
nonprofit groups whose main purpose is to provide
their members and the community with good, inexpensive food and basic household needs. At first
glance, supermarkets such as Lane Grocer may appear
to be cheaper because they offer so many specials,
which they emphasize heavily through ads and in-
store promotions. These special deals, known as "loss-
leaders" in the retail industry, are more than made up
for by the extremely high markups on other products.
For example, around Thanksgiving Lane Grocer might
have a sale on flour and shortening and then set up the
displays with utmost care so that as customers reach
for the flour they will be drawn to colorful bottles of pie
spices, fancy jars of mincemeat, or maybe an inviting
bin of fresh-roasted holiday nuts, all of which may be
marked up 100% or more—way above what is being
lost on the flour and shortening.

The Fort Collins Co-op rarely bothers with such
pricing gimmicks; instead, it tries to have a consistent
markup—just enough to meet overhead expenses. The
flour at the co-op may cost an extra few cents, but that

examples of co-op
prices

same fancy spice bottle that costs over $1.00 from the
supermarket display can be refilled at the co-op for less
than 25¢. The nuts, considered by regular groceries as
a seasonal "gourmet" item, are sold at the co-op for
about two thirds the price. Great savings like these are
achieved by buying in bulk and having customers bag
their own groceries. Recycled containers are used as
much as possible, cutting down substantially on overhead. Buying in bulk may seem awkward at first, but
the extra time spent bagging and weighing their own
food results in welcome savings for co-op members.

Point two:
atmosphere

Once people have gotten accustomed to bringing
their own containers and taking part in the work at the
co-ops, they often find that it's actually more fun to

Description of Lane
Grocer's atmosphere
contrasted to
description of the co-
op's atmosphere

shop in the friendly, relaxed atmosphere of the co-ops.
At Lane Grocer, for example, I often find shopping a
battle of tangled metal carts wielded by bored customers who are frequently trying to manage one or more
cranky children. The long aisles harshly lit by rows of
cold fluorescent lights and the bland commercial
music don't make the chore of shopping any easier
either. On the other hand, the Fort Collins Co-op may

not be as expertly planned, but at least the chaos is carried on in a friendly way. Parents especially appreciate that they can safely let their children loose while they shop because in the small, open-spaced co-op even toddlers don't become lost as they do in the aisles of towering supermarket shelves. Moreover, most members are willing to look after the children of other members if necessary. And while they shop, members can choose to listen to the FM radio or simply to enjoy each other's company in relative quiet.

Point three: benefits to local producers

As well as benefitting member consumers, co-ops also help small local producers by providing a direct market for their goods. Large chain stores may require minimum wholesale quantities far beyond the capacity of an individual producer, and mass markets like Lane Grocer often feel they are "too big" to negotiate with small local producers.

No benefits at Lane Grocer contrasted to two benefits at the co-op

But because of their small, independent nature co-ops welcome the chance to buy direct from the grower or producer. Direct selling offers two advantages for producers: they get a better price for their wares than by selling them through a middleman, and at the same time they establish an independent reputation for their business, which can be immensely valuable to their success later on. In Fort Collins, for example, Soywaze tofu (bean curd) stands out as an excellent illustration of this kind of mutual support. Several years ago my friend Carol Jones began making tofu in small batches to sell to the co-op as a way to earn a part-time income as well as to contribute to the co-op. Her enterprise has now grown so well that last year her husband quit his job to go into business with her full time. She currently sells to distributors and independent stores from here to Denver; even Lane Grocer, who earlier would not consider selling her tofu even on a trial basis, is now thinking about changing its policy.

Conclusion: summarizing the advantages of co-ops over chain stores

Of course, not all co-ops are like the one here in Fort Collins, but that is one of their best features. Each one reflects the personalities of its members, unlike the supermarket chain stores that vary only slightly. Most importantly, though, while each has a distinctive character, co-ops share common goals of providing members with high-quality, low-cost food in a friendly, cooperative spirit.

Professional Essay

Prufrock[5] Before the Television Set

Michael J. Arlen

Michael J. Arlen is a television critic and staff writer for *The New Yorker* magazine. He won the Screen Directors' Guild for television criticism in 1968 and the National Book Award for contemporary affairs in 1976. Arlen is also the author of seven books, including *Living-Room War* (1969), *Passage to Ararat* (1975), and *The Camera Age* (1981). This selection was taken from one of Arlen's *New Yorker* columns.

A few days ago, while seated snugly in an airplane seat on my way back to **1** New York from Chicago, with a drink in front of me, and last week's copy of *Sports Illustrated* on my lap, and the soothing hum of the engines washing over my ears (and with the memory of the taxi ride and traffic jam and ticket-counter chaos already receding), it occurred to me that there was a rather striking similarity between what I was experiencing then, flying in a modern airliner, and what I've felt often happens as I watch television. To begin with, both are largely passive experiences; or, rather, they have been made into passive experiences. But this passivity is, itself, interesting and complicated, for not only does it involve obvious conditions of quietude and inaction, as well as the illusion of privacy; it also implies, and sometimes makes explicit, a quite formal undertaking of non-aggressive behavior on the part of the passenger or viewer. In fact, there is something to be said for the notion that much of the "pleasure" involved with riding in a commercial airliner, or in watching an evening's television schedule, has to do as much with this subjective state of non-aggression (in contrast with the aggressions of the "outside world") as it has with the supposedly greater and more evident pleasure of the trip or the actual programs.

Consider, for example, the airplane journey. In many ways, levels of ordi- **2** nary comfort for passengers have been, if anything, decreasing since the days of the old Pan American "Yankee Clipper." Even so, there is undoubted pleasure to be had in a routine jetliner trip of reasonable length (and admittedly one without crying babies or furious grandparents on one's lap). As an extreme example of this, I mention the experience of a friend who, being harried to exhaustion by a project in New York, determined suddenly to fly to California for a few days by the sea. As soon as he was airborne on the way out, he began to relax. Five hours later in California, however, as soon as he was on the ground, dealing with baggage and car rentals and freeways and finally his motel-by-the-sea, he began again to unravel. The same evening, he drove back to the airport, took a return flight to

[5]Prufrock is the protagonist of a well-known poem by T. S. Eliot, "The Love Song of J. Alfred Prufrock." In the poem Prufrock is presented as a passive man who wonders if he should take actions to control his life ("Do I dare/Disturb the universe?").

Reprinted by permission of Farrar, Straus and Giroux, Inc. "Prufrock Aloft; Prufrock Before the Television Set" from *The Camera Age* by Michael J. Arlen. Copyright © 1977, 1981 by Michael J. Arlen. This essay first appeared in *The New Yorker*.

New York, and, after five more hours of airplane massage, was in a suitable condition for resuming work.

People still talk of the romance of travel, and perhaps it is still romance for 3 fashionable visitors to Ethiopian ruins, or even for cruise-ship passengers. Indeed, travel was once an active and difficult undertaking, with the pleasure therein consisting in actively engaging in the difficulties and surmounting them—though even surmounting them wasn't always all that important. The important thing was to participate, to experience. But in much travel nowadays, it seems to me, the key element is non-participation. Not only is aggressive behavior discouraged or proscribed but non-aggressive behavior is formally encouraged as the norm. Thus, the pleasure of much of modern travel lies in the restful illusion that non-aggressive behavior is "being oneself."

On an airplane, for instance, the passenger lumpishly settles into his narrow 4 seat, usually dishevelled in mind or spirit from the hurly-burly of the outside world, sometimes still quivering from the hazards of actually getting to the airplane. The stewardess has already relieved him of his coat and briefcase, his downtown symbols. Sometimes, wifelike, she will have given him an initial, token reward for having reached her: a cup of coffee, a ginger ale, a Bloody Mary. Prufrock has arrived home. Prufrock need do nothing more, except buckle himself to his seat, and follow modest instructions "for his own safety," and act unaggressively. In fact, for doing so, he will be rewarded: by great speed and forward motion (i.e., by progress), by the benign smiles of the stewardess, by the loan of a magazine, by the outright gift of an airline magazine ("Yours to keep"), by drinks, by the hospitality of a meal, even by the appurtenances of an overnight guest—a pillow and blanket. A shower of benefits is rained upon the passenger by the authorities of the airplane (including periodic descriptions of the unseen ground being traversed, delivered over loudspeaker by the unseen captain), who ask in return only that the passenger do nothing, stay quiet, keep still. Bathroom privileges are given, but can easily be revoked. Primary addictive substances, such as cigarettes, are permitted more rapidly and easily than secondary substances, such as alcohol, which might cause disquiet or might "spill." When all the right conditions are met, modest walking about is allowed, but since there is usually no place to walk to, it is a privilege rarely accepted. Even when the seat-belt sign has been turned off, so the captain has announced, one would do well to keep buckled.

In short, passivity reigns in the modern airliner. And when aggression 5 reappears, it is sternly chastised. For example, after the plane has landed but before it has arrived at the gate, several passengers—doubtless summoned again to aggressive behavior by the imminence of the outside world—will leap to their feet and begin reaching for coats and bags like children who have been held too long in school. At this point, the formerly benign stewardess becomes severe and quickly reprimands the aggressive passengers. If these passengers do not abandon their aggressive behavior and return to the passivity of their seats, she says, they will be deprived of the one thing they still lack: further forward motion. Thereupon, the misbehaving passengers feign non-aggressive behavior until the second the plane has docked at the gate and they have been released from passivity. Immediately, aggression returns and now all the passengers push past each other down the airport corridors and once again start fighting over baggage, taxis, buses, or parking space.

The experience of watching most commercial television seems to involve a 6 similar voyage and a similar stylized passivity. Here, of course, the seat belts are figurative rather than actual, though I notice that there are a variety of "TV lounge chairs" now on the market, whose chief function seems to be safely to enclose the viewer during his nightly journey. Also, it is an interesting (if taste-numbing) coincidence that the TV dinner and the standard airline meal are made the same way, with the same technology and the same results. With television, the forward motion is through time, not space; but the effect is somewhat the same, since in the modern world final destinations rarely exist. The end of each day's program schedule, as with O'Hare Airport, is as much a beginning as a terminus.

Rewards for good behavior flow ceaselessly throughout the evening, accord- 7 ing to a set routine. In return for sitting still in front of his television set, the viewer is rewarded not only by the vague, general, forward-seeming flow of the entertainment but, more specifically, by periodic "messages" from the authority of the television station which promise him two levels of benefits. On the higher, symbolic level, there is the romantic promise of an upward alteration or enhancement of his life, by the acquisition of a new car, or a new deodorant, or a new kind of floor tile. This is deeply moving but it is remote, as is the promise of romance in travel. On a more immediate level, then, the viewer is rewarded by a trip to the bathroom or another bottle of beer from the refrigerator: these are stand-ins for the larger, dreamlike rewards.

Aggressive behavior is not actively prohibited, but it is discouraged. There are 8 almost no viewer phone-in programs, as on radio. Live audiences are few. Real audience participation is almost nonexistent, save for the inflated hysteria of a few game shows. Indeed, even some of the new game shows have become quite stylized and remote, with earnest, sedate couples trying to guess the authorship of "Hamlet" in the company of a lonely host and much electronic paraphernalia. On what are described as comedy or drama or adventure programs, there remains scarcely any nourishment of the viewer's active participation, in the form of emotionally involving stories. Thus, a middling detective series such as "Baretta" becomes oddly noticeable, as if it contained a certain gritty substance that somehow spoke to the still-awake part of the viewer's mind—that part persistently untouched by the noisiest bang-bang of cop-show revolvers or even by the sight of artillery explosions in foreign lands. In recent years, many news programs have taken steps toward greater informality and a semblance of involvement on the part of the newscasters. But the involvement of these newsmen has been mostly with each other. The audience continues voyaging, buckled into its Barcaloungers, attending no longer to the voice of a single, solemn captain but to the equally distant, cheery chitchat of two or three of them.

What is strange about this new passivity, regarding both travel and broadcast- 9 ing, is that not so long ago the reverse was considered normal. That is, flying was once a highly participatory activity—as was automobile driving, as was broadcasting. Thirty-five years ago, the driver of an ordinary car was intimately involved with the event of driving, by means of direct access to his steering wheel, brakes, transmission, and the outside environment. In the same period, a listener to Edward R. Murrow's broadcasts from London was directly involved with the event of broadcasting as well as the events of the Second World War that Murrow was describing. Since then, however, the automobile driver has given up his direct involvement in favor of power controls, automatic transmission, and sealed-in passenger interiors, while the television audience has largely given up its involvement with drama and news in favor of undemanding, mechanical entertainment and uninvolving news. Nowadays, only aggressive people insist on direct, or participatory, driving, by means of sports cars; at least, they are owned by people who are willing to appear aggressive. And only an aggressive minority, perhaps of a different cultural nature, appears to prefer participatory television, such as the music and serious drama programs that now and then are shown on public television.

The question remains: Have we somehow demanded this period of passivity 10 for ourselves (one in which we may, so to speak, draw a breath in order to reach the summit of this peculiar century), or has it been foisted upon us by the onrush of technical systems? Certainly it's true that technical systems assert a logic of their own, as well as clearly seeming to "prefer" a passivity on the part of their components, whether semiconductors or passengers or viewers. At the same time, if fear of flying evoked the seat belt and the stewardess, then fear of another kind has surely evoked our present uninvolving programs, news and entertainment both. Is it fear of communication, of "too much"? Or fear of ourselves? Are we the people meekly buckled in by seat belts or the people rushing pell-mell down the airport corridors and fighting over taxis? Or is there any difference?

At least, nowadays when one has something to think about one can usually 11 find the time and space for it, either by flying to Chicago or by turning on the television set.

Questions on Content, Style, and Structure

1. What is Arlen's thesis and where is it stated?
2. In his discussion of the airplane journey and television viewing, does Arlen primarily compare the two activities or contrast them? Does he use the point-by-point method or the block method to present his discussion?
3. How does Arlen use examples in paragraph 4 to illustrate his point that "passivity reigns in the modern airliner"? How does paragraph 5 also support this point?
4. How does Arlen smoothly make the transition from his discussion of airplane trips to television watching?
5. What are some of the similarities Arlen sees between airplane rides and television viewing?
6. Does Arlen provide enough points of comparison between his two subjects, and are all his examples persuasive? Select two or three of his examples and tell why you agree or disagree with Arlen's claims.
7. For what reason does Arlen criticize television in paragraph 8? What

supporting evidence does he provide? Do you agree with his assessment of television shows and news broadcasts? Why/why not?

8. In paragraph 9 Arlen contrasts air travel and television broadcasting to what subjects? What is his purpose in such a contrast?

9. Why does Arlen ask a series of questions in paragraph 10? Are they an appropriate way to lead into the conclusion of this essay? Does the concluding sentence effectively wrap up Arlen's essay?

10. Write a brief evaluation of Arlen's essay. Did he persuade you to accept his thesis? Why/why not? Which of his points were stronger or weaker than others, in your opinion?

Vocabulary

To understand this essay completely, you should know the meanings of the following words:

passivity (1)	chastised (5)
explicit (1)	imminence (5)
harried (2)	reprimands (5)
dishevelled (4)	feign (5)
benign (4)	semblance (8)
appurtenances (4)	foisted (10)

STRATEGY FOUR: DEVELOPMENT BY DEFINITION

Frequently in conversation we must stop to ask, "What do you mean by that?", because in some cases our failure to comprehend just one particular term may lead to total misunderstanding. Suppose, for example, in a discussion with a friend, you refer to a new law as a piece of "liberal legislation"; if you and your friend do not share the same definition of "liberal," your remark may be completely misinterpreted. Take another example: you tell your parents that the Police are the New Wave group of the decade; if they don't know what New Wave is, they miss the point entirely. In other words, definition of terms is often essential to meaningful communication.

Sometimes a dictionary definition or a one- or two-sentence explanation is all a term needs (Hemingway, for example, once defined courage as "grace under pressure").[6] Occasionally, however, you will find it necessary to provide an *extended definition*—that is, a longer, more detailed explanation that thoroughly defines the subject. Essays of extended definitions are quite common; think, for instance, of the articles you've seen lately on "mercy killing" that try to define death, or the arguments on abortion that define "life" in a variety of ways. Other recent essays have grappled with such complex concepts as the liberated woman/man, pornography, discrimination, and "reverse" discrimination. And the controversial verdict in the trial of John Hinckley, accused of the attempted assassina-

[6] Even graffiti employs definition. One bathroom wall favorite: "Death is Nature's way of telling you to slow down."

tion of President Ronald Reagan in 1981, produced many articles and editorials debating the meaning of criminal "insanity."

Essays of extended definition are usually written for one or more of the following reasons:

1. to provide an interpretation of a vague, controversial, or misunderstood term (such as "obscenity," "welfare," "political prisoner," "euthanasia")
2. to explain an abstract term or concept (such as "heroic," "success," "jealousy," "moral," "symbolism")
3. to define a new or unusual term, found in slang, dialect, or the jargon of a particular field of study or industry (such as "grody to the max," "objective correlative," or "floppy discs")

Developing Your Essay

Here are three suggestions to help you prepare your essay of extended definition:

Present a Thesis That Clearly Expresses <u>Your</u> Attitude Toward Your Subject. Your definition of "conservative," for example, may differ radically from that of newspaper columnist William Buckley, just as his probably differs from those of political activists Jane Fonda and Tom Hayden. One way to introduce your thesis is to explain the previous use, misuse, or misunderstanding of the term; then present your new or different interpretation of the term or concept. An introduction and thesis defining a slang word, for instance, might state: "Despite the visions of cornbread dressing and cranberries it conjures up for most Americans, the word 'turkey' does not always refer to the Thanksgiving bird. Today, 'turkey' is also a common slang expression designed primarily to tease or even insult someone." Or take this introduction and thesis aimed at a word the writer feels is unclear to many readers: "When the credits roll at the end of a movie, much of the audience may be perplexed to see the job of 'best boy' listed. No, the 'best boy' doesn't stand up with the groom at a wedding of children—he (or she) is, in fact, the key electrician's first assistant, who helps rig the lights for the movie's director of photography."

Keep Your Audience in Mind To Anticipate and Avoid Problems of Clarity. Because you are trying to present a new or improved definition, you must strive above all for clarity. You don't help your audience, for example, by defining one unfamiliar slang expression in terms of other bits of unfamiliar slang. If, in other words, you define "bummed out" as "turned off," you're probably confusing your audience more than you are informing them. If your assignment doesn't specify an audience, it may be useful to imagine a specific one. You might pretend you're defining a campus or slang expression to your parents, or that you're explaining an ambiguous term to a foreign visitor. After all, your definition is effective only if your explanation is clear not just to you but to those unfamiliar with the term or concept under discussion.

Use as Many Strategies as Necessary To Clarify Your Definition. Depending on your subject, you may use any number of the following methods in your essay to define your term:

1. give some synonyms
2. state some examples
3. compare and contrast to similar terms
4. explain an operation or process
5. present the history
6. describe the parts
7. define by negation (i.e., tell what the term doesn't mean)
8. discuss causes or effects

To illustrate some of the methods suggested above, let's suppose you wanted to write an extended definition of modern country music. You might choose one or more of these methods:

- describe the parts: music, lyrics, and typical subject matter
- compare or contrast to other kinds of music, such as bluegrass and western swing
- give some examples of famous country songs
- trace its historical development from traditional country music to its present state

In the paper on country music or in any definition essay, you should, of course, use only those methods that will best define your term. Never include methods purely for the sake of exhibiting a variety of techniques. You, the writer, must decide which method or methods work best, which should receive the most emphasis, and in which order the chosen methods of definition should appear.

Problems To Avoid

Here is a list of "don'ts" for the writer of extended definition essays:

Don't Present an Incomplete Definition. An inadequate definition is often the result of choosing a subject too broad or complex for your essay. You probably can't, for instance, do a good job of defining "twentieth-century painting" in all its varieties in a short essay; you might, however, acquaint your reader with some specific school of modern art, such as impressionism, cubism, expressionism, surrealism, or pop. Therefore, narrow your subject to a manageable size and then define it as thoroughly as possible.

Don't Introduce Your Essay with a Quote from Webster. In fact, try to avoid direct quotes from dictionaries or encyclopedias altogether. If you must include a standard definition of the term, put the dictionary's definition in your own words. Dictionary definitions are generally so dull and overused that they often drive composition teachers to seek more interesting jobs, such as measuring spaghetti in a pasta factory. Don't bore your audience to death; it's a terrible way to go.

Don't Define Vaguely or by Using Generalities. As always, use specific, vivid details to explain your subject. If, for example, you define a chair as "something with four legs," you have also described a dog, cat, horse, and cow, none of which are remotely akin to your subject. Consequently, you must select details that will make your subject distinct from any other. Including concrete samples is frequently useful in any essay but especially so when you are defining an abstract term such as "pride," "faith," or "prejudice." To make your definition both interesting and clear, always add as many precise details as possible. (For a review of using specific, colorful language, see pp. 57, 64–66, and 88–91.)

Don't Offer Circular Definitions. To identify a poet as "one who writes poetry" or the American Dream as "the dream most Americans hold dear" is about as helpful as a doctor telling a patient, "Your illness is primarily a lack of good health." Explain your subject; don't just rename it.

Essay Topics

Below are several suggestions for terms whose meanings are often unclear. Narrow any topic that seems too broad for your assignment. (Student writers, by the way, often note that abstract concepts are harder to define than the more concrete subjects, so proceed at your own risk and remember to use plenty of specific detail in your essay.)

1. any current slang, campus, or local expression
2. a term from your field of study
3. conceit or hypocrisy
4. success or failure
5. a good/bad teacher, class, coach, friend, parent, or date
6. heroism or cowardice
7. Army brat (or some other stereotype)
8. any kind of music, painting, architecture, or dance
9. feminists, the "New Right," or some other political group
10. any current fad or style
11. a rebel or conformist
12. power
13. a good/bad restaurant, store, restaurant attendant, or salesperson
14. nostalgia
15. sex appeal
16. a freshman

Sample Student Essay

A student studying to become a veterinarian wrote the following essay to illustrate her understanding of an important term in her field, equine encephalomyelitis. Note that she uses a variety of methods to explain the disease.

EQUINE ENCEPHALOMYELITIS: A POTENTIAL KILLER

Introduction: the importance of the term and a general definition (including origin of the term)

Because of its potential as an epidemic killer, equine encephalomyelitis, sleeping sickness in horses caused by a virus, must be understood by both veterinarians and horse owners. Carried by two types of mosquitoes, the *Culex tarsallis* and the *Culiseta melanura,* encephalomyelitis attacks the horse through the bloodstream, affecting the spinal column and the brain. The word "encephalomyelitis" comes from the Greek "encephalos" or brain, and the Greek word for marrow, since the disease attacks the core of the spinal column and inflames the brain.

Description of the types of the disease

Three types of encephalomyelitis have been pinpointed in the United States: two discovered in North America, the eastern in Kentucky and the western in Texas, and one South American strain discovered in Venezuela. The Venezuelan strain was first diagnosed in that country in 1936 but didn't appear in the U.S., in Texas, until 1971; especially virulent, it has a mortality rate of 80–90% and may attack humans. The other two types have caused the deaths of nearly a million horses in this country since 1930; eastern sleeping sickness has a mortality rate of more than 90%, while the western type isn't as bad—50% or less.

Effects of the disease

Once an animal has been infected, usually by mosquitoes, the disease follows a definite sequence: The virus travels through the bloodstream to the brain, where it attacks the cells; the brain's blood vessels are engorged with blood and the animal becomes very excitable; body temperature rises, and then lethargy sets in. The animal may wander aimlessly, crashing into things, and become increasingly sleepy, even resting its head on nearby objects. Grinding of teeth, inability to swallow, paralysis of the lips, blindness, and unconsciousness precede death. If affected animals don't recover—and the mortality rates cited above show that few do—death occurs in about four days.

Treatment of the diseased horse

Medically, treatment of a horse with the disease is nearly impossible, and the animal should be put to sleep to minimize suffering. There are steps to take to make the horse more comfortable, though, if treatment is attempted. It should be put into a dark place away from other animals and protected from excitement and noise. Cold packs should be placed on the skull, and a sedative should be given, along with easily swallowed, easily digested foods. With the nearly inevitable death comes the problem of disposal of the carcass; experts say it should be burned to avoid contamination of other animals and migratory birds.

Conclusion: how to avoid the disease

Horses of any age can be effectively protected from all three strains of this disease by proper annual vaccination with chick-embryo vaccines. For all areas, especially where blood-sucking insects are prevalent year round, it is best to vaccinate in late winter or very early spring. Since the insect larvae abound in marshy areas and stagnant waters, it is crucial when animals are raised in such areas to use screened stables and insect repellents, and pasture the horses in the daytime when such insects are less numerous. With such preventive measures, horse owners and veterinarians working together can halt the spread of one of the world's most serious equine diseases.

Professional Essay

Gobbledygook

Stuart Chase

Stuart Chase, a long-time consultant to various government agencies, has written many books, including *Democracy Under Pressure* and *The Tyranny of Words*. This essay is an excerpt from *Power of Words*.

Said Franklin Roosevelt, in one of his early presidential speeches: "I see one- 1 third of a nation ill-housed, ill-clad, ill-nourished." Translated into standard bureaucratic prose his statement would read:

It is evident that a substantial number of persons within the Continental boundaries of the United States have inadequate financial resources with which to purchase the products of agricultural communities and industrial establishments. It would appear that for a considerable segment of the population, possibly as much as 33.3333[7] percent of the total, there are inadequate housing facilities, and an equally significant proportion is deprived of the proper types of clothing and nutriment.

[7]Not carried beyond four places. [Chase's note]

From *Power of Words*, copyright © 1953, 1954, by Stuart Chase. Reprinted by permission of Harcourt Brace Jovanovich, Inc.

This rousing satire on gobbledygook—or talk among the bureaucrats—is 2
adapted from a report[8] prepared by the Federal Security Agency in an attempt to
break out of the verbal squirrel cage. "Gobbledygook" was coined by an exasperated Congressman, Maury Maverick of Texas, and means using two, or three, or
ten words in the place of one, or using a five-syllable word where a single syllable
would suffice. Maverick was censuring the forbidding prose of executive departments in Washington, but the term has now spread to windy and pretentious
language in general.

"Gobbledygook" itself is a good example of the way a language grows. There 3
was no word for the event before Maverick's invention; one had to say: "You know,
that terrible, involved, polysyllabic language those government people use down
in Washington." Now one word takes the place of a dozen.

A British member of Parliament, A. P. Herbert, also exasperated with 4
bureaucratic jargon, translated Nelson's[9] immortal phrase, "England expects
every man to do his duty":

England anticipates that, as regards the current emergency, personnel will
face up to the issues, and exercise appropriately the functions allocated to
their respective occupational groups.

A New Zealand official made the following report after surveying a plot of 5
ground for an athletic field:[10]

It is obvious from the difference in elevation with relation to the short depth of
the property that the contour is such as to preclude any reasonable development potential for active recreation.

Seems the plot was too steep.
An office manager sent this memo to his chief: 6

Verbal contact with Mr. Blank regarding the attached notification of promotion has elicited the attached representation intimating that he prefers to
decline the assignment.

---

[8]This and succeeding quotations from F.S.A. report by special permission of the
author, Milton Hall. [Chase's note]
[9]Horatio Nelson (1758–1805), English naval hero, victor over the French at
Trafalgar.
[10]This item and the next two are from the piece on gobbledygook by W. E. Farbstein,
New York Times, March 29, 1953. [Chase's note]

Seems Mr. Blank didn't want the job.

A doctor testified at an English trial that one of the parties was suffering from "circumorbital haematoma."

Seems the party had a black eye.

In August 1952 the U.S. Department of Agriculture put out a pamphlet entitled: "Cultural and Pathogenic Variability in Single-Condial and Hyphaltip Isolates of Hemlin-Thosporium Turcicum Pass."

Seems it was about corn leaf disease.

On reaching the top of the Finsteraarhorn in 1845, M. Dollfus-Ausset, when 7 he got his breath, exclaimed:

The soul communes in the infinite with those icy peaks which seem to have their roots in the bowels of eternity.

Seems he enjoyed the view.

A government department announced: 8

Voucherable expenditures necessary to provide adequate dental treatment required as adjunct to medical treatment being rendered a pay patient in in-patient status may be incurred as required at the expense of the Public Health Service.

Seems you can charge your dentist bill to the Public Health Service. Or can you? . . .

Reducing the Gobble

As government and business offices grow larger, the need for doing something 9 about gobbledygook increases. Fortunately, the biggest office in the world is working hard to reduce it. The Federal Security Agency in Washington,[11] with nearly 100 million clients on its books, began analyzing its communication lines some years ago, with gratifying results. Surveys find trouble in three main areas: correspondence with clients about their social security problems, office memos, official reports.

Clarity and brevity, as well as common humanity, are urgently needed in this 10

---

[11]Now the Department of Health, Education, and Welfare. [Chase's note]

vast establishment which deals with disability, old age, and unemployment. The surveys found instead many cases of long-windedness, foggy meanings, clichés, and singsong phrases, and gross neglect of the reader's point of view. Rather than talking to a real person, the writer was talking to himself. "We often write like a man walking on stilts."

Here is a typical case of long-windedness: 11

> *Gobbledygook as found:* "We are wondering if sufficient time has passed so that you are in a position to indicate whether favorable action may now be taken on our recommendation for the reclassification of Mrs. Blank, junior clerk-stenographer, CAF 2, to assistant clerk-stenographer, CAF 3?"
>
> *Suggested improvement:* "Have you yet been able to act on our recommendation to reclassify Mrs. Blank?"

Another case:

> Although the Central Efficiency Rating Committee recognizes that there are many desirable changes that could be made in the present efficiency rating system in order to make it more realistic and more workable than it now is, this committee is of the opinion that no further change should be made in the present system during the current year. Because of conditions prevailing throughout the country and the resultant turnover in personnel, and difficulty in administering the Federal programs, further mechanical improvement in the present rating system would require staff retraining and other administrative expense which would seem best withheld until the official termination of hostilities, and until restoration of regular operations.

The F.S.A. invites us to squeeze the gobbledygook out of this statement.   12 Here is my attempt:

> The Central Efficiency Rating Committee recognizes that desirable changes could be made in the present system. We believe, however, that no change should be attempted until the war is over.

This cuts the statement from 111 to 30 words, about one-quarter of the   13 original, but perhaps the reader can do still better. What of importance have I left out?

Sometimes in a book which I am reading for information—not for literary   14 pleasure—I run a pencil through the surplus words. Often I can cut a section to half its length with an improvement in clarity. Magazines like *The Reader's Digest* have reduced this process to an art. Are long-windedness and obscurity a cultural lag from the days when writing was reserved for priests and cloistered scholars? The more words and the deeper the mystery, the greater their prestige and the firmer the hold on their jobs. And the better the candidate's chance today to have his doctoral thesis accepted.

The F.S.A. surveys found that a great deal of writing was obscure although 15 not necessarily prolix. Here is a letter sent to more than 100,000 inquirers, a classic example of murky prose. To clarify it, one needs to *add* words, not cut them:

> In order to be fully insured, an individual must have earned $50 or more in covered employment for as many quarters of the coverage as half the calendar quarters elapsing between 1936 and the quarter in which he reaches age 65 or dies, whichever first occurs.

Probably no one without the technical jargon of the office could translate this; nevertheless, it was sent out to drive clients mad for seven years. One poor fellow wrote back: "I am no longer in covered employment. I have an outside job now."

Many words and phrases in officialese seem to come out automatically, as if 16 from lower centers of the brain. In this standardized prose people never *get jobs*, they "secure employment"; *before* and *after* become "prior to" and "subsequent to"; one does not *do*, one *"performs"*; nobody *knows* a thing, he is "fully cognizant"; one never *says*, he "indicates." A great favorite at present is "implement."

Some charming boners occur in this talking-in-one's-sleep. For instance: 17

> The problem of extending coverage to all employees, regardless of size, is not as simple as surface appearances indicate.

> Though the proportions of all males and females in ages 16–45 are essentially the same . . .

> Dairy cattle, usually and commonly embraced in dairying . . .

In its manual to employees, the F.S.A. suggests the following: 18

Instead of	*Use*
give consideration to	consider
make inquiry regarding	inquire
is of the opinion	believes
comes into conflict with	conflicts
information which is of a confidential nature	confidential information

Professional or office gobbledygook often arises from using the passive rather 19 than the active voice. Instead of looking you in the eye, as it were, and writing "This act requires . . ." the office worker looks out of the window and writes: "It is required by this statute that . . ." When the bureau chief says, "We expect Congress to cut your budget," the message is only too clear; but usually he says, "It is expected that the departmental budget estimates will be reduced by Congress."

> *Gobbled*: "All letters prepared for the signature of the Administrator will be single spaced."

Ungobbled: "Single space all letters for the Administrator." (Thus cutting 13 words to 7.)

Only People Can Read

The F.S.A. surveys pick up the point . . . that human communication 20 involves a listener as well as a speaker. Only people can read, though a lot of writing seems to be addressed to beings in outer space. To whom are you talking? The sender of the officialese message often forgets the chap on the other end of the line.

A woman with two small children wrote the F.S.A. asking what she should 21 do about payments, as her husband had lost his memory. "If he never gets able to work," she said, "and stays in an institution would I be able to draw any benefits? . . . I don't know how I am going to live and raise my children since he is disable to work. Please give me some information. . . ."

To this human appeal, she received a shattering blast of gobbledygook, 22 beginning, "State unemployment compensation laws do not provide any benefits for sick or disabled individuals . . . in order to qualify an individual must have a certain number of quarters of coverage . . ." et cetera, et cetera. Certainly if the writer had been thinking about the poor woman he would not have dragged in unessential material about old-age insurance. If he had pictured a mother without means to care for her children, he would have told her where she might get help—from the local office which handles aid to dependent children, for instance.

Gobbledygook of this kind would largely evaporate if we thought of our 23 messages as two way—in the above case, if we pictured ourselves talking on the doorstep of a shabby house to a woman with two children tugging at her skirts, who in her distress does not know which way to turn.

Results of the Survey

The F.S.A. survey showed that office documents could be cut 20 to 50 24 percent, with an improvement in clarity and a great saving to taxpayers in paper and payrolls.

A handbook was prepared and distributed to key officials.[12] They read it, 25 thought about it, and presently began calling section meetings to discuss gobbledygook. More booklets were ordered, and the local output of documents began to improve. A Correspondence Review Section was established as a kind of laboratory to test murky messages. A supervisor could send up samples for analysis and suggestions. The handbook is now used for training new members; and many employees keep it on their desks along with the dictionary. Outside the Bureau some 25,000 copies have been sold (at 20 cents each) to individuals, governments, business firms, all over the world. It is now used officially in the Veterans Administration and in the Department of Agriculture.

The handbook makes clear the enormous amount of gobbledygook which 26 automatically spreads in any large office, together with ways and means to keep it

[12]By Milton Hall. [Chase's note]

under control. I would guess that at least half of all the words circulating around the bureaus of the world are "irrelevant, incompetent, and immaterial"—to use a favorite legalism; or are just plain "unnecessary"—to ungobble it.

My favorite story of removing the gobble from gobbledygook concerns the 27 Bureau of Standards at Washington. I have told it before but perhaps the reader will forgive the repetition. A New York plumber wrote the Bureau that he had found hydrochloric acid fine for cleaning drains, and was it harmless? Washington replied: "The efficacy of hydrochloric acid is indisputable, but the chlorine residue is incompatible with metallic permanence."

The plumber wrote back that he was mighty glad the Bureau agreed with 28 him. The Bureau replied with a note of alarm: "We cannot assume responsibility for the production of toxic and noxious residues with hydrochloric acid, and suggest that you use an alternate procedure." The plumber was happy to learn that the Bureau still agreed with him.

Whereupon Washington exploded: "Don't use hydrochloric acid; it eats hell 29 out of the pipes!"

Questions on Content, Style, and Structure

1. As explained by Chase, what is gobbledygook? What are its main characteristics?
2. What is Chase's attitude toward gobbledygook?
3. Where did the term originate and why?
4. To define his term, Chase relies primarily upon what means of development? Cite evidence to support your answer. Does he successfully explain his definition?
5. What, according to the F.S.A. surveys, is one of the main reasons people produce gobbledygook? What should people think about before they write?
6. Does all gobbledygook come from government bureaucrats? What are some other common sources?
7. What are some of the specific ways Chase and the F.S.A. suggest to clear up murky prose?
8. In paragraph 2, Chase refers to the F.S.A.'s "attempt to break out of the verbal squirrel cage." What does this phrase mean? Is it effective?
9. How does the conclusion successfully summarize Chase's thesis?
10. Can you find or think of other examples of gobbledygook? Do you think that gobbledygook is under control—or is it spreading? What evidence can you cite to support your opinion?

Vocabulary

To understand this essay completely, you should know the meanings of the following words:

ill-clad (1)	exasperated (2)
satire (2)	censuring (2)

polysyllabic (3)   prolix (15)
jargon (4)   cognizant (16)
cloistered (14)   implement (16)

STRATEGY FIVE: DEVELOPMENT BY CLASSIFICATION

We classify knowledge to make it easier to comprehend. Without some sort of imposed system of order, a body of information would be only a jumble of facts and figures. For example, at some point you've probably turned to the classified ads in the newspaper; if the ads were not classified into categories such as "houses to rent," "cars for sale," and "help wanted," you would have to search through countless ads to find the service or item you needed. Classification, then, means approaching a subject by separating it into groups, types, or categories.

Classification occurs everywhere around you. As a student, you may be classified as a freshman, sophomore, junior, or senior; you may also be classified by your major. If you vote, you may be categorized as a Democrat, Republican, Socialist, or whatever; if you attend religious services, you may be classified as Baptist, Methodist, Catholic, Jewish, and so on. The car you drive may be classified as luxury, family size, compact, or economy; the movies you see have already been typed as "G," "GP," "R," or "X." Professionals classify almost every kind of knowledge: ornithologists classify birds; etymologists classify words by origins; botanists classify plants; zoologists classify animals, and so on. The list of classification examples is practically endless.

Developing Your Essay

A classification paper is generally easy to develop. Each class or category is identified and described in a major part of the body of the essay. Frequently, one body paragraph will be devoted to each category. Here are three additional rules for classification essays:

Select One Principle of Classification and Stick To It. If you are classifying students by major, for instance, don't suddenly switch to classification by college: French, economics, psychology, *arts and sciences*, math, and chemistry. A similar error occurs in this classification of dogs by breeds because it includes a physical characteristic: spaniels, terriers, *long-haired*, hounds, and retrievers. Decide on what basis of division you will classify your subject and then be consistent throughout your essay.

State the Purpose of Your Classification. Don't just announce, "There are three kinds of 'X.'" Instead, tell the readers why it's important they know about this classification or why this particular classification is meaningful. Here are some sample theses for classification essays:

By recognizing the three kinds of poisonous snakes in this area, campers and backpackers may be able to take the proper medical steps if they are bitten.

Knowing the four types of spinning reels will enable novice fishermen to purchase the equipment best suited to their needs.

While karate has become a popular form of exercise as well as of self-defense, few people actually know what the six levels of achievement—or "belts," as they are called—really stand for.

Don't just classify for the sake of classifying; organize your material for a particular reason and then explain to your reader what that reason is.

Account for All the Parts in Your Classification. Don't, for instance, claim to classify all the trees native to your hometown and then leave out one or more species. For a short essay, narrow your ruling principle rather than omit categories. You couldn't, for instance, classify all the architectural styles in America in a short paper, but you could discuss the *major* styles on your campus. In the same manner, the enormous task of classifying all types of mental illness could be narrowed to the most common forms of schizophrenia. However you narrow your topic, remember that in a formal classification, all the parts must be accounted for.

Like most rules, the one above has an exception. If your instructor permits, you can also write a satirical or humorous classification. In this sort of essay, you make up your own categories as well as your thesis. One writer, for example, recently wrote about the kinds of moviegoers who spoil the show for everyone else, such as "the babbling idiot," "the laughing hyena," and "the wandering dawdler." Another female student described blind dates to avoid, including "Mr. Neanderthal," "Timothy Timid," "Red, the Raging Rebel," and "Frat-Rat Freddie," among others. Still another student classified the various kinds of people who frequent the school library at two A.M. In this kind of informal essay, the thesis rule still holds true: though you start by making a humorous or satirical point about your subject, your classification must be more than mere silliness. Effective humor should ultimately make good sense, not nonsense.

Problems To Avoid

Avoid Underdeveloped Categories. A classification is not a mechanical list; each category should contain enough specific details to make it clearly recognizable and interesting. To present each category, you may draw upon the methods of development you already know, such as example, comparison and contrast, and definition.

Avoid Indistinct Categories. Each category should be a separate unit; there should be no overlap between categories. For example, in a classification of shirts by fabric, the inclusion of flannel with silk, nylon, and cotton is an overlap because flannel is a kind of cotton. Similarly, in a classification of soft drinks by flavor, to include sugar-free with cola, root beer, orange, grape, etc., is misleading because sugar-free drinks come in many different flavors. In other words, make each category unique.

Avoid Too Few or Too Many Categories. A classification essay should have at least three categories, avoiding the either-or dichotomy. On the other hand, too many categories give a short essay the appearance of a list rather than a discussion; for a 500–800-word essay, three to five categories seems about right. (Whatever the number, don't forget to use transition devices for an easy movement from category to category.)

Essay Topics

Narrow your subject by selecting an appropriate principle of classification. Some of the suggestions are intended for humorous essays.

1. kinds of plants, insects, animals
2. teachers
3. T.V. game shows
4. doctors or dentists
5. methods of advertising for a particular product, such as cigarettes or perfume
6. bad dates
7. fast-food restaurants
8. approaches to studying a subject or theories on "X"
9. roommates
10. salespersons/waiters/waitresses
11. sports fans or amateur athletes
12. hitchhikers
13. people who accost you on campus
14. ways of accomplishing a task (such as three ways to conduct an experiment, four ways to introduce a bill into Congress, etc.)
15. people who play video games

Sample Student Essay

In the essay below, the student writer divided the Mesa Verde Indian Era into three time periods that correspond to changes in the people's domestic skills, crafts, housing, etc. Note the writer's use of description and examples to help the reader see the advances from one time period to another.

THE INDIAN ERA AT MESA VERDE

Introduction: establishing a reason for knowing the classification

Visiting Mesa Verde National Park is a trip back in time to two and a half centuries before Columbus. The Park, located in southwestern Colorado, is the setting of a silent stone city, ten ruins built into protective seven-hundred-foot cliffs that housed hundreds of Indians from the pre-Columbian era to the end of the thirteenth century. If you visit the Park, you'll enjoy its architec-

Principle of classification of the Indian Era

ture and history more if you know a little about the various people who lived there. The Indian Era may be divided into three time periods that show growing sophistication in such activities as crafts, hunting, trade, and housing: Basket Maker (A.D. 1–450), Modified Basket Maker (A.D. 450–750), and Pueblo (A.D. 750–1300).

Time period one: the beginnings

The earliest Mesa Verdeans, the Basket Makers, whose forefathers had been nomads, sought shelter from the dry plains in the cliff caves and became farmers. During growing seasons they climbed up toeholds cut in the cliffs and grew beans and squash on the green mesa above. Settling down also meant more time for crafts. They didn't make pottery yet, but instead wove intricate baskets that held water. Instead of depending on raw meats and vegetables, they could now cook food in these baskets by dropping heated rocks into the water. Because the Basket Makers hadn't invented the bow and arrow yet, they had to rely on the inaccurate spear, which meant little fresh meat and few animal skins. Consequently, they wore little clothing but liked bone, seed, and stone ornaments.

Time period two: advances in skills, trade, and housing

The second period, A.D. 450–750, saw the invention of pottery, the bow and arrow, and houses. Pottery was apparently learned from other tribes. From crude clay baked in the sun, the Indians advanced to clay mixed with straw and sand and baked in kilns. Paints were concocted from plants and minerals, and the Indians produced a variety of beautifully decorated mugs, bowls, jars, pitchers, and canteens. Such pots meant that water could be stored for longer periods, and perhaps a water supply encouraged more trade with neighboring tribes. These Mesa Verdeans also acquired the bow and arrow, a weapon that improved their hunting skills, and enlarged their wardrobes to include animal skins and feather blankets. Their individual living quarters, called pithouses, consisted of twenty-foot wide holes in the ground with log, grasses, and earthen framework over them.

Time period three: more advances in community living, trade, and skills

The third period lasted until A.D. 1300 and saw the innovation of pueblos, or groups of dwellings, instead of single-family units. Nearly eight hundred dwellings show the large number of people who inhabited the complex, tunneled houses, shops, storage rooms, courtyards, and community centers whose masonry walls, often elaborately decorated, were three and four stories high. At the spacious Balcony House pueblo, for example, an adobe court lies beneath another vaulted roof: on three sides stand two-story houses with balconies that lead from one room to the next. In back of the court is a spring, and along the front side is a low wall that kept the children from falling down the seven-hundred-foot cliff to the canyon floor below. Balcony House also contains two *kivas,* circular sub- terranean ceremonial chambers that show the impor- tance of fellowship and religion to the Indians of this era. During this period the Indians were still farmers and potters, but cotton cloth and other non-native products found at the ruins suggest a healthy trade with the south. But despite the trade goods, sophisticated pottery, and such innovations in clothing as the "dis- posable" juniper-bark diapers of babies, life was still primitive; the Indians had no system of writing, no wheel, and no metal.

Conclusion: decline of the Indian Era

Near the end of the thirteenth century, the cliff dwellings became ghost towns. Archaeologists don't know for certain why the Indians left their elaborate homes, but they speculate that a drought that lasted some twenty years may have driven them south into New Mexico and Arizona, where strikingly similar crafts and tools have been found. Regardless of their reason for leaving, the Indians left an amazing archi- tectural and cultural legacy. Learning about the people who lived in Mesa Verde centuries ago provides an even deeper appreciation of the cliff palaces that awe thousands of National Park visitors every year.

Professional Essay

Friends, Good Friends—and Such Good Friends

Judith Viorst

Judith Viorst is a contributing editor and a regular columnist for *Redbook Magazine,* from which this essay was taken. She is the author of eight books for children, four books of poetry, and two books of prose. Her latest book, a collection of poems for children, is called *If I Were in Charge of the World.*

Women are friends, I once would have said, when they totally love and support and trust each other, and bare to each other the secrets of their souls, and   1

Copyright © 1977 by Judith Viorst.

run—no questions asked—to help each other, and tell harsh truths to each other (no, you can't wear that dress unless you lose ten pounds first) when harsh truths must be told.

Women are friends, I once would have said, when they share the same 2 affection for Ingmar Bergman, plus train rides, cats, warm rain, charades, Camus, and hate with equal ardor Newark and Brussels sprouts and Lawrence Welk and camping.

In other words, I once would have said that a friend is a friend all the way, but 3 now I believe that's a narrow point of view. For the friendships I have and the friendships I see are conducted at many levels of intensity, serve many different functions, meet different needs and range from those as all-the-way as the friendship of the soul sisters mentioned above to that of the most nonchalant and casual playmates.

Consider these varieties of friendship: 4

1. Convenience friends. These are the women with whom, if our paths 5 weren't crossing all the time, we'd have no particular reason to be friends: a next-door neighbor, a woman in our car pool, the mother of one of our children's closest friends or maybe some mommy with whom we serve juice and cookies each week at the Glenwood Co-op Nursery.

Convenience friends are convenient indeed. They'll lend us their cups and 6 silverware for a party. They'll drive our kids to soccer when we're sick. They'll take us to pick up our car when we need a lift to the garage. They'll even take our cats when we go on vacation. As we will for them.

But we don't, with convenience friends, ever come too close or tell too much; 7 we maintain our public face and emotional distance. "Which means," says Elaine, "that I'll talk about being overweight but not about being depressed. Which means I'll admit being mad but not blind with rage. Which means that I might say that we're pinched this month but never that I'm worried sick over money."

But which doesn't mean that there isn't sufficient value to be found in these 8 friendships of mutual aid, in convenience friends.

2. Special-interest friends. These friendships aren't intimate, and they 9 needn't involve kids or silverware or cats. Their value lies in some interest jointly shared. And so we may have an office friend or a yoga friend or a tennis friend or a friend from the Women's Democratic Club.

"I've got one woman friend," says Joyce, "who likes, as I do, to take 10 psychology courses. Which makes it nice for me—and nice for her. It's fun to go with someone you know and it's fun to discuss what you've learned, driving back from the classes." And for the most part, she says, that's all they discuss.

"I'd say that what we're doing is *doing* together, not *being* together," Suzanne 11 says of her Tuesday-doubles friends. "It's mainly a tennis relationship, but we play together well. And I guess we all need to have a couple of playmates."

I agree.   12

My playmate is a shopping friend, a woman of marvelous taste, a woman who 13 knows exactly *where* to buy *what*, and furthermore is a woman who always knows beyond a doubt what one ought to be buying. I don't have the time to keep up with what's new in eyeshadow, hemlines and shoes, and since I don't *want* to wear smocks if the smock look is finished, I'm very glad to have a shopping friend.

3. Historical friends. We all have a friend who knew us when . . . maybe way 14 back in Miss Meltzer's second grade, when our family lived in that three-room flat in Brooklyn, when our dad was out of work for seven months, when our brother Allie got in that fight where they had to call the police, when our sister married the endodontist from Yonkers and when, the morning after we lost our virginity, she was the first, the only, friend we told.

The years have gone by and we've gone separate ways and we've little in 15 common now, but we're still an intimate part of each other's past. And so whenever we go to Detroit we always go to visit this friend of our girlhood. Who knows how we looked before our teeth were straightened. Who knows how we talked before our voice got un-Brooklyned. Who knows what we ate before we learned about artichokes. And who, by her presence, puts us in touch with an earlier part of ourself, a part of ourself it's important never to lose.

"What this friend means to me and what I mean to her," says Grace, "is 16 having a sister without sibling rivalry. We know the texture of each other's lives. She remembers my grandmother's cabbage soup. I remember the way her uncle played the piano. There's simply no other friend who remembers those things."

4. Crossroads friends. Like historical friends, our crossroads friends are 17 important for *what was*—for the friendship we shared at a crucial, now past, time of life. A time, perhaps, when we roomed in college together; or worked as eager young singles in the Big City together; or went together, as my friend Elizabeth and I did, through pregnancy, birth and that scary first year of new motherhood.

Crossroads friends forge powerful links, links strong enough to endure with 18 not much more contact than once-a-year letters at Christmas. And out of respect for those crossroads years, for those dramas and dreams we once shared, we will always be friends.

5. Cross-generational friends. Historical friends and crossroads friends seem 19 to maintain a special kind of intimacy—dormant but always ready to be revived— and though we may rarely meet, whenever we do connect, it's personal and intense. Another kind of intimacy exists in the friendships that form across generations in what one woman calls her daughter-mother and her mother-daughter relationships.

Evelyn's friend is her mother's age— "but I share so much more than I ever 20 could with my mother"—a woman she talks to of music, of books and of life. "What I get from her is the benefit of her experience. What she gets—and enjoys—from me is a youthful perspective. It's a pleasure for both of us."

I have in my own life a precious friend, a woman of 65 who has lived very 21 hard, who is wise, who listens well; who has been where I am and can help me understand it; and who represents not only an ultimate ideal mother to me but also the person I'd like to be when I grow up.

In our daughter role we tend to do more than our share of self-revelation; in 22 our mother role we tend to receive what's revealed. It's another kind of pleasure— playing wise mother to a questing younger person. It's another very lovely kind of friendship.

6. Part-of-a-couple friends. Some of the women we call our friends we never 23 see alone—we see them as part of a couple at couples' parties. And though we share interests in many things and respect each other's views, we aren't moved to deepen the relationship. Whatever the reason, a lack of time or—and this is more likely—a lack of chemistry, our friendship remains in the context of a group. But the fact that our feeling on seeing each other is always, "I'm *so* glad she's here" and the fact that we spend half the evening talking together says that this too, in its own way, counts as a friendship.

(Other part-of-a-couple friends are the friends that came with the marriage, 24 and some of these are friends we could live without. But sometimes, alas, she married our husband's best friend; and sometimes, alas, she *is* our husband's best friend. And so we find ourself dealing with her, somewhat against our will, in a spirit of what I'll call *reluctant* friendship.)

7. Men who are friends. I wanted to write just of women friends, but the 25 women I've talked to won't let me—they say I must mention man-woman friendships too. For these friendships can be just as close and as dear as those that we form with women. Listen to Lucy's description of one such friendship:

"We've found we have things to talk about that are different from what he 26 talks about with my husband and different from what I talk about with his wife. So sometimes we call on the phone or meet for lunch. There are similar intellectual interests—we always pass on to each other the books that we love—but there's also something tender and caring too."

In a couple of crises, Lucy says, "he offered himself, for talking and for 27 helping. And when someone died in his family he wanted me there. The sexual, flirty part of our friendship is very small, but *some*—just enough to make it fun and different." She thinks—and I agree—that the sexual part, though small, is always *some*, is always there when a man and a woman are friends.

It's only in the past few years that I've made friends with men, in the sense of a 28 friendship that's *mine*, not just part of two couples. And achieving with them the ease and the trust I've found with women friends has value indeed. Under the dryer at home last week, putting on mascara and rouge, I comfortably sat and talked with a fellow named Peter. Peter, I finally decided, could handle the shock of me minus mascara under the dryer. Because we care for each other. Because we're friends.

8. There are medium friends, and pretty good friends, and very good friends 29 indeed, and these friendships are defined by their level of intimacy. And what we'll reveal at each of these levels of intimacy is calibrated with care. We might tell a medium friend, for example, that yesterday we had a fight with our husband. And we might tell a pretty good friend that this fight with our husband made us so mad that we slept on the couch. And we might tell a very good friend that the reason we got so mad in that fight that we slept on the couch had something to do with that girl who works in his office. But it's only to our very best friends that we're willing to tell all, to tell what's going on with that girl in his office.

The best of friends, I still believe, totally love and support and trust each 30 other, and bare to each other the secrets of their souls, and run—no questions asked—to help each other, and tell harsh truths to each other when they must be told.

But we needn't agree about everything (only 12-year-old girl friends agree   31
about *everything*) to tolerate each other's point of view. To accept without judgment. To give and to take without ever keeping score. And to *be* there, as I am for
them and as they are for me, to comfort our sorrows, to celebrate our joys.

Questions on Content, Style, and Structure

1. What is Viorst's purpose in this essay? What former definitions of friends
   is she now refuting?
2. What is the principle of classification in this essay?
3. Is each of Viorst's categories distinct and clearly presented? Does Viorst
   use enough detail and examples to explain each variety of friends?
   Support your answer with reference to the essay.
4. What does Viorst gain by quoting various women (Elaine, Joyce,
   Suzanne, Grace, Evelyn) throughout her essay?
5. What role do Viorst's own personal experiences play in her explanation
   of these categories?
6. What simple device does Viorst use to show the transition from one
   category to the next? What other kinds of transition devices might she
   have used instead?
7. Why does Viorst often use the first-person plural "we" point of view
   instead of the first-person singular "I" when she discusses various kinds of
   friends?
8. Pick out some examples of Viorst's occasional use of fragment sentences.
   Are her fragments effective? Why or why not?
9. Analyze Viorst's use of parallelism (see paragraphs 14, 15, and 29 for
   examples). What effects do such similar sentence constructions produce?
10. Evaluate Viorst's conclusion. Why does paragraph 30 repeat some lines
    from paragraph 1? How does the last paragraph emphasize Viorst's new
    view of best friends?

Vocabulary

To understand this essay completely, you should know the meanings of the
following words:

ardor (2)	dormant (19)
nonchalant (3)	reluctant (24)
convenience (5)	

STRATEGY SIX: DEVELOPMENT BY CAUSAL ANALYSIS

Causal analysis explains the cause-and-effect relationship between two (or more)
elements. When you discuss the condition producing something, you are analyzing *cause*; when you discuss the result produced by something, you are analyzing
effect. To find examples of causal analysis, you need only look around you. If your
car stops running on the way to class, for example, you may discover the cause was

an empty gas tank. On campus, you may study the causes of the Civil War in your history class, the effects of teenage spending on the cosmetics market in your economics class, and both the causes and effects of heart disease in your biology class. Over dinner you may discuss the effects of some crisis in the Middle East on American foreign policy, and as you drift to sleep, you may ponder the effects of your studying—or *not* studying—for your chemistry test tomorrow.

To express it most simply, *cause* asks:

—why did "X" happen?
or, why does "X" happen?
or, why will "X" happen?

Effect, on the other hand, asks:

—what did "Y" produce?
or, what does "Y" produce?
or, what will "Y" produce?

Some essays of causal analysis focus on the cause(s) of something; others analyze only the effect(s); still others discuss both causes and effects. If, for example, you wanted to concentrate on the causes of the Wall Street crash of 1929, you might begin by briefly describing the effects of the crash on the economy, then devote your thesis and the rest of your essay to analyzing the causes, perhaps allotting one major section (or one paragraph, depending on the complexity of the reasons) to each cause. Conversely, an effect paper might briefly describe the causes of the crash and then detail the effects. An essay covering both the causes and effects of something usually demands a longer paper so that each part will be clear. (If you can select your own essay topic, ask your teacher which kind of causal analysis essay you should write.)

Developing Your Essay

Whether you are writing an essay that primarily discusses either causes or effects, or one that focuses on both equally, you should follow these rules:

Present a Reasonable Thesis Statement. If your thesis makes dogmatic, unsupportable claims ("Medicare will lead to a complete collapse of quality medical treatment") or overly broad assertions ("Boredom is the cause of alcoholism among housewives"), you won't convince your reader. Limit or qualify your thesis whenever necessary by using such phrases as "may be," "a contributing factor," "one of the main reasons," "two important factors," and so on ("Boredom is *one of the major causes* of alcoholism among housewives").

Convince Your Reader that a Causal Relationship Exists by Showing How the Relationship Works. Let's suppose you are writing an essay in which you want to discuss the three major changes you've undergone since coming to college. Don't just state the changes and describe them; your job is to show the reader how college has brought about these changes. If, for instance, your study habits have improved, then you must show the reader how the academic demands of your college courses caused you to change your habits; a simple description of your new study techniques is not enough. Remember that a causal analysis essay should stress *how* (and sometimes *why*) "X" caused "Y," rather than merely "Y" as it now exists.

Limit Your Essay to a Discussion of Recent, Major Causes or Effects. In a short paper you generally don't have space to discuss minor or remote causes or effects. If, for example, you analyzed your car wreck, you might find that the two major causes included running a stop sign and speeding. The minor, or remote, causes might include being rushed because of oversleeping, oversleeping because of staying out too late the night before, staying out late because of an out-of-town visitor, and so on—back to the womb. In some cases you may want to mention a few of the indirect causes or effects, but do be reasonable. Concentrate on the most immediate, most important factors. Often, a writer of a 500–800-word essay will discuss no more than two, three, or four major causes or effects of something; to try to cover more frequently results in an underdeveloped essay. (Special organizational note: Sometimes you may discover that you can't isolate "the three main causes/effects of 'X'"; some essays do in fact demand a narrative explaining a chain reaction of causes and effects. For example, a paper on the rebellion of the American colonies might show how one unjust British law or restriction after another led to the war for independence. In this kind of causal analysis essay, be careful to explain how each step led to the next and continue, as always, to focus on the major causes and effects.)

Problems To Avoid

Don't Oversimplify by Assigning One All-Encompassing Cause to Some Effect. Most complex subjects have more than one cause (or effect), so make your analysis as complete and objective as you can, especially when dealing with your own problems or beliefs. Did you, for example, flunk English only because the professor disliked your style – or also because you failed to turn in the last two essays? Did your best friend wreck his parents' car because of icy streets—or was it a combination of icy streets and his own carelessness? Before judging a situation too quickly, investigate your own biases. Then provide a thoughtful, thorough analysis, effectively organized to convince your readers of the validity of your viewpoint.

Avoid the <u>post hoc</u> Fallacy. This error in logic (from the Latin phrase *post hoc, ergo propter hoc,* meaning "after this, therefore because of this") results when we mistake a temporal connection for a causal relationship—or, in other words, when we assume that because one event follows another in time, the first event caused the second. Most of our superstitions are *post hoc* fallacies; we now realize that tripping after walking under a ladder is a matter of coincidence, not cause and effect. The *post hoc* fallacy provided the basis for a rather popular joke in the 1960s' debates over decriminalizing marijuana. Those against argued that marijuana led to heroin because most users of the hard drug had first smoked grass. The proponents retorted that milk, then, was the real culprit, because both marijuana and heroin users had drunk milk as babies. The point is this: in any causal analysis, you must be able to prove that one event *caused* another, not just that it preceded it in time.

Avoid Circular Logic. Often causal essays seem to chase their own tails when they include such circular statements as "There aren't enough parking spaces for students on campus because there are too many cars." Such a statement merely presents a second half that restates what is already implied in the first half. A revision might say, "There aren't enough parking spaces for students on campus because the parking permits are not distributed fairly." This kind of assertion can be argued specifically and effectively; the other is a dead end.

Essay Topics

The suggestions below may be developed into essays emphasizing cause, or effect, or both.

1. a pet peeve or bad habit
2. a change of mind about some important issue or belief
3. an accident
4. a family tradition
5. the popularity of some sport, hobby, fad, or style
6. a trend in T.V. shows or movies (horror, science fiction, cops-and-robbers, etc.)
7. a change in your appearance (losing or gaining weight, dyeing your hair)
8. a form of pollution or crime
9. cheating or dishonesty
10. an important decision
11. popularity of a politician or celebrity (movie star, rock star, athlete, etc.)
12. an important idea or discovery in your field of study
13. a superstition or irrational fear
14. a place that is special to you
15. a disappointment or a success
16. sexism (in your experience) or some kind of discrimination or prejudice
17. a friendship or influential person
18. a political action (campus, local, state, national) or historical event

Sample Student Essay

In the following lighthearted personal essay, the student writer explains the three main causes of his habit of saving old papers or documents. Note that the writer tries to provide enough detail in each paragraph so that the reader understands how this bad habit developed and why it flourishes still.

TIMELESS ACCUMULATION

Introduction: the habit of saving things

Thesis and essay map: the three causes of his habit

Throughout history people have continued to save things that seem to have little or no value. Cavemen would save their old broken clubs, sultans would hold on to their old wives, and preppies would never think of discarding an old Izod shirt. I, in a similar fashion, indefinitely hold on to every piece of paper given to me. Saving all these papers is not just a bad habit picked up from my father; I also hoard papers because I often think of them as awards and because I'm convinced that one day each one will serve some useful, valuable purpose.

Cause one: imitation of father

While I was growing up, Dad would constantly warn me of the vices of life; however, not throwing away items like church bulletins, ticket stubs, and newspaper clippings was never mentioned as a vice because he saved these scraps of paper himself. Because I wanted to grow up just like my father, I imitated everything he did. Since my dad's desk was crammed with bills, receipts, and office memos, I had to stuff my desk full of paper (that is, if there was any that had slipped past him). Not only did he save little pieces of paper, but every periodical like *Time*, *National Geographic*, and *People* that entered our house stayed there. So whenever I purchased a *Sports Illustrated* or *Backpacker* magazine, it was soon jammed into a drawer or shoved into my magazine-laden bookshelf. Thus, by the age of twelve my habit of not throwing anything away was well established through my efforts to be just like my father.

Cause two: viewing of papers as ego-pleasing awards

Once I began to collect papers in my youth, I found I could not part with them because so many of them seemed like awards. For example, looking at highly scored old tests and well-written reports from school is like looking over a collection of medals and ribbons; viewing them strokes my ego. Surely no one would be expected to toss his Medal of Valor into the trash can! Even though I wrote my first term paper on the American Federation of Labor when I was in the eighth grade, it is still stashed away in one of the many boxes of old papers that seem to grow exponentially in my closet. When I occasionally dig through those boxes and find that report, I am reminded that my hours spent writing about enormously boring unions were rewarded with an "A" and the memory swells my head. (Not only does pride swell my head, but my enlarged ego usually results in an enlarged collection of papers.) In addition to the boxes full of papers, my bulletin board is another place where little ego-building tidbits tend to crop up. For example, pictures of my chromosomes, which adorn a corner of the board, remind me of all the extra time spent in the biology lab drawing blood, mixing it up, and taking pictures. Because only an elite few were allowed to participate in the nauseating experiment, the resulting photographs help to build my conceit. Consequently, because so many of my papers are conducive to my vanity, there is no way I can bring myself to throw them out.

Even though papers like my old bank statements and cash register receipts are not cherished, I hold on to them, too, because I feel strongly that someday they will serve some useful purpose. For instance, if the Internal Revenue Service decided to audit me, their investigation could be thwarted by my simply producing the myriad of receipts, which are buried someplace in my desk, glove box, and other convenient places. Deductions could be verified for anything from pens to boxer shorts to my car battery. Without these receipts I might be continuing my collection in jail. Old papers such as class notes might be extremely helpful if a friend enrolls in a class I have taken before. For a nominal fee, I would be more than willing to allow him to peruse my notes if he thought it would help him with the class. Because of this potential loss of revenue, throwing out old notes would not be very practical.

Despite the opinions of neatness fanatics, my utter disdain toward throwing away papers is not the product of a warped mind but has been caused by several sensible desires for a better life. My only problem now is that I've either got to become more selective about what to keep or plan to make lots of money to buy a bigger house. I wonder what the caveman did with all those broken clubs. . . .

Cause three: view of papers as potentially valuable

Conclusion: reference to thesis ending on humorous note

Professional Essay

Mystery!

Nicholas Meyer

Nicholas Meyer is a screenwriter and a novelist. Having worked for Warner Brothers as a story editor early in his career, he later wrote and directed the 1979 film *Time After Time*. He is the author of five books, two of which—*The Seven-Per-Cent Solution* (1974) and *The West End Horror* (1976)—were mysteries made into successful movies. Meyer is well known as a fan of the great detective Sherlock Holmes.

Reading mysteries is a bedtime recreation for all segments of society—high, **1** low and middle brow. It is the *divertissement*[13] of prime ministers and plumbers. Mysteries, whether they are on television, paper or movie screens, delight almost all of us. Everyone likes to "curl up" with a good mystery, and that makes this particular kind of literature unique in its ubiquitous appeal. No other genre so transcends what might otherwise appear to be significant differences in the social, educational and economic backgrounds of its audience.

Why, for heaven's sake? What is there about mystery and detective stories that **2** fascinate so many of us, regardless of age, sex, color and national origin?

On the surface, it seems highly improbable that detective novels should **3** provide such broad-based satisfaction. Their jacket blurbs and ad copy contain plenty of violent, even gory, references: "The body lay inert, the limbs dangling at unnatural angles, the head bashed in, clearly the result of a blunt instrument . . ." Who wants to read this stuff? Even assuming that there is a certain segment of society that delights in sadistic imagery and rejoices in thrills and chills and things that go bump in the night, it is hard to imagine that these sensibilities are in the majority.

As the Great Detective[14] himself might have observed, "It is a singular **4** business, Watson, and on the surface, most unlikely." Yet as Holmes was wont to remark, evidence that appears to point in one unerring direction may, if viewed from a slightly altered perspective, admit of precisely the opposite interpretation. People do, in fact, like to "curl up" with a good mystery. They take the corpses and the murderers to bed with them as favorite nighttime reading. One could hardly imagine a more intimate conjunction!

But the phrase "curling up" does not connote danger; say rather the reverse. It **5** conjures up snug, warm, secure feelings. Curling up with a good mystery is not exciting or thrilling; it is in fact oddly restful. It is reassuring.

Now why should this be? How is it possible that detective stories, with all the **6**

---

[13]A French word that originally referred to a ballet suite presented as an interlude in a performance, *divertissement* is used here to mean diversion or entertainment.

[14]Sherlock Holmes

Reprinted with permission from TV GUIDE® Magazine. Copyright © 1980 by Triangle Publications, Inc., Radnor, Pennsylvania.

murder and blackmail and mayhem and mystery that pervades them, should provide us with feelings of security, coziness and comfort?

Well, detective stories have other things in them besides violence and blood. 7 They have solutions, for one thing. Almost invariably, the murderer is caught, or at the very least identified. *As sure as God made little green apples, it all adds up to something.* If it doesn't, we aren't happy with the piece. A good detective story ties up all the loose ends; we resent motives and clues left unconnected.

Yes, detective stories have solutions. But life does not. On the contrary, life is 8 an anarchic proposition in which meaningless events conspire daily to alter our destiny without rhyme or reason. Your plane crashes, or the one you were booked on crashes but you missed it; a flat tire, a missed phone call, an open manhole, a misunderstanding—these are the chaotic commonplaces of everyday existence. But they have no place in the mystery novel. In detective novels, nothing happens without a reason. Detective literature, though it may superficially resemble life, in fact has effected at least one profound alteration: mystery stories *organize* life and provide it with meaning and answers. The kind of confusion in which real people are forced to exist doesn't occur in detective stories. Whatever the various people's problems, the only serious difficulty confronting them in detective stories is the fact that they are suspected of committing the crime involved. Once cleared of that lowering cloud, they are free to pursue their lives with, presumably, successful results.

So we see that the coziness of detective and mystery stories is not entirely 9 incomprehensible or inappropriate, after all. If we like to take such literature to bed with us and cuddle up with it, what we are really cuddling up to is a highly stylized literary formula, which is remarkably consistent in delivering to us that reassuring picture we all crave of an ordered world.

Sherlock Holmes, Philip Marlowe, Miss Marple or Columbo—the stories in 10 which these characters appear all manage to delight us by reassuring us. The victim is usually only slightly known or not very well liked. The world seems better off without him, or else he is so sorely missed that tracking his (or her) murderer will be, in Oscar Wilde's[15] words, more than a duty, it will be a pleasure.

And pleasurable indeed is the process of watching the tracking. There are 11 some highfalutin apologists of the detective genre who would have us believe it is the intellectual exercise of following the clues along with the detective—the reader's or viewer's participation in a kind of mental puzzle—that provides the satisfaction associated with detective stories. I believe such participation is largely illusory. We don't really ever have all the pieces at our disposal and most of us are not inclined to work with them very thoroughly, even in those rare cases when the author has been scrupulously "fair" in giving them to us. We enjoy the *illusion* of participation without really doing any of the mental legwork beyond the normal wondering "Whodunit?"

---

[15]Oscar Wilde (1854 – 1900) was an English wit and author; his well-known novel *The Picture of Dorian Grey* tells the story of a man who appears to remain ageless and innocent while his portrait reflects his evil deeds.

In any event, such a theory to justify the fascination exerted by detective and 12
mystery stories is elitist and falsely elitist into the bargain. It distracts our attention
with a pretentious and tenuous explanation in place of a much more interesting
and persuasive one; namely, that detective stories are appealing because they
depict life not as it is but in some sense as it ought to be.

Questions on Content, Style, and Structure

1. In this essay Meyer tries to solve a mystery himself. He is trying to find the
   cause of our enjoyment of what activity?
2. Why does Meyer begin his essay wondering about the popularity and
   appeal of this activity? Is this an effective way to begin this essay?
3. What is the purpose of the questions in paragraph 6?
4. What is Meyer's thesis? Where does it first become clear?
5. How do mystery stories differ from life? What examples does Meyer
   provide to help the reader see the contrast?
6. Meyer plays on the cliché of "curling up with a good mystery" several
   times in this essay; in his opinion, what are we really cuddling up to when
   we take a good mystery to bed?
7. According to Meyer and Oscar Wilde, mysteries provide another, secondary, source of pleasure. What is that?
8. What other explanation for the mystery's popularity does Meyer reject?
   Why does he reject this explanation?
9. Meyer often uses informal diction like "stuff" (3) and "highfalutin" (11),
   and clichés such as "thrills and chills and things that go bump in the
   night" (3) and "as sure as God made little green apples" (7). Are these
   choices effective? Why/why not?
10. How does Meyer conclude his essay? Does the ending successfully wrap
    up his causal analysis? Why/why not?

Vocabulary

To understand this essay completely, you should know the meanings of the
following words:

ubiquitous (1)	scrupulously (11)
genre (1)	elitist (12)
mayhem (6)	pretentious (12)
anarchic (8)	tenuous (12)

9

Argumentation

At some time during your childhood or adolescence, you probably decided that nagging and whining did not get you what you wanted. You may have realized, for example, that you had a much better chance of successfully borrowing the car, staying out late, or finagling a raise in your allowance if you presented your argument to your parents in a calm, logical fashion, giving them sound reasons for your position. Similarly, in discussions with your friends, you probably try to sway them to your viewpoint by arguing with as many facts, examples, and reasons as you can muster. And that, in effect, is what a good argumentative essay does: it presents logical reasoning to convince your audience of a particular point of view.

An argumentative essay may present your stand or position on some subject ("Capital punishment does not deter murder," "Gun control laws help stop crime"), or it may urge your readers to take some action ("Capital punishment should be abolished," "Our state should adopt gun control proposal #10"). In either case, the body of your essay then offers reasons to support your beliefs and to persuade your readers to agree with you.

DEVELOPING YOUR ESSAY

The way you present your reasons determines, to a large degree, how convincing your argument is. Therefore, you should consider the following suggestions carefully:

Anticipate Opposing Views. An argument assumes that there is more than one side to an issue. In a verbal argument, for example, you and a friend may trade comments, each one responding by countering the other's points. But in an essay, there is no opposition voice—only yours. Nevertheless, to be convincing, you must first be aware of your opposition's views on the subject and then organize your essay to answer or correct those views. If you don't have a good idea of the opposing arguments, you can't effectively persuade your readers to dismiss their objections and see matters your way. Therefore, before you begin your rough draft, write down all the opposing views you can think of and formulate an answer to each of them so that you will know your subject thoroughly.

Refer to the Opposition's Argument. In many persuasive essays, you may find it helpful to present, in addition to your own thesis, arguments against the opposition's major points; not only does this technique help you organize your own ideas, it also suggests to the reader that you are trying to argue fairly and thoroughly. While there is no one model of organization for argumentative essays, here are some common patterns: (1) present your thesis, your major points, refutation of the opposition's points, conclusion; (2) reverse of pattern one—present your thesis, your refutation, the points for your side, conclusion; (3) present your thesis, followed by a paragraph-by-paragraph discussion of your major points that also refute the opposition's major points. (For example, in an essay in which you are advocating mandatory deposits on bottles and cans, you might write a paragraph showing the consumer saving money because of lower taxes for highway trash clean-up that would refute the opposition's major point, that the program costs too much.

The outlines below illustrate each of the three plans. Note that for the sake of simplicity, the first three outlines present two of the writer's points and two opposing ideas. Naturally, your essay may contain any number of points and refuted points, depending upon the complexity of your subject and the assigned length of your essay:

Pattern 1: Thesis
            Your point one
            Your point two
            Refutation of opposition point one
            Refutation of opposition point two
            Conclusion
Pattern 2: Thesis
            Refutation of opposition point one
            Refutation of opposition point two
            Your point one
            Your point two
            Conclusion
Pattern 3: Thesis
            Your point one that also refutes opposition point one
            Your point two that also refutes opposition point two
            Conclusion

If your position as yet has no opposition ("There should be a stop sign at Fifth and Elm"), your essay outline might appear like this:

Thesis
Major point one
Major point two
Major point three . . . and so on
Conclusion

Most arguments, however, have at least two sides, so you might present, in addition to your main points, a body paragraph that offers hypothetical objections and then answers them ("The City Council may say that a stop light at Fifth and Elm costs too much, but the cost in lives is much greater").

Support Your Argument Effectively. To convince your readers, you should provide sufficient reasons for your assertions. You must give more than mere opinion—you must offer logical evidence to back up your position. Some of the possible methods of arguing should already be familiar to you from writing expository essays; listed below are several examples:

1. definition
   Example: If "angel dust" is an addictive narcotic, it should be legally classified as one.
2. comparison
   Example: If "Feathers" Balboa was sentenced to ten years for bank robbery, then his partner should go to jail, too.
3. cause and effect
   Example: Because Senator Mudwater has served well for twenty-six years as chairman of the Senate Committee on the Preservation of Muskrats, he should be returned to Congress.

In some essays you may also want to use the following kinds of evidence:

1. factual information
2. personal experience
3. statistics (Make sure your source is reliable and unbiased and that the figures are current.)
4. testimony from an authority (For a strong argument, the testimony must come from someone who knows the field, who is respected by his/her peers—beware remarks of a prestigious person from an entirely unrelated field. A football player, for example, doesn't necessarily know any more about panty hose or popcorn poppers than anyone else.)

Maintain a Coolly Rational Tone. You want to convince your audience, not alienate them. Instead of laying on insults or sarcasm, present your ideas in a moderate let-us-reason-together spirit. Such a tone will persuade your readers that you are sincere in your attempts to argue as truthfully and fairly as possible. If your readers do not respect you as a reasonable person, they certainly won't be swayed to your side of an issue. Don't preach or pontificate either; no one likes—or respects—a writer with a holier-than-thou attitude. Write in your natural "voice"; don't adopt a pseudointellectual tone. In short, to argue effectively you should sound logical, sincere, and informed. (For additional comments on audience and tone, review pp. 9–10, 61–62, 83–85, 91–93.)

Problems To Avoid

Here is a list of common logical fallacies—the errors most frequently found in reasoning. Always check your rough draft carefully to avoid any of the following:

Hasty Generalization: The Writer Bases the Argument on Insufficient or Unrepresentative Evidence. Suppose, for example, you have owned two poodles and they have both attacked you. If you declare that all poodles are vicious dogs, you are making a hasty generalization. There are, of course, thousands of poodles who have not attacked anyone. Similarly, you're in error if you interview only campus athletes and then declare, "University students favor a new stadium." What about the opinions of the students who aren't athletes? In other words, when the generalization is drawn from an unrepresentative or insufficient sample, your conclusion isn't valid.

Non sequitur ("it doesn't follow"): The Writer's Conclusion Is Not Necessarily a Logical Result of the Facts. An example of a *non sequitur* occurs when you conclude, "Professor Smith is a famous historian, so he will be a brilliant history teacher." As you may have realized by now, just that someone knows a subject well does not automatically mean that he or she can communicate the information clearly; hence, the conclusion is not necessarily valid.

Begging the Question: The Writer Presents as Truth What Is Supposed To Be Proven by the Argument. For example, in the statement, "All useless laws such as Reform Bill 13 should be repealed," the writer has already assumed the bill is useless without assuming responsibility for proving that accusation. Similarly, the statement "Japan's immoral slaughter of whales ought to be condemned by the United Nations" begs the question (that is, tries like a beggar to get something for nothing from the reader) because the writer gives no evidence for what must first be argued, not merely asserted—that Japan's killing of whales is immoral.

Red Herring: The Writer Introduces an Irrelevant Point To Divert the Readers' Attention from the Main Issue. This term originates from the old tactic, used by escaped prisoners, of dragging a smoked herring, a strong-smelling fish, across their trail to confuse tracking dogs by making them follow the wrong scent. If a writer arguing the merits of a particular politician who was seeking reelection suddenly broke into a description of the drinking habits of the politician's brother, such a description would be a red herring; the politician's brother has nothing to do with an evaluation of the incumbent's political merit.

Post hoc, ergo propter hoc: See pp. 163–164.

Argument ad hominem ("to the man"): The Writer Attacks the Opponent's Character Rather than the Opponent's Argument. The statement "Professor Bloom can't be a competent philosophy teacher since he's divorced" is illogical, because Bloom's marital status has nothing to do with his ability to teach his course well.

Argument <u>ad populum</u> ("to the people"): The Writer Evades the Issues by Appealing to Readers' Emotional Reactions to Certain Subjects. For example, instead of arguing the facts of an issue, a writer might play upon the readers' negative response to such words as "communism" and "fascism" or their positive response to words and concepts like "God," "country," and "liberty." In the statement "If you are a true American, you will vote against the referendum on busing," the writer avoids any discussion of the merits or weaknesses of the bill and merely substitutes an emotional appeal. (Advertisers, of course, play on consumers' emotions by filling their ads with pictures of babies, animals, status objects, and sexually attractive men and women.)

Circular Thinking: See p. 164.

Either/or: The Writer Tries To Convince the Readers that There Are Only Two Sides to an Issue—One Right, One Wrong. The statement "If you don't go to war against Iceland, you don't love your country" is irrational because it doesn't consider the other possibilities, such as patriotic people's right to oppose war as an expression of love for their country. A classic example of this sort of oversimplification was illustrated in the 1960s' bumper sticker that was popular during the debate over the Vietnam War: "America: Love It or Leave It." Obviously, there are other choices ("Change It or Lose It," for instance).

Hypostatization: The Writer Uses an Abstract Concept as if It Were a Concrete Reality. Always be suspicious of a writer who uses statements beginning, "History has taught us . . . , " "Science has proven . . . , " or "Medicine has discovered . . . . " The implication in each case is that history or science or medicine has only one voice, one opinion. On the contrary, "history" is written by a multitude of historians who hold a variety of opinions; doctors and scientists also frequently disagree. Instead of generalizing about a particular field, quote a respected authority or simply qualify your statement by referring to "many" or "some" scientists, historians, or whatever.

Bandwagon Appeal: The Writer Tries To Validate a Point by Intimating that "Everyone Else Believes in This." Such a tactic evades discussion of the issue itself. Advertising often uses this technique: "Everyone who demands real taste smokes Phooey cigarettes"; "Discriminating women use Smacky-Mouth lipstick." (The ultimate in "bandwagon" humor may have appeared on a recent Colorado bumper sticker: "Eat lamb—could 1000s of coyotes be wrong?")

Faulty Analogy: The Writer Uses an Extended Comparison as Proof of a Point. Look closely at all extended comparisons and metaphors to see if the two things being compared are really similar. For example, in a recent editorial a woman protested the new laws requiring parents to use car seats for small children, arguing that if the state could require the seats they could just as easily require mothers to breastfeed instead of using formula. Are the two situations alike? Car accidents are the leading cause of death of children under four; is formula dangerous? Or perhaps you've read that Politician X's plan for aid to Transylvania (or somewhere) is just like Russia's control of Poland. If the opinion isn't supported by factual evidence, then the analogy isn't persuasive. Remember that even though an analogy might suggest similarities, it alone cannot *prove* anything.

Practicing What You've Learned

Errors in reasoning can cause your reader to doubt your credibility and sincerity. In the mock essay below, for example, the writer includes a variety of fallacies that undermine his argument; see if you can identify all his errors.

BAN THOSE BOOKS!

A serious problem faces America today, a problem of such grave importance that our very existence as a nation is threatened. We must either cleanse our schools of evil-minded books or we must reconcile ourselves to seeing our children become welfare moochers and bums.

History has shown time and time again that placement of immoral books in our schools is part of a *bona fide* Communist plot designed to weaken the moral fiber of our youth from coast to coast. In Wettuckett, Ohio, for example, the year after books by Mark Twain such as *Tom Sawyer* and *Huckleberry Finn* were introduced into the school library by liberal free-thinkers and radicals, the number of students cutting classes rose by ten percent. And in that same year the number of high school seniors going on to college dropped from thirty to twenty-two.

The reason for this could either be a natural decline in intelligence and morals or the influence of those dirty books that teach our beloved children disrespect and irresponsibility. Since there is no evidence to suggest a natural decline, the conclusion is inescapable: once our children read about Twain's characters skipping school and running away from home, they had to do likewise. If they hadn't read about such undesirable characters as Huckleberry Finn, our innocent children would never have behaved in those ways.

Now, I am a simple man, a plain old farm boy—the pseudointellectuals call me redneck just like they call you folks. But I can assure you that, redneck or not, I've got the guts to fight the Communist conspiracy everywhere I find it, and I urge you to do the same. For this reason I want all you good folks to come to the ban-the-books rally this Friday so we can talk it over. I can promise you all your right-thinking neighbors will be there.

Essay Topics

Write a convincing argument attacking or defending one of the following statements. Narrow the topic when necessary.

1. The penalties for drunken driving (or any crime) are too lenient/ severe.
2. All college students should live their freshman year in a dorm.
3. Throwaway bottles and cans should be outlawed.
4. The foreign language requirement (or any requirement) at this school is worthwhile/useless.
5. Space exploration is a waste of time and money/our best hope for a brighter future.
6. High school competency tests in math and English should be adopted across the country.
7. Education in computer literacy should begin in grade school.
8. Women are still denied equal pay for equal work.
9. Lie detector tests for employees should be prohibited in all states.
10. Vitamin C (or herbal healing or any kind of nontraditional treatment) can help relieve illness.
11. In the event of a compulsory military draft, men and women should be equally liable.
12. Couples under twenty-five should be required by law to live together six months before marriage.
13. Prostitution should not be legalized.
14. Persons over twelve should have the right to see the movies of their choice.
15. Student evaluations should be a major consideration in the promotion of a professor.
16. Students should be employed for two years before they are admitted to college.
17. Nuclear energy (or solar energy) should be the primary power source of the future.
18. Conscientious objectors should/should not have the right to object to a particular war.

(See also the controversial statements on pp. 45−46.)

Sample Student Essay

In the essay the student writer argues for adoptees' rights to see their birth and adoption records. To argue her case, the writer uses Pattern 2, in which she presents and addresses two opposition points and then gives another point in favor of her own position. Notice that she employs a variety of persuasive techniques, including hypothetical examples, statistics, and testimony.[1] Does this writer persuade you to her point of view?

---

[1]If you decide to use quoted or paraphrased material from books, articles, interviews, or other sources to support your argument, turn to pages 249−257 for help on the proper ways to document your evidence.

BIRTHRIGHT

Introduction:
presenting the
problem

Thesis

Opposition point one

Rebuttal of
opposition point one

Many adoptees search for something that everyone else takes for granted: the story of their birth, the missing link in their identity. These people are faced with much pain and frustration as they are rebuffed with the typical response, "I'm sorry, your files are confidential." The usual reasons for this confidentiality concern the supposedly traumatic disruption that they may cause to the biological parents and adoptive parents involved. But despite these concerns, mature adoptees should have full access to their birth and adoption records, especially when adoptees have extreme medical needs.

Many opponents of open-access adoption records are the adopting parents. Too often these parents fear that if their adopted child should find his or her birth parents, their family's relationship will be disrupted or perhaps even severed completely. As one adoptee noted, with the mere hint of a search, "the danger flag is up, as if the adoptive parents believe that the very mention of those original parents will make them materialize on the spot and snatch their child away."[2] Such fears are usually unfounded. In the first place, parents who adopt should remember that laws prevent children from being removed from their homes if the birth parents change their minds.[3] Secondly, most adoptees searching for their roots are not trying to return to the homes of their birth parents; they simply want some answers about their past. They understand that their "real" parents are those who have raised them. As Anne Wade, a counselor for Colorado Adoption Services, points out, if strong relationships have already been established, adoptive parents shouldn't fear that their children will transfer their sentiments from those who have cared for them all of their lives to the new-found parents who gave them away years ago.[4] Instead of being concerned, the adoptive parents should also realize that just as they could love more

[2]Betty Jean Lifton, "My Search for My Roots," *Seventeen*, March 1977, p. 133.
[3]John H. Stang, *The Adoption Process* (New York: Hallmark Press, 1980), p. 56.
[4]Telephone interview with Anne Wade, counselor for Colorado Adoption Services, Denver, Colorado, on March 3, 1982.

than one child, their child could love more than one set of parents. In short, many adoptive parents do too much unnecessary worrying.

Opposition point two

Stronger resistance to open records comes from those who fear that the lives of the birth parents will be disrupted by a confrontation with a child from the past. One or both of the birth parents may have a family to protect, or they may have begun a new family or career they do not want disturbed. They may wish to keep people from knowing that they had a child out of wedlock or that they gave up a child. However, birth

Rebuttal of opposition point two

parents who wish to remain anonymous should realize that they do not have to respond if they are contacted by their child. Open records would allow those parents who do wish to meet their children to do so; in one survey of 162 parents located in 246 agency searches, only 24 refused to see their children.[5] Subsequent studies showed that 80 to 90 percent of the reunions were successful.[6] The closed-records policy of today discourages such searches and reunions.

Another point for the writer's position

The adoptee's rights should also be weighed in this argument. In addition to wanting to know about heritage, there can be important medical reasons for knowing about one's parents. Consider the hypothetical case of a young man who is in an accident or who develops a serious illness. He may need medical information, donor organs, blood transfusions, or bone marrow transplants from biological relatives—whose names he cannot obtain in time to save himself. The adoptee's welfare is sacrificed because of the laws of confidentiality.

Conclusion: summary of writer's position

In many cases, the birth parents' wishes to remain undisturbed should be respected; however, the rights of mature adoptees should be extended to include access to information surrounding their birth and their medical history. Sealed records are, ultimately, an infringement upon basic human rights, including those promising equal protection under the law, and therefore should be abolished.

[5]Nancy Kupersmith, "The Fight to Open Up Adoption Records," *The Reader's Digest,* June 1978, p. 29.

[6]Kupersmith, p. 32.

Bibliography

Kupersmith, Nancy. "The Fight To Open Up Adoption Records." *The Reader's Digest,* June 1978, pp. 27–32.

Lifton, Betty Jean. "My Search for My Roots." *Seventeen,* March 1977, pp. 132–38.

Stang, John H. *The Adoption Process.* New York: Hallmark Press, 1980.

Wade, Anne, Counselor for Colorado Adoption Services, Denver, Colorado. Telephone interview, March 3, 1982.

Professional Essay

Away with Big-Time Athletics

Roger M. Williams

Roger M. Williams has been published in *Time* and in *Sports Illustrated* and has been an editor for *Saturday Review*. This essay first appeared in *Saturday Review* in 1976.

At their mid-January annual meeting, members of the National Collegiate 1 Athletic Association were locked in anguished discussion over twin threats to big-time college athletic programs: rapidly rising costs and federal regulations forcing the allocation of some funds to women's competition. The members ignored, as they always have, the basic issue concerning intercollegiate athletics. That is the need to overhaul the entire bloated, hypocritical athletic system and return athletics to a sensible place in the educational process.

A complete overhaul of the athletic programs, not the fiscal repair now being 2 attempted by the NCAA, is what is necessary. For decades now big-time football, and to a lesser degree basketball, have commanded absurdly high priorities at our colleges and universities. Football stands at the center of the big-time system, both symbolically and financially; the income from football has long supported other, less glamorous sports.

Many American universities are known more for the teams they field than for 3 the education they impart. Each year they pour hundreds of thousands of dollars apiece into athletic programs whose success is measured in games won and dollars earned—standards that bear no relation to the business of education and offer nothing to the vast majority of students.

The waste of resources is not the only lamentable result of the overemphasis 4 of intercollegiate athletics. The skewing of values is at least as damaging. Everyone involved in the big-time system—players, coaches, alumni and other boosters, school officials, trustees, even legislators—is persuaded that a good football team is a mark of the real worth of an educational institution. Some of the most successful coaches elevate that bizarre notion to a sort of philosophy. Woody Hayes of Ohio State has said that the most important part of a young man's college education is the football he plays. Jim Kehoe, athletic director at the University of

Maryland, has said of the games played by Maryland: "You do anything to win. I believe completely, totally, and absolutely in winning."

Anyone doubtful of the broad psychic satisfaction provided by winning teams 5 need only observe who it is that shouts, "We're number one!" It is seldom the players and only sometimes other students. The hard core of team boosters is composed of middle-aged men—mainly alumni but also legions of lawyers, doctors, and businessmen with no tangible connection to the school.

In the South, where football mania rides at a shrill and steady peak, winning 6 seems to offer a special reward: an opportunity to claim the parity with other regions that has been so conspicuously lacking in more important areas of endeavor. In Alabama in the late sixties, when Coach Bear Bryant was fielding the first of his remarkable series of national championship teams, both Bear and team were the objects of outright public adulation: that is, *white* public adulation. White Alabamians, reacting to the assaults on George Wallace[7] and other bastions of segregation, took a grim, almost vengeful pride in "their" team. During those years, when I covered the South as a reporter, one could hardly meet a white Alabamian who didn't talk football or display, on an office or den wall, a picture of Bryant and the Crimson Tide squad.

The disease of bigtime-ism seems to run rampant in provincial places where 7 there is little else to do or cheer for: Tuscaloosa and Knoxville, Columbus and Lincoln, Norman and Fayetteville. But everywhere, always, it feeds on a need to win—not just win a fair share of games but win almost all of them, and surely all of the "big" ones.

At the University of Tennessee last fall, coach Bill Battle nearly lost his job 8 because the Volunteers won a mere seven out of twelve games. Never mind that Battle's Tennessee teams had previously amassed a five-year record of forty-six victories, twelve defeats, and two ties and had been to a bowl in each of those years. Although Battle was eventually rehired, he received no public support from a university administration which seemed to agree with the fanatics that, outstanding as his record was, it was not good enough.

Everyone knows something about the excess of recruiting high-school players 9 and something about the other trappings of the big-time system: the athletic dormitory and training table; where the "jocks" or "animals" are segregated in the interests of conformity and control; the "brain coaches" hired to keep athletes from flunking out of school; the full scholarships ("grants in aid"), worth several thousand dollars apiece, that big-time schools can give to 243 athletes each year. (Conference regulations restrict the size of football traveling squads to about sixty, while the NCAA permits ninety-five players to be on football scholarships. This means that some three dozen football players at each big-time school are getting what's called a full ride without earning it.)

What a few people realize is that these are only the visible workings of a 10

[7]George Wallace is currently the governor of Alabama. During his former terms as governor (1963–1966, 1971–1974, 1975–1978), he was known as a staunch segregationalist.

system that feeds on higher education and diverts it from its true purposes. The solution, therefore, is not to deliver slaps on the wrist to the most zealous recruiters, as the NCAA often does, or to make modest reductions in the permissible number of athletic scholarships, as it did last year. The solution is to banish big-time athletics from American colleges and universities.

Specifically, we should: 11

1. Eliminate all scholarships awarded on the basis of athletic ability and those 12 given to athletes in financial need. Every school should form its teams from a student body drawn there to pursue academic interests.

2. Eliminate athletic dormitories and training tables, which keep athletes out 13 of the mainstream of college life and further their image as hired guns. Also eliminate special tutoring, which is a preferential treatment of athletes, and "red shirting," the practice of keeping players in school an additional year in the hope that they'll improve enough to make the varsity.

3. Cut drastically the size and the cost of the coaching staffs. Football staffs at 14 Division I schools typically number twelve or fourteen, so that they are larger than those employed by professional teams. With practice squads numbering eighty or fifty, the present staff size creates a "teacher-pupil" ratio that permits far more individualized instruction on the playing field than in the classroom. The salaries paid to assistant coaches should be spent to hire additional faculty members. The salaries of head coaches, who in some states earn more than the governor, should be reduced to a point where no head coach is paid more than a full professor.

4. Work to eliminate all recruiting of high-school athletes. It has produced 15 horrendous cases of misrepresentation, illegal payments, and trauma for the young men involved.

The worst of the abuses is the athletic scholarship, because it is central to all 16 the others. If members of a college team are not principally athletes, there is no need to lure them to the school by offering special treatment and platoons of coaches. They should be students to whom football or basketball is the season's major extracurricular activity.

What will happen if these changes are made? The games will go on. In fact, 17 they may well be more like real games than the present clashes between hired, supertrained, and sometimes brutalized gladiators. Will the caliber of play suffer? Of course, but every school will be producing the same lower caliber. Given a certain proficiency, which the best of any random selection of student-athletes always possesses, the games will be as competitive and as exciting for spectators as they are today. Is a 70-yard run by a nonscholarship halfback less exciting than the same run by Bear Bryant's best pro prospect? For spectators who crave top athletic performance, it is available from a myriad of professional teams. We need not demand it of students.

Certainly, the counter-argument runs, alumni and other influential support- 18 ers would not stand for such changes. There would indeed be ill feeling among— and diminished contributions from—old grads who think of their alma mater primarily as a football team. Let them stew in their own pot of distorted values. Those legislators whose goodwill toward a state university depends on winning seasons and free tickets can stew with them. A serious institution is well rid of such "supporters." They may discover the pleasures of a game played enthusiastically by moderately skilled students who are not in effect paid performers.

Will athletic-program revenues drop? They undoubtedly will, at least for a   19 while; not many people will pay seven dollars to see games of admittedly lower quality, nor will the TV networks pay fancy fees for the right to televise them. The fans and the networks will eventually return, because these will be the only college games available. And think of the financial savings, as the costs of the typical big-time athletic program drop by hundreds of thousands of dollars a year. If a revenue gap persists, let it be made up out of general funds. The glee club, the intramural athletic program, and innumerable other student activities do not pay for themselves. Why should intercollegiate athletics have to do so?

Supporters of big-time programs often say piously that, thanks to those   20 programs, many young men get a college education who otherwise would have no chance for one. That is true. But there are even more young men, of academic rather than athletic promise, who deserve whatever scholarship money is available. If somebody has to pay an athlete's way to college, let it be the professional teams that need the training that college competition provides.

The president of a good Southern university once told me privately that he   21 would like to hire outright a football team to represent his school and let the educational process proceed. George Hanford of the College Entrance Examination Board, who has made a study of intercollegiate athletics, would keep the present system but legitimize the preparation of players for professional sports. Hanford would have a college teach athletes such skills as selecting a business agent and would permit student-athletes to play now and return later to do the academic work required for a degree.

While Hanford's suggested changes would remove the mask of hypocrisy   22 from big-time college athletic programs, they would not solve the fundamental problem: the intrusions the programs make on the legitimate functions and goals of an educational institution. For institutions with a conscience, this problem has been persistently vexing. Vanderbilt University football coach Art Guepe summed it up years ago, when he characterized Vanderbilt's dilemma as "trying to be Harvard five days a week and Alabama on Saturday."

Because of pressures from alumni and others who exalt the role of football,   23 Vanderbilt is still attempting to resolve this dilemma; and it is still failing. Now it is time for all the Vanderbilts and all the Alabamas to try to be Harvard whenever they can and Small-Time State on Saturday.

Questions on Content, Style, and Structure

1. What is Williams' thesis?
2. Why does he object to "big-time" college athletic programs? What reasons does he give?
3. What in the past has been the solution to the excesses of big-time athletics?

4. What steps would Williams take to accomplish his solution to the problem?
5. What, according to Williams, is the worst abuse in college athletics? Do you agree?
6. What tactic does Williams take in paragraphs 18–20? Is it effective?
7. What does Williams gain by paraphrasing or directly quoting the opinions of several coaches? Why, for instance, does he include the comments of Jim Kehoe and Woody Hayes in paragraph 4? Why does he quote Art Guepe in paragraph 22?
8. How does Williams conclude his essay? Is his ending effective?
9. Describe the pattern of organization of Williams' essay. Which of the patterns outlined on p. 172 is most similar to Williams' organization?
10. Evaluate Williams' essay in terms of its strengths and weaknesses. Did he respond persuasively to the opposition's arguments? Were his own arguments convincing? Why/why not?

Vocabulary

To understand this essay completely, you should know the meanings of the following words:

anguished (1)
lamentable (4)
tangible (5)
parity (6)
adulation (6)
bastions (6)

rampant (7)
zealous (10)
preferential (11)
myriad (13)
exalt (19)

Description

The writer of description creates a word-picture of persons, places, objects, and emotions, using a careful selection of details to make an impression on the reader. If you have already written expository or argumentative essays in your composition course, then you almost certainly have written some descriptive prose. Nearly every essay, after all, calls for some kind of description; for example, in the student comparison/contrast essay (pp. 134–136), the writer describes two kinds of stores; in the student classification essay (pp. 155–157), the writer describes Indian dwellings; in the process essay (pp. 123–125), the writer describes the proper ways to plow and plant a garden. To help you write better description in your other essays, however, you may want to practice writing descriptive paragraphs or a short description essay.

HOW TO WRITE EFFECTIVE DESCRIPTION

Regardless of the kind of description you are writing, you should follow the three basic suggestions below:

Recognize Your Purpose. Description is not free-floating; it appears in your writing for a particular reason—to help you explain, persuade, create a mood, or whatever. In some essays you will want your description as *objective* as you can make it; for example, you might describe a scientific experiment or a business transaction in straight factual detail. Most of the time, however, you will want to convey a particular attitude toward your subject; this approach to description is called *subjective* or *impressionistic*. Note the differences between the following two descriptions of a tall, thin boy: The objective writer sticks to the facts by saying, "The eighteen-year-old boy was 6'1" and weighed 125 pounds," whereas the subjective writer gives an impressionistic description, "The young boy was as tall and scrawny as a birch tree in winter." Therefore, before you begin describing anything, you must decide first your purpose and then whether it calls for objective or subjective reporting.

Select Appropriate Details. In any description the choice of details depends largely on the writer's purpose and audience. However, many descriptions—especially the more subjective ones—will present a *dominant impression*; that is, the writer selects only those details that communicate a particular mood or feeling to the reader. The dominant impression is the controlling focus of a description; for example, if you wrote a description of your grandmother to show her thoughtfulness, then you would select only those details that convey an impression of a sweet, kindly old lady. Below are two brief descriptions illustrating the concept of dominant impression. The first writer tries to create a mood of mystery:

> Down a black winding road stands the abandoned old mansion, silhouetted against the cloud-shrouded moon, creaking and moaning in the wet chill wind.

The second writer tries to present a feeling of joy and innocence:

> A hundred kites filled the spring air, and around the bright picnic tables spread with hot dogs, hamburgers, and slices of watermelon, Tom and Annie played away the warm April day.

In the description of the deserted mansion, the writer would have violated the impression of mystery had the sentence read:

> Down the black winding road stands the abandoned old mansion, surrounded by bright, multicolored tulips in early bloom.

Including the cheerful flowers as a detail in the description destroys the dominant mood of bleakness and mystery. Similarly, example two would be spoiled had the writer ended it this way:

> . . . Tom and Annie played away the warm April day until Tom got so sunburned he became ill and had to go home.

Therefore, remember to select only those details that advance your descriptive purpose. Omit any details you consider unimportant or distracting.

See if you can determine the dominant impression of each description below:

> The wind had curled up to sleep in the distant mountains. Leaves hung limp and motionless from the silent trees, while birds perched on the branches like little statues. As I sat on the edge of the clearing, holding my breath, I could

hear a squirrel scampering through the underbrush. Somewhere far away a dog barked twice, and then the woods were hushed once more.

The mayor's eyebrows fell in at the center, pointing down toward the nose. A red stain filled his meaty cheeks, and his broad lips tightened into a thin hard line. His hands on the table before him clenched into fists, the knuckles white as bare bone. Sparks seemed to fly from his narrowed eyes as the police chief finished his report.

Describe Clearly and Vividly. To improve any kind of writing, follow the rules for a good prose style outlined in Chapters 5 (on sentences) and 6 (on words). As explained in detail there, you should always prefer active, vigorous verbs and strong nouns to strings of modifiers. For example, the sentence "The Glutmobile spun around and around in shrieking circles before slamming into the wall" is stronger than the wordy sentence "The Glutmobile moved quickly and noisily in circles many times before hitting the wall very hard." In addition to the advice given in the chapters on effective words and sentences, here are three other ways to enliven and clarify your descriptions

Use specific details. The reader cannot imagine your subject clearly if your description is couched in vague generalities. The sentence below, for example, presents only a hazy picture:

Larry is so overweight that his clothes don't fit him right.

Revised, the picture is now sharply in focus:

Larry is so fat that his shirt constantly bulges over his belt, his trousers will not stay snapped, and his countless chins spill over his collar like dough rising out of a too-small pan.

Specific details can turn cloudy prose into crisp, clear images that can be reproduced in the mind like photographs.

Use sensory details. Another method of clarifying description is by presenting images that appeal to your readers' five senses. If, for example, you are describing your broken leg and the ensuing stay in a hospital, tell your readers how the place smelled, how it looked, what your cast felt like, how your pills tasted, and what noises you heard. Below are some specific examples using sensory details:

Sight: The clean white corridors of the hospital resembled the set of a sci-fi movie, with everyone scurrying around in identical starched uniforms.

Hearing:	At night, the only sounds I heard were the quiet squeakings of sensible white shoes as the nurses made their rounds.
Smell:	The green beans on the hospital cafeteria tray smelled stale and waxy, like crayons.
Touch:	The hospital bed sheet felt as rough and heavy as a feed sack.
Taste:	Every four hours they gave me an enormous gray pill whose aftertaste reminded me of the castor oil my grandmother insisted on giving me when I was a kid.

By appealing to the readers' senses, you better enable them to identify with and imagine the subject you are describing. Joseph Conrad, the famous nineteenth-century novelist, agreed, believing that all art "appeals primarily to the senses, and the artistic aim when expressing itself in written words must also make its appeal through the senses, if its highest desire is to reach the secret spring of responsive emotions." In other words, to make your readers feel, first make them "see."

Use figurative language when appropriate. As you may recall from Chapter 6, figurative language produces images or pictures in the readers' minds, helping them to understand unfamiliar or abstract subjects. The two most common figures of speech—the metaphor and simile—have already been discussed (see p. 94), but here are four other devices you might use to clarify or spice up your prose:

1. personification: the attribution of human characteristics and emotions to inanimate objects, animals, or abstract ideas
   Example: The old stuffed teddy bear sat in a corner, dozing before the fireplace.
2. hyperbole: intentional exaggeration or overstatement
   Example: The overworked composition teacher struggled to grade the mile-high stack of essays on her desk.
3. understatement: intentional representation of a subject as less important than the facts would warrant (see also irony, pp. 83–84)
   Example: "Last week I saw a woman flayed, and you will hardly believe how much it altered her person for the worse."—Jonathan Swift, eight-eenth-century satirist
4. synecdoche: a part of something is used to represent the whole.
   Example: A hundred tired feet hit the dance floor for one last jitterbug. [Here "feet" stand for the dancing couples themselves.]

Using figures of speech can make your descriptions clear, lively, and memorable.

Problems To Avoid

Besides remembering to use vivid, specific details, keep in mind these three other bits of advice to solve problems that frequently arise in description:

Avoid an Erratic Organization of Details. Too often descriptions are a hodge-podge of details, jotted down randomly. When you write a lengthy description, you should select a plan that will arrange your details in an orderly fashion. Depending upon your subject matter and your purpose, you might adopt a plan calling for a description of something from top to bottom, left to right, front to back, etc. For example, a description of a woman might begin at the head and move to the feet; furniture in a room might be described as your eyes move from one side of the room to another. A second plan for arranging details presents the subject's outstanding characteristics first and then fills in the lesser information; a woman's red hair, for example, might be her most striking feature and therefore would be described first. A third plan presents details in the order you see them approaching: dust, then a car, then details about the car, its occupants, and so on. Or you might describe a subject as it unfolds chronologically, as in some kind of a process or operation. Regardless of which plan of organization you choose, the reader should feel a sense of order in your description.

Avoid Any Sudden Change in Perspective. If, for example, you are describing the White House from the outside, don't suddenly include details that could be seen only from inside. Similarly, if you are describing a car from a distance, you might be able to tell the car's model, year, and color, but you could hardly describe the upholstery or reveal the mileage. It is, of course, possible for you—or your observer—to approach or move around the subject of your description, but the reader must be aware of this movement. Any shift in point of view must be presented clearly and logically, with no sudden, confusing leaps from a front to a back view, from outside to inside, and so on.

Don't Use Figurative Language Unwisely. Don't include too many figures of speech; don't mix your images; don't repeat clichés. Make your figurative language fresh, insightful, and arresting. (For more information on clichés and mixed metaphors, see pp. 90–91 and 94–95.)

Essay Topics

Here are some suggestions for a descriptive essay or paragraph; narrow your topic to fit your assignment. Don't forget that every description, whether objective or subjective, has a purpose and that every detail should support that purpose.

1. a campus character
2. your room or roommate
3. a piece of equipment important to your major
4. a building or place you're fond of (such as a "haunted" house in your neighborhood or even a childhood tree house)
5. a sports event
6. a family member or family pet

7. your most unforgettable character
8. a striking landscape
9. your favorite painting or art work
10. registration at your school
11. a doctor's or dentist's waiting room
12. the woman/man of your dreams
13. your face—or your face after plastic surgery
14. a special day in your life (birthday, holiday, graduation, etc.)
15. a dead cockroach
16. a business transaction
17. a germ, cell, or virus
18. a laboratory experiment
19. some part of the human body, such as the heart or brain
20. a computer, calculator, or some other machine

Sample Student Paragraphs

Although description is one of the four kinds of prose, as noted earlier, it is the one most frequently found in other kinds of essays. Consequently, instead of one sample essay, here are several paragraphs that are primarily descriptive. In these three *subjective* paragraphs, each describing something worn out, study the uses of detail and figurative language.

The old covered bridge sagged in the middle, and the roof was full of jagged holes that let the sunlight pour through randomly in long crooked rays. Age had crept into the joints and beams like arthritis. The weight of a single automobile was enough to set the warped floorboards creaking. Each day the city's safety inspector drove out to stand and peer at the bridge like a doctor calmly waiting out a dying man.

Although the salesman swore that the pickup truck had been driven only occasionally, it looked remarkably worn to me. Dents waffled the top and the hood, as if the vehicle had been left out in a hailstorm. Someone had obviously sideswiped it, too, because the paint on one side had flaked off along a deep scar that ran from headlight to taillight. The radiator was caked with dried bugs. The front bumper was so rusted that its few remaining patches of chrome looked like shining islands in a narrow reddish sea. The back window was shattered around a tiny hole, the cracks spreading out like threads of a spider web.

This poor thing has seen better days, but one should expect the sofa in a fraternity house den to be well worn. The large, plump, brown corduroy pillows strewn lazily on the floor and propped comfortably against the threadbare arms bear the pencil-point scars of frustrated students and foam-bleeding cuts of multiple pillow wars. No less than four pairs of rotting Nikes stand twenty-four-hour guard at the corners of its carefully mended frame. Obviously the relaxed, inviting appearance masks the permanent odors of cheap cigars and Michelob from Thursday night poker parties; at least two or three guests each weekend sift through the popcorn kernels and Doritos crumbs, sprawl facedown, and pass out for the duration. However, frequent inhabitants have learned to avoid the dark stains courtesy of the house pup and the red-punch designs of the chapter klutz. Habitually, they strategically lunge over the back of the sofa to an unsoiled area easily identifiable in flight by the large depression left by previous regulars. The quiet *hmmph* of the cushions and harmonious squeal of the exhausted springs signal a perfect landing and utter a warm greeting from an old and faithful friend.

In the three *objective* paragraphs below, note that each of the writers uses specific detail to convey accuracy:

The liver is a person's largest internal organ, containing 300 billion cells and weighing an average of three pounds. Located on the right side of the abdominal cavity under the ribs, the liver is reddish brown and shaped like a five-sided pyramid. It is divided into two lobes, with the right lobe almost six times larger than the left lobe. The liver has a double blood supply: the portal vein carries blood from the stomach, intestines, and the spleen, and the hepatic artery brings arterial blood from the heart. Forty fluid ounces of blood flow through the liver every minute.

A vaulting horse is a piece of equipment used by gymnasts during competition to help propel them into the air when they perform any of a variety of leaps known as vaults. The gymnasts usually approach the vaulting horse from a running start and then place their hands on the horse for support or for a push off as they perform their vaults. The horse itself resembles a carpenter's sawhorse but the main beam is composed of padded leather rather than wood. The rectangular beam is approximately five feet three inches long and thirteen and a half inches wide. Supported by four legs usually made of steel, the padded leather beam is approximately four feet, one half inch above the floor in men's competitions and three feet, seven inches in women's competitions. The padded leather beam has two white lines marking off three sections on top: the croup, the saddle, and the neck. The two end sections—the croup and the neck—are each fifteen and one half inches long. Gymnasts place their hands on the neck or croup depending on the type of vault they are attempting.

Austin, Texas, is located in Travis County on the Edwards Plateau. The city
was founded in 1835 by Jacob M. Harrell on the banks of the Colorado River.
The altitude is 455 feet by the river and 1,000 feet in the hills of the northwest
area of the town. The average normal temperature is 68.3 degrees, with a
winter temperature range of 42°−62° and a summer range of 73°−94°.
Average annual rainfall is 32.49 inches. Population within the city limits in
1975 was 306,000.

Professional Essay

Down in the Coal Mines

George Orwell

George Orwell is the pseudonym of Eric Arthur Blair, a British novelist and essayist.
Some of his best-known works include *Down and Out in Paris and London*, *Animal
Farm*, *Nineteen Eighty-Four*, and *Shooting an Elephant*. This essay is an excerpt from
The Road to Wigan Pier.

When you go down a coal mine it is important to try and get to the coal face   1
when the "fillers" are at work. This is not easy, because when the mine is working
visitors are a nuisance and are not encouraged, but if you go at any other time, it is
possible to come away with a totally wrong impression. On a Sunday, for instance,
a mine seems almost peaceful. The time to go there is when the machines are
roaring and the air is black with coal dust, and when you can actually see what the
miners have to do. At those times the place is like hell, or at any rate like my own
mental picture of hell. Most of the things one imagines in hell are there—heat,
noise, confusion, darkness, foul air, and above all, unbearably cramped space.
Everything except the fire, for there is no fire down there except the feeble beams
of Davy lamps[1] and electric torches which scarcely penetrate the clouds of coal
dust.

When you have finally got there—and getting there is a job in itself: I will   2
explain that in a moment—you crawl through the last line of pit props and see
opposite you a shiny black wall three or four feet high. This is the coal face.
Overhead is the smooth ceiling made by the rock from which the coal has been cut;

---

[1]One of the earliest safety lamps designed to prevent explosions in the British mines.
Named for its inventor, Sir Humphrey Davy (1778−1829), the English chemist who
discovered sodium and potassium.

From *The Road to Wigan Pier* by George Orwell. Reprinted by permission of Harcourt
Brace Jovanovich, Inc.

underneath is the rock again, so that the gallery you are in is only as high as the ledge of coal itself, probably not much more than a yard. The first impression of all, overmastering everything else for a while, is the frightful, deafening din from the conveyor belt which carries the coal away. You cannot see very far, because the fog of coal dust throws back the beam of your lamp, but you can see on either side of you the line of half-naked kneeling men, one to every four or five yards, driving their shovels under the fallen coal and flinging it swiftly over their left shoulders. They are feeding it on to the conveyor belt, a moving rubber belt a couple of feet wide which runs a yard or two behind them. Down this belt a glittering river of coal races constantly. In a big mine it is carrying away several tons of coal every minute. It bears it off to some place in the main roads where it is shot into tubs holding half a ton, and thence dragged to the cages and hoisted to the outer air.

It is impossible to watch the "fillers" at work without feeling a pang of envy for 3 their toughness. It is a dreadful job that they do, an almost superhuman job by the standards of an ordinary person. For they are not only shifting monstrous quantities of coal, they are also doing it in a position that doubles or trebles the work. They have got to remain kneeling all the while—they could hardly rise from their knees without hitting the ceiling—and you can easily see by trying it what a tremendous effort this means. Shoveling is comparatively easy when you are standing up, because you can use your knee and thigh to drive the shovel along; kneeling down, the whole of the strain is thrown upon your arm and belly muscles. And the other conditions do not exactly make things easier. There is the heat—it varies, but in some mines it is suffocating—and the coal dust that stuffs up your throat and nostrils and collects along your eyelids, and the unending rattle of the conveyor belt, which in that confined space is rather like the rattle of a machine gun. . . .

Probably you have to go down several coal mines before you can get much 4 grasp of the processes that are going on round you. This is chiefly because the mere effort of getting from place to place makes it difficult to notice anything else. In some ways it is even disappointing, or at least is unlike what you have expected. You get into the cage, which is a steel box about as wide as a telephone box and two or three times as long. It holds ten men, but they pack it like pilchards in a tin, and a tall man cannot stand upright in it. The steel door shuts upon you, and somebody working the winding gear above drops you into the void. You have the usual momentary qualm in your belly and a bursting sensation in the ears, but not much sensation of movement till you get near the bottom, when the cage slows down so abruptly that you could swear it is going upward again. In the middle of the run the cage probably touches sixty miles an hour; in some of the deeper mines it touches even more. When you crawl out at the bottom you are perhaps four hundred yards underground. That is to say you have a tolerable-sized mountain on top of you; hundreds of yards of solid rock, bones of extinct beasts, subsoil, flints, roots of growing things, green grass and cows grazing on it—all this suspended over your head and held back only by wooden props as thick as the calf of your leg. But because of the speed at which the cage has brought you down, and the complete darkness through which you have traveled, you hardly feel yourself deeper down than you would at the bottom of the Piccadilly tube.[2]

What *is* surprising, on the other hand, is the immense horizontal distances 5 that have to be traveled underground. Before I had been down a mine I had vaguely imagined the miner stepping out of the cage and getting to work on a ledge of coal a few yards away. I had not realized that before he even gets to his work he may have to creep through passages as long as from London Bridge to Oxford Circus. In the beginning, of course, a mine shaft is sunk somewhere near a seam of coal. But as that seam is worked out and fresh seams are followed up, the workings get farther and farther from the pit bottom. If it is a mile from the pit bottom to the coal face, that is probably an average distance; three miles is a fairly normal one; there are even said to be a few mines where it is as much as five miles. But these distances bear no relation to distances above ground. For in all that mile or three miles as it may be, there is hardly anywhere outside the main road, and not many places even there, where a man can stand upright.

You do not notice the effect of this till you have gone a few hundred yards. 6 You start off, stooping slightly, down the dim-lit gallery, eight or ten feet wide and about five high, with the walls built up with slabs of shale, like the stone walls in Derbyshire.[3] Every yard or two there are wooden props holding up the beams and girders; some of the girders have buckled into fantastic curves under which you have to duck. Usually it is bad going underfoot—thick dust or jagged chunks of shale, and in some mines where there is water it is as mucky as a farmyard. Also there is the track for the coal tubs, like a miniature railway track with sleepers[4] a foot or two apart, which is tiresome to walk on. Everything is gray with shale dust; there is a dusty fiery smell which seems to be the same in all mines. You see mysterious machines of which you never learn the purpose, and bundles of tools slung together on wires, and sometimes mice darting away from the beam of the lamps. They are surprisingly common, especially in mines where there are or have been horses. It would be interesting to know how they got there in the first place; possibly by falling down the shaft—for they say a mouse can fall any distance uninjured, owing to its surface area being so large relative to its weight. You press yourself against the wall to make way for lines of tubs jolting slowly toward the shaft, drawn by an endless steel cable operated from the surface. You creep through sacking curtains and thick wooden doors which, when they are opened, let out fierce blasts of air. These doors are an important part of the ventilation system. The exhausted air is sucked out of one shaft by means of fans, and the fresh

---

[2]"Tube" is the common name for London's underground subway system, the largest in the world; Piccadilly is the name of a popular subway station located near the famous landmark Piccadilly Square. The average depth of London's subways is no more than forty-five feet.

[3]A county in north central England known for its formations of carboniferous rocks. Derbyshire contains fields divided by stone walls, which give the county a checkerboard appearance.

[4]The British word for railroad ties.

air enters the other of its own accord. But if left to itself the air will take the shortest way round, leaving the deeper workings unventilated; so all shortcuts have to be partitioned off.

At the start to walk stooping is rather a joke, but it is a joke that soon wears off. 7 I am handicapped by being exceptionally tall, but when the roof falls to four feet or less it is a tough job for anybody except a dwarf or a child. You have not only got to bend double, you have also got to keep your head up all the while so as to see the beams and girders and dodge them when they come. You have, therefore, a constant crick in the neck, but this is nothing to the pain in your knees and thighs. After half a mile it becomes (I am not exaggerating) an unbearable agony. You begin to wonder whether you will ever get to the end—still more, how on earth you are going to get back. Your pace grows slower and slower. You come to a stretch of a couple of hundred yards where it is all exceptionally low and you have to work yourself along in a squatting position. Then suddenly the roof opens out to a mysterious height—scene of an old fall of rock, probably—and for twenty whole yards you can stand upright. The relief is overwhelming. But after this there is another low stretch of a hundred yards and then a succession of beams which you have to crawl under. You go down on all fours; even this is a relief after the squatting business. But when you come to the end of the beams and try to get up again, you find that your knees have temporarily struck work and refuse to lift you. You call a halt, ignominiously, and say that you would like to rest for a minute or two. Your guide (a miner) is sympathetic. He knows that your muscles are not the same as his. "Only another four hundred yards," he says encouragingly; you feel that he might as well say another four hundred miles. But finally you do somehow creep as far as the coal face. You have gone a mile and taken the best part of an hour; a miner would do it in not much more than twenty minutes. Having got there, you have to sprawl in the coal dust and get your strength back for several minutes before you can even watch the work in progress with any kind of intelligence.

Coming back is worse than going, not only because you are already tired out 8 but because the journey back to the shaft is probably slightly uphill. You get through the low places at the speed of a tortoise, and you have no shame now about calling a halt when your knees give way. Even the lamp you are carrying becomes a nuisance and probably when you stumble you drop it; whereupon, if it is a Davy lamp, it goes out. Ducking the beams becomes more and more of an effort, and sometimes you forget to duck. You try walking head down as the miners do, and then you bang your backbone. Even the miners bang their backbones fairly often. This is the reason why in very hot mines, where it is necessary to go about half naked, most of the miners have what they call "buttons down the back"—that is, a permanent scab on each vertebra. When the track is downhill the miners some-times fit their clogs,[5] which are hollow underneath, on to the trolley rails and slide

[5]Heavy shoes that have thick wooden soles.

down. In mines where the "traveling" is very bad all the miners carry sticks about two and a half feet long, hollowed out below the handle. In normal places you keep your hand on top of the stick and in the low places you slide your hand down into the hollow. These sticks are a great help, and the wooden crash-helmets—a comparatively recent invention—are a godsend. They look like a French or Italian steel helmet, but they are made of some kind of pith and very light, and so strong that you can take a violent blow on the head without feeling it. When finally you get back to the surface you have been perhaps three hours underground and traveled two miles, and you are more exhausted than you would be by a twenty-five-mile walk above ground. For a week afterward your thighs are so stiff that coming downstairs is quite a difficult feat; you have to work your way down in a peculiar sidelong manner, without bending the knees. Your miner friends notice the stiffness of your walk and chaff you about it. ("How'd ta like to work down pit, eh?" etc.) Yet even a miner who has been long away from work—from illness, for instance—when he comes back to the pit, suffers badly for the first few days.

Questions on Content, Style, and Structure

1. What is Orwell's purpose in writing this description? Is his description primarily objective or subjective?
2. What is the dominant impression Orwell tries to convey? Point out words and passages to support your answer.
3. What is Orwell's attitude toward the coal miners? Again select words and passages to support your opinion.
4. Analyze Orwell's use of specific detail. Are there enough details to give you a clear understanding of what is being described? In paragraph 4, for example, how does Orwell use specific detail to make you aware of the true depth—and possible danger—of the mine?
5. Many of Orwell's descriptive passages affect the senses. Point out specific examples of language that are meant to trigger your sense of smell, sight, touch, or hearing.
6. Orwell often uses figurative language. Select some examples of metaphors and similes and explain how each one helps you to understand his description more clearly.
7. Notice Orwell's frequent choice of active verbs (for instance, in paragraph 2: "driving," "flinging," "races," "shot," "dragged," "hoisted"). How do these verbs contribute to the vividness of his descriptions?
8. Orwell describes the trip into the mine largely in terms of "you" rather than "I." What effect is he trying to produce by using the second-person point of view?
9. By what organizational plan does Orwell order his details in paragraphs 4 through 8?
10. This description may also be viewed as an essay developed by what expository strategy?

Vocabulary

To understand this essay completely, you should know the meanings of the following words:

trebles (3)

pilchards (4)

qualm (4)

girders (6)

shale (6)

ignominiously (7)

vertebra (8)

pith (8)

chaff (8)

11

Narration

Not all narratives begin "Once upon a time," nor are they limited to the kinds of fiction found in novels and short stories. In this chapter we are not concerned with "how to write best-selling fiction"—that's a skill taught in creative writing classes—but rather with those narratives, or stories, that may be used in your essays to explain or prove a point. Some narratives will support your essay's thesis; for example, if you wanted to show how registration is a dehumanizing process, you might tell your readers the story of your (or a friend's) horrible experience. Other shorter narratives may be used to support a particular point in an expository, argumentative, or descriptive essay; if, for instance, you were writing an essay on a nearby ghost town, you might tell, briefly, the story of the town's founding or of its demise. Or you might want to begin one of your essays with a brief incident that will lead the reader to your thesis. Regardless of how you use it, though, narration is frequently an informative, persuasive means of swaying the readers to your opinion. (By the way, don't let the word "narration" fool you into thinking that all stories are fictional; some of the best stories are true, and more often than not you'll probably be writing about your own experiences or those of friends.)

HOW TO WRITE EFFECTIVE NARRATION

While narratives differ according to each writer's purpose and imagination, here are some general hints for writing successful stories or anecdotes (these are short narratives that reveal the character of a person, place, or event; they are frequently humorous).

Know Your Purpose. As mentioned previously, narratives in most essays are designed to support or illustrate a specific point or thesis. Don't allow your story to run on pointlessly so that the reader must wonder, "Where is this going? What is the meaning of this story?" Tailor your narrative to fit your purpose. On the other hand, don't turn your narrative into a sermonette—support your thesis with an entertaining story that informs rather than preaches.

Maintain a Consistent Point of View. This subject is complex, and teachers of literature courses often spend much time explaining it in detail. For your purposes, however, a brief treatment will suffice. In the first place, you should decide whether the story will be told by you in the first person, by a character involved in the plot, or by an omniscient ("all-knowing") narrator who may reveal the thoughts, feelings, and actions of any character. The selection of a point of view is important because it determines whose thoughts or actions will be described. If, for example, one of your female characters narrates the story, she is limited to giving only the information that she can know; that is, she cannot reveal another character's thoughts or describe an event that took place across town, out of her sight. Once you have decided which point of view is best for your purpose, be consistent; don't abruptly change point of view in mid-story.

Follow a Logical Time Sequence. Most narrative essays—or stories used in other kinds of essays—follow a chronological order, presenting events as they occur in the story. Occasionally, however, a writer will use the flashback technique, which takes the readers back in time to reveal an incident that occurred before the opening scene of the story. Many novelists and short story writers use a variety of techniques to alter time sequences in their fiction; Joseph Heller's famous novel *Catch-22*, for example, contains chaotic time shifts to emphasize the absurd nature of war. Most stories used in essays, however, follow a strictly chronological order.

Use Details To Present the Setting. Most stories are set in particular times and places. If the setting plays an important role in your story, you must describe it in vivid terms so that your readers can imagine it easily. For example, let's suppose you are pointing out the necessity of life preservers on sailboats by telling the story of how you spent a horrible, stormy night in the lake, clinging to your capsized boat. To convince your readers, let them "feel" the stinging rain and the icy current trying to drag you under; let them "see" the black waves, the dark, menacing sky; let them "hear" the howling wind and the gradual splitting apart of the boat. Effective narration often depends upon effective description, and effective description depends upon vivid, specific detail. (For more help on writing description, see Chapter 10.)

Make Your Characters Believable. Again, the use of detail is crucial. Your readers should be able to visualize your characters clearly; if your characters are drawn too thinly, or if they seem phony or stereotyped, your readers will not fully grasp the intensity of your story, and thus its meaning will be lost. Show the readers a realistic picture of the major characters by commenting unobtrusively on their appearances, speech, and actions. In addition, a successful narrative depends upon the reader's understanding of characters' motives—why they act the way they do in certain situations. A story in which a grouchy miser suddenly donates a large sum of money to a poor family isn't very believable unless we know the motive behind the action. In other words, let your readers know what is happening to whom by explaining *why*.

Use Dialogue Realistically. If your story calls for dialogue, be sure the word choice and the manner of speaking are in keeping with the character's education, background, age, location, and so forth. Don't, for example, put a sophisticated philosophical treatise into the mouth of a ten-year-old boy or the latest campus slang into the speeches of an auto mechanic from Two Egg, Florida. Also, make sure that your dialogue doesn't sound "wooden" or phony. The right dialogue can help make your characters more realistic and interesting, provided that the conversations are essential to the plot and are not merely substituted for dramatic action. (For help in punctuating dialogue, see pp. 237–238 in Part Three.)

Problems To Avoid

Unconvincing, boring narratives are often the result of poor choices of subject matter and/or bad pacing; therefore, you should keep in mind the following advice:

Don't Write on Unfamiliar Subjects. In narrative essays most of the best stories come from personal experience, and the reason is fairly obvious: it's difficult to write convincingly about something you've never seen or done. You probably couldn't, for instance, write a realistic account of a bullfight unless you'd seen one or at least had studied the subject in great detail. The simplest, easiest, most interesting narrative you can write is likely to be about an event with which you are personally familiar. This doesn't mean that you can't improvise many details or give your story some imaginative twists, but, in general, try to write about something or someone you know well.

Don't Let Your Story Lag with Insignificant Detail. At some time you've probably listened to a storyteller who became stuck on some insignificant detail ("Was it Friday or Saturday the letter came? Let's see now . . . " "Then Joe said to me—no, it was Sally—no, wait, it was . . . "). And you've probably also heard bores who insist on making a short story long by including too many unimportant details or digressions. These mistakes ruin the *pacing* of their stories; in other words, the story's tempo or movement becomes bogged down until the reader is bored witless. To avoid putting your reader to sleep, dismiss all unessential details and focus your attention—and use of detail—on the important events, people, and places. Skip uneventful periods of time by using such phrases as "A week went by before Mr. Smith called . . . " or "Later that evening, around nine o'clock . . . " In short, keep the story moving quickly enough to hold the reader's interest. More-over, you should use a variety of transition devices to move the reader from one action to another; don't rely continuously on the childish "and then . . . and then . . . " method.

Essay Topics

Use one of the topics below to suggest an essay that is at least partially, if not entirely, supported by narration. Remember that each essay must have a purpose or thesis.

1. a loyal pet or friend
2. the worst mix-up of your life
3. your best Christmas (birthday or any holiday)
4. your first/worst auto accident
5. an act of courage
6. your most frightening childhood experience
7. a memorable vacation incident
8. meeting a celebrity
9. an event that changed your thinking on a particular subject
10. your first/worst date
11. a person who influenced your choice of career (or some other important decision)
12. your first introduction to prejudice or sexism
13. being hired or fired from your first or most important job
14. a triumph in sports or in some artistic endeavor

Student Essay

In this narrative a student uses a story about a sick but fierce dog to show how she learned a valuable lesson in her job as a veterinarian's assistant. Notice the student's good use of vivid details that makes this well-paced story both clear and interesting.

NEVER UNDERESTIMATE THE LITTLE THINGS

Introduction: a
misconception

When I went to work as a veterinarian's assistant for Dr. Sam Holt and Dr. Jack Gunn last summer, I was under the false impression that the hardest part of veterinary surgery would be the actual performance of an operation. What might transpire before or after this feat didn't occur to me as being of any importance. As it happened, I had been in the veterinary clinic only a total of four hours before I met a little animal who

Thesis

convinced me that the operation itself was probably the easiest part of treatment. This animal, to whom I owe thanks for so enlightening me, was a chocolate-colored chihuahua of tiny size and immense perversity named Smokey.

Description of the
story's main
character:
his appearance

Now Smokey could have very easily passed for some creature from another planet. It wasn't so much his gaunt little frame and overly large head, or his bony paws with nearly saberlike claws, as it was his grossly infected eyes. Those once-shining eyes were now distorted and swollen into grotesque balls of septic, sightless flesh. The only vague similarity they had to what we'd normally think of as the organs of vision was a slightly upraised dot, all that was left of the pupil, in the center of a pink and purply marble. As if that were not enough, Smokey had a temper to match his ugly sight. He also had surprisingly good aim, considering his largely diminished vision, toward any moving object that happened to place itself unwisely before his ever-inquisitive nose, and with sudden and wholly vicious

his personality

intent he would snap and snarl at whatever blocked the little light that could filter through his swollen and ruptured blood vessels. Truly, in many respects, Smokey was a fearful dog to behold.

Beginning of the
story: dog in the cage

Such an appearance and personality did nothing to encourage my already flagging confidence in my capabilities as a vet's assistant. How was I supposed to get that little demon out of his cage? Jack had casually requested that I bring Smokey to the surgery room, but did he really expect me to put my hands into the mouth of the cage of that devil dog? I suppose it must have been my anxious expression that saved me, for as I turned uncertainly toward the kennel, Jack chuckled nonchalantly and accompanied me to demonstrate how professionals in his line of business dealt with professionals in Smokey's. He took a small rope about four feet long with a slipnoose at one end and began to unlatch Smokey's cage. Then cautiously he reached in and dangled the noose before the dog's snarling jaws. Since Smokey could only barely see what he was biting at, his attacks were directed haphazardly in a semicircle around his body. The tiny area of his cage led to his capture, for during one of Smokey's forward lunges, Jack dropped the noose over his head and dragged the struggling creature out onto the floor. The fight had only just begun for Smokey, however, and he braced his feet against the slippery linoleum tiling and forced us to drag him, like a little pull toy on a string, to the surgery.

In the surgery room

Once in the surgery, however, the question that hung before our eyes like a veritable presence was how to get the dog from floor to table. Simply picking him up and plopping him down was out of the question. One glance at the quivering little figure emitting ominous and throaty warnings was enough to assure us of that. Realizing that the game was over, Jack grimly handed me the rope and reached for a muzzle. It was a doomed attempt from the start; the closer Jack dangled the tiny leather cup to the dog's nose the more violent did Smokey's contortions and rage-filled cries become and the more frantic our efforts became to try to keep our feet and fingers clear of the angry jaws. Deciding that a firmer method had to be used, Jack instructed me to raise the rope up high enough so that Smokey'd have to stand on his hind legs. This greatly reduced his maneuverability but served to increase his tenacity, for at this the little dog nearly went into paroxysms of frustration and rage. In his struggles, however, Smokey caught his forepaw on his swollen eye, and the blood that had been building up pressure behind the fragile cornea burst out and dripped to the floor. In the midst of our surprise and the twinge of panic startling the three of us, Jack saw his chance and swiftly muzzled the animal and lifted him to the operating table.

During the operation

Even at that point it wasn't easy to put the now terrified dog to sleep. He fought even the local anesthesia and caused Jack to curse as he was forced to give Smokey far more of the drug than should have been necessary for such a small beast. After what seemed an eternity, Smokey lay prone on the table, breathing deeply and emitting soft snores and gentle whines. We also breathed deeply in relief, and I relaxed to watch fascinated, while Jack performed a very delicate operation quite smoothly and without mishap.

Conclusion: restatement of thesis

Such was my harrowing induction into the life of a veterinary surgeon. But Smokey did teach me a valuable lesson that has proven its importance to me many times since, and that is that wherever animals are concerned, even the smallest detail should never be taken for granted.

Professional Essay
_____

Shame

Dick Gregory

Dick Gregory is a comedian, civil-rights activist, lecturer, and author of a number of books, including *The Shadow That Scares Me, From the Back of the Bus,* and *Dick Gregory's Political Primer.* This story is taken from *nigger: An Autobiography.*

I never learned hate at home, or shame. I had to go to school for that. I was 1 about seven years old when I got my first big lesson. I was in love with a little girl named Helene Tucker, a light-complected little girl with pigtails and nice manners. She was always clean and she was smart in school. I think I went to school mostly to look at her. I brushed my hair and even got me a little old handkerchief. It was a lady's handkerchief, but I didn't want Helene to see me wipe my nose on my hand. The pipes were frozen again, there was no water in the house, but I washed my socks and shirt every night. I'd get a pot, and go over to Mr. Ben's grocery store, and stick my pot down into his soda machine. Scoop out some chopped ice. By evening the ice melted to water for washing. I got sick a lot that winter because the fire would go out at night before the clothes were dry. In the morning I'd put them on, wet or dry, because they were the only clothes I had.

Everybody's got a Helene Tucker, a symbol of everything you want. I loved 2 her for her goodness, her cleanliness, her popularity. She'd walk down my street and my brothers and sisters would yell, "Here comes Helene," and I'd rub my tennis sneakers on the back of my pants and wish my hair wasn't so nappy and the white folks' shirt fit me better. I'd run out on the street. If I knew my place and didn't come too close, she'd wink at me and say hello. That was a good feeling. Sometimes I'd follow her all the way home, and shovel the snow off her walk and try to make friends with her Momma and her aunts. I'd drop money on her stoop late at night on my way back from shining shoes in the taverns. And she had a Daddy, and he had a good job. He was a paper hanger.

I guess I would have gotten over Helene by summertime, but something 3 happened in that classroom that made her face hang in front of me for the next twenty-two years. When I played the drums in high school it was for Helene and when I broke track records in college it was for Helene and when I started standing behind microphones and heard applause I wished Helene could hear it, too. It wasn't until I was twenty-nine years old and married and making money that I really got her out of my system. Helene was sitting in that classroom when I learned to be ashamed of myself.

From *nigger: An Autobiography* by Dick Gregory with Robert Lipsyte. Copyright © 1964 by Dick Gregory Enterprises, Inc. Reprinted by permission of the publisher, E. P. Dutton, Inc.

It was on a Thursday. I was sitting in the back of the room, in a seat with a 4
chalk circle drawn around it. The idiot's seat, the troublemaker's seat.

The teacher thought I was stupid. Couldn't spell, couldn't read, couldn't do 5
arithmetic. Just stupid. Teachers were never interested in finding out that you
couldn't concentrate because you were so hungry, because you hadn't had any
breakfast. All you could think about was noontime, would it ever come? Maybe
you could sneak into the cloakroom and steal a bite of some kid's lunch out of a
coat pocket. A bite of something. Paste. You can't really make a meal out of paste,
or put it on bread for a sandwich, but sometimes I'd scoop a few spoonfuls out of
the paste jar in the back of the room. Pregnant people get strange tastes. I was
pregnant with poverty. Pregnant with dirt and pregnant with smells that made
people turn away, pregnant with cold and pregnant with shoes that were never
bought for me, pregnant with five other people in my bed and no Daddy in the next
room, and pregnant with hunger. Paste doesn't taste too bad when you're hungry.

The teacher thought I was a troublemaker. All she saw from the front of the 6
room was a little black boy who squirmed in his idiot's seat and made noises and
poked the kids around him. I guess she couldn't see a kid who made noises because
he wanted someone to know he was there.

It was on a Thursday, the day before the Negro payday. The eagle always flew 7
on Friday. The teacher was asking each student how much his father would give to
the Community Chest. On Friday night, each kid would get the money from his
father, and on Monday he would bring it to the school. I decided I was going to buy
me a Daddy right then. I had money in my pocket from shining shoes and selling
papers, and whatever Helene Tucker pledged for her Daddy I was going to top it.
And I'd hand the money right in. I wasn't going to wait until Monday to buy me a
Daddy.

I was shaking, scared to death. The teacher opened her book and started 8
calling out names alphabetically.

"Helene Tucker?"   9

"My Daddy said he'd give two dollars and fifty cents."   10

"That's very nice, Helene. Very, very nice indeed."   11

That made me feel pretty good. It wouldn't take too much to top that. I had 12
almost three dollars in dimes and quarters in my pocket. I stuck my hand in my
pocket and held onto the money, waiting for her to call my name. But the teacher
closed her book after she called everybody else in the class.

I stood up and raised my hand.   13

"What is it now?"   14

"You forgot me."   15

She turned toward the blackboard. "I don't have time to be playing with you, 16
Richard."

"My Daddy said he'd . . ."   17

"Sit down, Richard, you're disturbing the class."   18

"My Daddy said he'd give . . . fifteen dollars."   19

She turned and looked mad. "We are collecting this money for you and your 20 kind, Richard Gregory. If your Daddy can give fifteen dollars you have no business being on relief."

"I got it right now, I got it right now, my Daddy gave it to me to turn in today,   21
my Daddy said . . ."

"And furthermore," she said, looking right at me, her nostrils getting big and   22
her lips getting thin and her eyes opening wide, "we know you don't have a
Daddy."

Helene Tucker turned around, her eyes full of tears. She felt sorry for me.   23
Then I couldn't see her too well because I was crying, too.

"Sit down, Richard."   24

And I always thought the teacher kind of liked me. She always picked me to   25
wash the blackboard on Friday, after school. That was a big thrill, it made me feel
important. If I didn't wash it, come Monday the school might not function right.

"Where are you going, Richard?"   26

I walked out of school that day, and for a long time I didn't go back very often.   27
There was shame there.

Now there was shame everywhere. It seemed like the whole world had been   28
inside that classroom, everyone had heard what the teacher had said, everyone had
turned around and felt sorry for me. There was shame in going to the Worthy Boys
Annual Christmas Dinner for you and your kind, because everybody knew what a
worthy boy was. Why couldn't they just call it the Boys Annual Dinner, why'd
they have to give it a name? There was shame in wearing the brown and orange and
white plaid mackinaw the welfare gave to 3,000 boys. Why'd it have to be the same
for everybody so when you walked down the street the people could see you were
on relief? It was a nice warm mackinaw and it had a hood, and my Momma beat
me and called me a little rat when she found out I stuffed it in the bottom of a pail
full of garbage way over on Cottage Street. There was shame in running over to
Mister Ben's at the end of the day and asking for his rotten peaches, there was
shame in asking Mrs. Simmons for a spoonful of sugar, there was shame in
running out to meet the relief truck. I hated that truck, full of food for you and your
kind. I ran into the house and hid when it came. And then I started to sneak
through alleys, to take the long way home so the people going into White's Eat
Shop wouldn't see me. Yeah, the whole world heard the teacher that day, we all
know you don't have a Daddy.

Questions on Content, Style, and Structure

1. What is Gregory's purpose in telling this story from his childhood? What information about himself is he trying to explain to the reader?

2. For Gregory, who was Helene Tucker, and why was it important to "buy" himself a Daddy? Why did Helene's face hang before Gregory until he was twenty-nine? How did he finally get her "out of his system"?

3. Are the events in this story told in strict chronological order? If not, where are the deviations and why are they included?

4. Does Gregory use enough vivid detail to help you visualize the people and events of his story? Support your answer by citing specific passages.

5. Which characters are most developed in this story? How does Gregory help you understand the motivations for their actions? Is there any one character more fully developed than the others? If so, why?
6. Evaluate Gregory's use of dialogue. What does it add to the story?
7. Comment on Gregory's use of parallel construction in paragraphs 5 and 28.
8. Point out examples of slang and colloquial language in this story. Why did Gregory use such language?
9. How effective is Gregory's conclusion?

Vocabulary

To understand this story completely, you should know the meanings of the following words:

nappy (2)
pregnant (5)
mackinaw (28)

PART

3

A CONCISE HANDBOOK

In this section you will learn to recognize and correct the most common errors in grammar, punctuation, and mechanics. Each error will be explained as simply as possible, with a minimum of technical language. Beside each rule you will find the mark most teachers use to indicate that error in your essays.

Chapter

Major Errors in Grammar

ERRORS WITH VERBS
Faulty Agreement   S-V Agr

Make your verb agree in number with its subject; a singular subject takes a singular verb, and a plural subject takes a plural verb.

> Incorrect: *Lester Peabody*, principal of the Kung Fu School of Grammar, *don't* agree that gum chewing should be banned in the classroom.
>
> Correct: *Lester Peabody*, principal of the Kung Fu School of Grammar, *doesn't* agree that gum chewing should be banned in the classroom.

> Incorrect: The *actions* of the new Senator *hasn't* been consistent with his campaign promises.
>
> Correct: The *actions* of the new Senator *haven't* been consistent with his campaign promises.

A compound subject takes a plural verb, unless the subject denotes a single person or a single unit.

> Examples: *Coconuts* and *bananas were* Mungo's favorite foods for years after his rescue from the desert island. ["Coconuts" and "bananas" are two elements in a compound subject; therefore, use a plural verb.]
>
> The *winner* and new *champion refuses* to give up the microphone at the news conference. ["Winner" and "champion" denote a single person; therefore, use a singular verb.]

211

Listed below are some of the most confusing subject-verb agreement problems:

1. With a collective noun: a singular noun referring to a collection of elements as a unit generally takes a singular verb.

Incorrect: After Dr. Hall's lectures, the *class* often *throw* spoiled fruit.
Correct: After Dr. Hall's lectures, the *class* often *throws* spoiled fruit.

Incorrect: The *army* of the new nation *want* shoes, bullets, and weekend passes.
Correct: The *army* of the new nation *wants* shoes, bullets, and weekend passes.

However, you sometimes use a plural verb when the collective noun refers to its members as parts rather than to the group as a unit.

Incorrect: After Sticky Fingers O'Hoolihan visited the Queen, a *number of the crown jewels was* missing.
Correct: After Sticky Fingers O'Hoolihan visited the Queen, a *number of the crown jewels were* missing.

Incorrect: A small *group of the actors has* forgotten their lines.
Correct: A small *group of the actors have* forgotten their lines.

2. With a relative pronoun ("that," "which," "who" used as a subject: the verb agrees with its antecedent.

Incorrect: The boss rejected a shipment of *shirts* that *was* torn.
Correct: The boss rejected a shipment of *shirts* that *were* torn.

3. With "each," "none," "everyone," "neither" as the subject: use a singular verb even when followed by a plural construction.

Incorrect: *Each* of the boys at Harriet Tubman Junior High *have* a distinct opinion on whether girls should play football.
Correct: *Each* of the boys at Harriet Tubman Junior High *has* a distinct opinion on whether girls should play football.

Incorrect: All the students saw the teacher pull out his hair, but *none know* why he did it.
Correct: All the students saw the teacher pull out his hair, but *none knows* why he did it.

Incorrect: *Neither have* a dime left by the second of the month.
Correct: *Neither has* a dime left by the second of the month.

4. With "either . . . or," "neither . . . nor": the verb agrees with the nearer item.

Incorrect: Neither rain nor dogs nor *gloom of night keep* the mailman from delivering bills.
Correct: Neither rain nor dogs nor *gloom of night keeps* the mailman from delivering bills.

Incorrect: Either Betty or her *neighbors is* hosting a come-as-you-are breakfast.
Correct: Either Betty or her *neighbors are* hosting a come-as-you-are breakfast.

5. With "here is (are)," "there is (are)": the verb agrees with the number indicated by the subject following the verb.

Incorrect: *There is* only two good *reasons* for missing this law class: death and jury duty.
Correct: *There are* only two good *reasons* for missing this law class: death and jury duty.

Incorrect: To remind you of your obligations, *here are* a *list* of people to whom you owe money.
Correct: To remind you of your obligations, *here is* a *list* of people to whom you owe money.

6. With plural nouns intervening between subject and verb: the verb still agrees with the subject.

Incorrect: The *jungle,* with its poisonous plants, wild animals, and biting insects, *make* Herman long for the sidewalks of Topeka.
Correct: The *jungle,* with its poisonous plants, wild animals, and biting insects, *makes* Herman long for the sidewalks of Topeka.

7. With nouns plural in form but singular in meaning: a singular verb is usually correct.

Examples: *News travels* slowly if it comes through the post office.
            Politics is often the rich person's hobby.

Subjunctive   V Sub

When you make a wish or a statement that is contrary to fact, use the subjunctive verb form "were."

Incorrect: My mother always wished she *was* queen so she could levy a tax on men who cursed.

Correct: My mother always wished she *were* queen so she could levy a tax on men who cursed. [This expresses a wish.]

Incorrect: If "Fightin' Henry" *was* a foot taller and thirty pounds heavier, we would all be in trouble.

Correct: If "Fightin' Henry" *were* a foot taller and thirty pounds heavier, we would all be in trouble. [This proposes a statement contrary to fact.]

Tense Shift   T

In most cases the first verb in a sentence establishes the tense of any later verb. Keep your verbs within the same time frame.

Incorrect: Talmadge *bought* his second wife a ring for her birthday, but she *hocks* it the next day.

Correct: Talmadge *bought* his second wife a ring for her birthday, but she *hocked* it the next day.

Incorrect: Horace *uses* an artificial sweetener in his coffee all day, so he *felt* a pizza and a hot-fudge sundae were fine for dinner.

Correct: Horace *uses* an artificial sweetener in his coffee all day, so he *feels* a pizza and a hot-fudge sundae are fine for dinner.

Incorrect: Rex the Wonder Horse *was* obviously very smart because he *taps* out the telephone numbers of the stars with his hoof.

Correct: Rex the Wonder Horse *was* obviously very smart because he *tapped* out the telephone numbers of the stars with his hoof.

Split Infinitive   Sp I

Many authorities insist that you never separate *to* from its verb; today, however, some grammarians allow the split infinitive except in the most formal kinds of writing. Nevertheless, because it offends some readers, it is probably best to avoid the construction unless clarity or emphasis is clearly served by its use.

Traditional: A swift kick is needed *to start* the machine properly.
Untraditional: A swift kick is needed *to* properly *start* the machine.

Traditional: The teacher wanted Lori *to communicate* her ideas clearly.
Untraditional: The teacher wanted Lori *to* clearly *communicate* her ideas.

Double Negatives   D Neg

Don't use a negative verb and a negative qualifier together.

Incorrect: I *can't hardly* wait until Jim Bob gets his jaw out of traction, so I can punch him again.

Correct: I *can hardly* wait until Jim Bob gets his jaw out of traction, so (
            can punch him again.

Incorrect: He *didn't have scarcely* enough moonshine to pass around.
Correct: He *had scarcely* enough moonshine to pass around.

Passive Voice   Pass

For the most part, your prose style will improve if you choose strong active voice
verbs over weak passive voice verbs.

Weak passive verb: It is obvious that dirty words are being written on the
                     restroom walls by the company's junior executives.
Strong active verb: The company's junior executives obviously write dirty
                     words on the restroom walls.

Weak passive verb: Much protest is being voiced over the new Z.A.P.
                     bomb by members of the Fuse Lighters Association.
Strong active verb: Members of the Fuse Lighters Association are protest-
                     ing the new Z.A.P. bomb.

Weak passive verb: After the successful nose-transplant operation, the sur-
                     geon and his staff were given a round of applause by the
                     malpractice lawyers in attendance.
Strong active verb: After the successful nose-transplant operation, the
                     malpractice lawyers in attendance applauded the sur-
                     geon and his staff.

(For more examples of active and passive voice verbs, see pp. 65−66.)

Practicing What You've Learned

Errors with Verbs

Correct the sentences below, identifying each error you see. Skip any correct
sentence.

1. The ichthyologist's references to goldfish, the common household
   pet that once were an object of worship in ancient China, reminds
   Allison to feed her cat.
2. Each of our feet contain one fourth of all the bones in the human
   body.
3. Eighty percent of all auto accidents causing serious injury or death
   involves cars traveling under forty miles per hour.
4. Neither Clyde nor his friends knows that tomatoes originated in
   Peru.
5. For centuries tomatoes were thought to be dangerous by Europeans.

6. Either Jim Brown or O. J. Simpson win the honor of being known as the fastest man in football.

7 Everyone who has driven a car in a rainstorm is grateful to Mary Anderson, who invented the windshield wiper in 1903.

8. The team from Houston College are considering switching from baseball to volleyball because passing athletics are required for graduation.

9. Observation of Cuban land crabs show that they can run faster than horses.

10 None of his biographers believe that billionaire Cornelius Vander-bilt slept with the legs of his bed in dishes of salt to keep away evil spirits.

ERRORS WITH NOUNS   N

Possessive with "-ing" Nouns

When the emphasis is on the action, use the possessive form plus the "-ing" noun.

Example: He hated *my* singing around the house, so I made him live in the garage. [The emphasis is on *singing*.]

When the emphasis is not on the action, you may use a noun or pronoun plus the "-ing" noun.

Example: He hated *me* singing around the house, so I made him live in the garage. [The emphasis is on the person singing—*me*—not the action; he might have liked someone else singing.]

Misuse of Nouns as Adjectives

Some nouns may be used as adjectives modifying other nouns: "horse show," "movie star," "theater seats," etc. But some nouns used as adjectives sound awkward or like jargon. To avoid such awkwardness, you may need to change the noun to an appropriate adjective or reword the sentence.

Awkward: She worked hard to win the *president* race.
Better: She worked hard to win the *presidential* race.

Jargon: The executive began a *cost estimation comparison study* of the two products.
Better: The executive began to *study a comparison* of the two products' costs.

(For more information on ridding your prose of jargon, see pp. 91–92.)

ERRORS WITH PRONOUNS

Faulty Agreement   P Agr

A pronoun should agree in number and gender with its antecedent (that is, the word the pronoun stands for).

> Incorrect: To get a temperamental *actress* to sign a contract, the director would lock *them* in their dressing room.
>
> Correct: To get a temperamental *actress* to sign a contract, the director would lock *her* in her dressing room.

Use the singular pronoun with "everyone," "anyone," and "each".

> Incorrect: When the belly dancer asked for a volunteer partner from the audience, *everyone* in the YMCA raised *their* hand.
>
> Correct: When the belly dancer asked for a volunteer partner from the audience, *everyone* in the YMCA raised *his* hand.

> Incorrect: *Each* of the new wives decided to keep *their* own name.
>
> Correct: *Each* of the new wives decided to keep *her* own name.

Grammarians, sociologists, linguists, Women's Liberation proponents, and a myriad of others are still debating the use of the masculine pronoun "he" when the gender of the antecedent is unknown, as in the following: "If the *spy* refuses to answer questions, *he* should be forced to watch James Bond movies until *he* cracks." Some authorities now accept "she/he" (or the abbreviated "s/he"); others staunchly stand by "he" to represent both sexes, claiming that the "she/he" construction is awkward when maintained over a stretch of prose. Perhaps the best solution is to use the impersonal "one" when possible or simply rewrite the sentence in the plural: "If *spies* refuse to answer questions, *they* should be forced to watch James Bond movies until *they* crack."

Vague Reference   Ref

Your pronoun references should be clear.

> Vague: If the trained seal won't eat its dinner, throw *it* into the lion's cage. [What goes into the lion's cage?]
>
> Clear: If the trained seal won't eat its dinner, throw *the food* into the lion's cage.

> Vague: I'm a lab instructor in the biology department and am also taking a composition course. *This* has always been difficult for me. [Which action is difficult?]
>
> Clear: I'm a lab instructor in the biology department and am also taking composition, *a course* that has always been difficult for me.

Shift in Pronouns   P Sh

Be consistent in your use of pronouns; don't shift from one person to another.

Incorrect: When *you* are giving a report *one* should speak clearly.
Correct: When you are giving a report *you* should speak clearly

Incorrect: *We* left-handed people are at a disadvantage because most of the
            time *they* can't rent left-handed golf clubs or bowling balls.
Correct: *We* left-handed people are at a disadvantage because most of the
            time *we* can't rent left-handed golf clubs or bowling balls.

(For additional examples, see p. 70.)

Incorrect Case   Ca

The case of a pronoun is determined by its function. If the pronoun is a subject,
use the nominative case: "I," "he," "she," "we," "they"; if the pronoun is an
object, use the objective case: "me," "him," "her," "us," "them." To check your
usage, however, all you need to do in most cases is isolate the pronoun in the
manner shown here and see if it makes sense alone.

Incorrect: Give the smashed cupcakes to Frankie and *I*.
Isolated: Give the smashed cupcakes to *I*.
Correct: Give the smashed cupcakes to Frankie and *me*.

Incorrect: Bertram and *her* suspect that the moon is hollow.
Isolated: *Her* suspects that the moon is hollow.
Correct: Bertram and *she* suspect that the moon is hollow.

In other cases, to determine the correct pronoun, you will need to add
implied but unstated sentence elements.

Examples: Mother always liked Dickie more than *me*. [Mother liked Dickie
            more than *she liked* me.]
            She is younger than *I* by three days. [She is younger than I *am* by
            three days.]

To solve the confusing *who/whom* pronoun problem, first determine the case
of the pronoun in its own clause in each sentence.
    1. If the pronoun is the subject of a clause, use "who" or "whoever."

Examples: I don't know *who* spread the peanut butter on my English paper.
            ["Who" is the subject of the verb "spread" in the clause "who
            spread the peanut butter on my English paper."]

Dolores is an exotic dancer *who* won't perform in front of strangers. ["Who" is the subject of the verb "won't perform" in the clause "who won't perform in front of strangers."]
He will sell secrets to *whoever* offers the largest sum of money. ["Whoever" is the subject of the verb "offers" in the clause "whoever offers the largest sum of money."]

2. If the pronoun is the object of a verb, use "whom" or "whomever."

Examples: *Whom* am I kicking? ["Whom" is the direct object of the verb "kicking."]
Sid is a man *whom* I distrust. ["Whom" is the direct object of the verb "distrust."]
Whomever he kicked will probably be angry. ["Whomever" is the direct object of the verb "kicked."]

3. If the pronoun occurs as the object of a preposition, use "whom," especially when the preposition immediately precedes the pronoun.

Examples: *With whom* am I dancing?
To whom does the credit belong for spreading peanut butter on my English paper?
Do not ask *for whom* the bell tolls.

Practicing What You've Learned

Errors with Nouns and Pronouns

Correct the sentences below. Skip any correct sentences.

1. Harpo Marx, Jack the Ripper, Gerald Ford, and me are left-handed.
2. The first movie to gross over one million dollars was *Tarzan of the Apes* (1932) starring Johnny Weissmuller, a former Olympic star who became an actor. This didn't happen often in the movie industry at that time.
3. At the meeting we discussed new projects, including the wind-tunnel effectiveness study implementation.
4. It was a shock to both Esther and I to learn that veal comes from a calf, not a lamb.
5. According to a 1981 Labor Department study, a woman working full-time will not earn as much in their lifetime as men in the same occupations.
6. Of whom did Oscar Wilde once say, "He hasn't a single redeeming vice"?
7. By becoming a hot-air balloon racer, she was not living up to the conformity compliance standards of her neighborhood.

8. He had to tell his father, who was a great scholar, about his grade point average, which upset him greatly.
9. She sent the wedding reception invitations to Clarence and I, but it didn't arrive on time.
10. Many people don't use seat belts because they are afraid of being trapped in a wrecked car, but the truth is that you are in more danger of being hurt if you're thrown from the car.

ERRORS WITH ADVERBS AND ADJECTIVES
Incorrect Usage   Adv   Adj

Incorrect use of adverbs and adjectives often occurs when you confuse the two modifiers. Adverbs qualify the meaning of verbs, adjectives, and other adverbs; they frequently end in "-ly," and they often answer the question "how?"

Incorrect: After Hal fired his guru, his ears hurt *bad*.
Correct: After Hal fired his guru, his ears hurt *badly*. [How did his ears hurt?]

Adjectives, on the other hand, describe or qualify the meanings of nouns only.

Example: The *superstitious* guru went back into the mountains to put a curse on his former employer's ears.

One of the most confusing pairs of modifiers is "well" and "good." We often use "good" as an adjective modifying a noun and "well" as an adverb modifying a verb.

Examples: *How To Steal Social Security Checks from Old Ladies* is not a *good* book.
A *good* person is hard to find and even harder to hold onto.
I'm not feeling *well*.
Did you do *well* on your English test?

If you cannot determine whether a word is an adverb or adjective, consult your dictionary.

Faulty Comparison   Comp

When you compare two elements to a higher or lower degree, you often add "-er" or "-r" to the adjective.

Incorrect: Of the two girls, Sara is *tallest*.
Correct: Of the two girls, Sara is *taller*.

When you compare more than two elements, you often add "-est" to the adjective.

Example: Sara is the *tallest* of all the girls in her class.

Other adjectives use the words "more," "most," "less," and "least" to indicate comparison.

Examples: Bela Lugosi is *more* handsome than Lon Chaney but *less* handsome than Vincent Price.
Boris Karloff is the *most* handsome and Christopher Lee is the *least* handsome of all the horror film stars.

ERRORS IN MODIFYING PHRASES
Dangling Modifiers   DM

A modifying—or descriptive—phrase must have a logical relationship to some specific words in the sentence. When those words are omitted, the phrase "dangles" without anything to modify. Dangling modifiers frequently occur at the beginnings of sentences and often may be corrected by adding the proper subjects to the main clauses.

Dangling: Not knowing how to swim, buying scuba gear was foolish.
Correct: Not knowing how to swim, *I decided that* buying scuba gear was foolish.

Dangling: Furious over the puddles on her new carpet, the dog was pitched out the door.
Correct: Furious over the puddles on her new carpet, *Ms. Potatohead* pitched the dog out the door.

Misplaced Modifiers   MM

When modifying words, phrases, or clauses are not placed near the word they describe, confusion or unintentional humor often results.

Misplaced: Joe Bob recalled the day he had married Louise while sipping beer at their favorite bar.
Correct: While sipping beer at their favorite bar, Joe Bob recalled the day he had married Louise.

Misplaced: The cook prepared turkey bamboo for his guests made primarily of spinach.
Correct: The cook prepared turkey bamboo, made primarily of spinach, for his guests.

(For additional examples, see pp. 67–68.)

Practicing What You've Learned

Errors with Adverbs, Adjectives, and Modifying Phrases

Correct the sentences below, skipping any that are already correct.

1. Crossing the threshold, the bridal suite was unlike anything the couple had ever seen.
2. He didn't think the car would make it over the mountains, being eight years old.
3. Of all the foods in the world, liver is the worse.
4. I can't see very (good, well) in the dark, but since I want to do (good, well) on my test, I'm going to study despite the power failure.
5. After boarding Hard Luck Airways, the meals we were offered convinced us to return by ship.
6. I've read that a number of modern sailors, like Thor Heyerdahl, have sailed primitive vessels across the ocean in a book from the public library.
7. The teacher told Harvey he could either type or print his essay, whichever was easiest for him.
8. Being the last straw, I decided to throw out my roommate after he stole my girl friend.
9. We are enclosing with this letter the new telephone number for notifying the fire department of any fires that may be attached to your telephone.
10. On taking a closer look, we saw that the house was obviously a shack about to collapse.

ERRORS IN SENTENCES

Fragments   Frag

A complete sentence must contain a subject and a verb. A fragment is an incomplete sentence; it is often a participial phrase or dependent clause that belongs to the preceding sentence. To check for fragments, try reading your prose, one sentence at a time, starting at the *end* of your essay. If you find a "sentence" that makes no sense alone, it's probably a fragment that should be either rewritten or connected to another sentence.

Incorrect: My father evidently had a hard childhood, walking to school during blizzards and doing his homework by candlelight. Also, working weekends to support his ten brothers and sisters.

Correct: My father evidently had a hard childhood, walking to school during blizzards, doing his homework by candlelight, *and* working weekends to support his ten brothers and sisters.

Incorrect: Bubba's parents refuse to send him to a psychiatrist. Although they both know he eats shoelaces and light bulbs.

Correct: Bubba's parents refuse to send him to a psychiatrist, *although* they both know he eats shoelaces and light bulbs.

Comma Splice   CS

A comma splice occurs when two sentences are linked with a comma. To correct this error, you can (1) separate the two sentences with a period, (2) separate the two sentences with a semicolon, (3) insert a coordinating conjunction (such as "and," "or," "nor," "so," "yet") after the comma, (4) subordinate one clause.

Incorrect: Grover won a stuffed gila monster at the church raffle, his mother threw it away the next day while he was in school.
Correct: Grover won a stuffed gila monster at the church raffle. His mother threw it away the next day while he was in school.
Correct: Grover won a stuffed gila monster at the church raffle; his mother threw it away the next day while he was in school.
Correct: Grover won a stuffed gila monster at the church raffle, but his mother threw it away the next day while he was in school.
Correct: Although Grover won a stuffed gila monster at the church raffle, his mother threw it away the next day while he was in school.

(For more help on correcting comma splices, please see pp. 229–230; subordination is discussed in detail on pp. 74–75.)

Run-on Sentence   R-O

Don't run two sentences together without any punctuation. Use a period, a semicolon, a comma plus a coordinating conjunction (if appropriate), or subordinate one clause.

Incorrect: The mayor decided the park needed pelicans he bought them without asking the City Council.
Correct: The mayor decided the park needed pelicans. He bought them without asking the City Council.
Correct: The mayor decided the park needed pelicans; he bought them without asking the City Council.
Correct: The mayor decided the park needed pelicans, so he bought them without asking the City Council.
Correct: When the mayor decided the park needed pelicans, he bought them without asking the City Council.

Faulty Parallelism   //

Parallel thoughts should be expressed in parallel constructions.

Awkward: Boa constrictors like *to lie* in the sun, *to hang* from limbs, and *swallowing* small animals.

Better: Boa constrictors like *to lie* in the sun, *to hang* from limbs, and *to swallow* small animals.

Awkward: Whether *working* on his greasy car, *fistfighting* at the hamburger joint, or *asleep* in bed, my brother always kept his hair combed.

Better: Whether *working* on his greasy car, *fistfighting* at the hamburger joint, or *sleeping* in bed, my brother always kept his hair combed.

False Predication   Pred

This error occurs when the predicate (that part of the sentence that says something about the subject) doesn't fit properly with the subject. Illogical constructions result.

Incorrect: The meaning of the sermon deals with love. [A "meaning" cannot deal with anything; the author, speaker, or work itself can, however.]

Correct: The sermon deals with love.

Incorrect: The reason I drink vinegar every morning is because my personality is too sweet. ["Because" implies a reason.]

Correct: I drink vinegar every morning because my personality is too sweet.

Incorrect: Energy is one of the world's biggest problems. ["Energy" itself is not a problem.]

Correct: The lack of fuel for energy is one of the world's biggest problems.

Incorrect: True failure is when you make an error and don't learn anything from it. [Avoid all "is when" and "is where" constructions. The subject does not denote a time, so the predicate is faulty.]

Correct: You have truly failed only when you make an error and don't learn anything from it.

Incorrect: Her first comment on being in a spaceship was exhilarating. [Her comment wasn't exhilarating; her feeling was.]

Correct: Her first comment on being in a spaceship expressed her exhilaration.

(For other examples of faulty predication, see p. 70.)

Mixed Structure   Mix S

"Mixed structure" is a catchall term that applies to a variety of sentence construction errors. Usually, the term refers to a sentence in which the writer begins with one kind of structure and then shifts to another in mid sentence. Such a shift often occurs when the writer is in a hurry and the mind has already jumped ahead to the next thought.

Confused: By the time one litter of cats is given away seems to bring a new one.

Clear: Giving away one litter of cats seems to tell the mother cat that it's time to produce a new batch.

Confused: The bank robber realized that in his crime spree how very little fun he was having.

Clear: The bank robber realized that he was having very little fun in his crime spree.

Confused: The novel is too hard for what the author meant.

Clear: The novel is too hard for me to understand what the author meant.

Confused: The fact that we had to keep a daily journal, this was a good method for finding theme topics.

Clear: Keeping daily journals helped us find theme topics.

Confused: How many people do you employ, broken down by sex?

Clear: How many people do you employ? Your answer also should indicate the number of female and male employees.

(For other examples of mixed structure, see pp. 70–71).

Practicing What You've Learned

Errors in Sentences

Correct the following sentences; skip any that are correct.

1. According to a study by the Fish and Wildlife Service, Americans' favorite animals are dogs, horses, swans, robins, and butterflies. Whereas their least favorites are cockroaches, mosquitoes, rats, wasps, and rattlesnakes.
2. The 1904 Olympic Games were considered a successful sideshow for the St. Louis World's Fair. Despite the fact that only twelve foreign countries participated.
3. Leon Spinks became the heavyweight boxing champion in 1978 by beating Muhammad Ali, however, he lost his title to Ali later that year. Thus making himself known as the fighter with the shortest reign as a title holder—a mere 212 days.
4. The oldest living thing on earth is a bristlecone pine, named Methuselah, has grown for 4,600 years in the White Mountains of California.
5. I had been driving my car for forty years when I fell asleep at the wheel and drove into the tree.
6. According to the 1938 Action Comics book, Superman could leap

an eighth of a mile, run faster than an express train, and bullets could not penetrate his skin.

7. An example of my irrational fear of water is the ocean at Santa Barbara, I hate beaches too.

8. The reason so many people died when the *Titanic* sank was because they could remain conscious in the frigid North Atlantic water for only two minutes.

9. People often forget how large the Soviet Union is, for example, they don't realize that it encompasses eleven time zones.

10. The digging sites are so scattered, coupled with transportation being so expensive, living conditions are very crude, there is an abundance of biting insects, and the shortness of the summer season, all combine to make the Antarctic a difficult place for archaeological excavations.

A Concise Guide to Punctuation

Punctuation marks do not exist, as one student recently complained, to make your life miserable. They are used to clarify your written thoughts so that the reader understands your meaning. Just as traffic signs and signals tell a driver to slow down, stop, or go faster or slower, so punctuation is intended to guide the reader through your prose. Look, for example, at the confusion in the sentences below when the necessary punctuation marks are omitted:

Confusing: Has the tiger been fed Bill? [Bill was the tiger's dinner?]
Clear: Has the tiger been fed, Bill?

Confusing: After we had finished raking the dog jumped into the pile of leaves. [Raking the dog?]
Clear: After we had finished raking, the dog jumped into the pile of leaves.

Confusing: Bubbles McGoo's diet called for a lunch of cottage cheese soup and salad. [Cottage cheese soup?]
Clear: Bubbles McGoo's diet called for cottage cheese, soup, and salad.

Because punctuation helps you communicate clearly with your reader, you should familiarize yourself with the following rules.

THE PERIOD (.)   P

1. Use a period to end a sentence.

Examples: Ralph quit school to go live with the Pygmies in Africa. He
returned shortly thereafter.

2. Use a period after initials and many abbreviations.

Examples: W. B. Yeats, 12 A.M., Dr., etc., M.A.

3. Only one period is necessary if the sentence ends with an abbreviation.

Examples: The elephant was delivered C.O.D.
To find a good job, you should obtain a B.S. or B.A.

THE QUESTION MARK (?)   P

1. Use a question mark after every direct question.

Examples: May I borrow your galoshes?
Is the sandstorm over now?

2. No question mark is necessary after an indirect question.

Examples: She asked him why he had wrecked her car.
He wondered how she had found out about the accident.

THE EXCLAMATION POINT (!)   P

The exclamation point follows words, phrases, or sentences to show strong
feelings.

Examples: Fire! Call the rescue squad!

THE COMMA (,)   P

1. Use a comma to separate two independent clauses[1] joined by a coordinating
conjunction ("but," "and," "or," "nor," "so," "yet," "for").

---

[1]An independent clause looks like a complete sentence; it contains a subject and a
verb, and it makes sense by itself.

Examples: You can bury your savings in the backyard, but don't expect
            Mother Nature to pay interest.
            All Sue inherited was a black limousine, so she started a chauf-
            feur service.
            I'm going home to my teddy bear, and I'm never coming back.

Do *not* join two sentences with a comma only; such an error is called a
comma splice. Use a comma plus one of the coordinating conjunctions listed
previously, a period, a semicolon, or subordination.

Comma splice: Beatrice washes and grooms the chickens, Samantha feeds
                the spiders.
Correct: Beatrice washes and grooms the chickens, and Samantha
                feeds the spiders.
Correct: Beatrice washes and grooms the chickens. Samantha feeds
                the spiders.
Correct: Beatrice washes and grooms the chickens; Samantha feeds
                the spiders.
Correct: When Beatrice washes and grooms the chickens,
                Samantha feeds the spiders.

Comma splice: I like ketchup on most food, however, even I can't stand it
                on fried eggs.
Correct: I like ketchup on most food, but even I can't stand it on fried
                eggs.
Correct: I like ketchup on most food. However, even I can't stand it
                on fried eggs.
Correct: I like ketchup on most food; however, even I can't stand it
                on fried eggs.
Correct: Although I like ketchup on most food, even I can't stand it
                on fried eggs.

(For additional help, see p. 223.)

2. Conjunctive adverbs, such as "however," "moreover," "thus," "consequently," and "therefore," are used to show continuity and are frequently set off by
commas when they appear in mid sentence.

Examples: She discovered, *however*, that he had stolen her mono-
            grammed towels in addition to her pet avocado plant.
            She felt, *consequently*, that he was not trustworthy.

When a conjunctive adverb occurs at the beginning of a sentence, it may be
followed by a comma, especially if a pause is intended. If no pause is intended, you
may omit the comma, but inserting the comma is never wrong.

Examples: *Thus*, she resolved never to speak to him again.
              Therefore, she resolved never to speak to him again.
              Therefore she resolved never to speak to him again.

Please note that "however" can never, never be used as a coordinating conjunction joining two independent clauses. Incorrect use of "however" most often results in a comma splice.

Comma splice: The police arrested the thief, *however*, they had to release him because the plant wouldn't talk.
Correct: The police arrested the thief; *however*, they had to release him because the plant wouldn't talk.
Also correct: The police arrested the thief. *However*, they had to release him because the plant wouldn't talk.

(For more information on avoiding the comma splice, see p. 223.)

3. Set off with a comma an introductory phrase or clause, unless it is very short.

Examples: When we came out of the store, Grandmother was gone.
           According to her son, there were no clues as to her whereabouts.
           After a week she called to say she had eloped with the postmaster.

4. Set off nonessential phrases and clauses. If the information can be omitted without changing the meaning of the main clause, then the phrase or clause is nonessential. Do *not* set off clauses or phrases that are essential to the meaning of the main clause.

Essential: Mrs. Mungo quickly identified the man *who had sold her the fake birth certificate.* [The "who" clause is essential to explain which man was identified, and why.]
               The storm *that destroyed Mr. Peartree's outhouse* left him speechless with anger. [The "that" clause is essential to explain why the storm angered Mr. Peartree.]
               The movie *showing now at the Ritz* is very obscene and very popular. [The participial phrase is essential to identify the movie.]
Nonessential: Joe Medusa, *who won the jalapeno-eating contest last year*, is this year's champion cow-chip tosser. [The "who" clause is nonessential because it only supplies additional information to the main clause.]
               Black widow spiders, *which eat their spouses after mating*, are easily identifiable by the orange hour glass design on their

abdomens. [The "which" clause is nonessential because it only supplies additional information.]

Bernie Patooka, *playing second base for the Dodgers,* broke his nose yesterday when he swatted a mosquito without letting go of the ball. [The participial phrase is nonessential because it only supplies additional information.]

5. Use commas to separate items in a series of words, phrases, or clauses.

Examples: Julio collects coins, stamps, bottle caps, erasers, and pocket lint.
Mrs. Jones chased her husband out the window, around the ledge, down the fire escape, and into the busy street.

While journalists and some grammarians permit the omission of the last comma before the "and," many authorities believe the comma is necessary for clarity. For example, how many pints of ice cream are listed in the sentence below:

Please buy the following pints of ice cream: strawberry, peach, coffee, vanilla and chocolate swirl.

Four or five pints? Without a comma before the "and," the reader doesn't know if vanilla and chocolate swirl are (is?) one item or two. By inserting the last comma, you clarify the sentence:

Please buy the following pints of ice cream: strawberry, peach, coffee, vanilla, and chocolate swirl.

6. Use commas to separate adjectives of equal emphasis that modify the same noun. To determine if a comma should be used, see if you can insert the word "and" between the adjectives; if the phrase still makes proper sense with the substituted "and," use a comma.

Examples: The vampire gazed at her long, pink, inviting neck.
The vampire gazed at her long and pink and inviting neck

I have a sweet, handsome husband.
I have a sweet and handsome husband.

I called from a convenient telephone booth.
But not: I called from a convenient and telephone booth.
["Convenient" modifies the unit "telephone booth," so there is no comma.]

Hand me some of that homemade salad dressing.
But not: Hand me some of that homemade and salad dressing.
["Homemade" modifies the unit "salad dressing," so there is no
comma.]

7. Set off direct address with commas.

Examples: Gentlemen, keep your seats.
Car fifty-four, where are you?
Not now, Eleanor, I'm busy.

8. Use commas to set off items in addresses and dates.

Examples: The sheriff followed me from Austin, Texas, to question me
about my uncle.
He found me on February 2, 1978, when I stopped for gas in
Fairbanks, Alaska.

9. Use commas to set off a degree or title following a name.

Examples: John Dough, M.D., was audited when he reported only $5.68
in taxable income last year.
The Neanderthal Award went to Samuel Lyle, Ph.D.

10. Use commas to set off dialogue from the speaker.

Examples: Alexander announced, "I don't think I want a second helping of
possum."
"Eat hearty," said Marie, "because this is the last of the food."

11. Use commas to set off "yes," "no," "well," and weak exclamations.

Examples: Yes, I think I understand your position.
Ah, now I see what you mean.
Well, perhaps you're wrong after all.

12. Set off interrupters or parenthetical elements appearing in the midst of a
sentence. A parenthetical element is additional information placed as explanation
or comment within an already complete sentence. This element may be a word
(such as "certainly" or "fortunately"), a phrase ("for example," "in fact"), or a
clause ("I believe," "you know"). The word, phrase, or clause is parenthetical if
the sentence parts before and after it fit together.

Examples: You are, I think, a fool.
            Jack, my roommate, is also a fool.
            I, unfortunately, am the biggest fool of all.

Practicing What You've Learned

Errors with Commas, Periods, Question Marks

The sentences below contain errors that may be corrected by changing, adding, or deleting commas, periods, and question marks.

1. Although the first ice cream soda was introduced in 1850 the first ice cream cone didn't appear until 1904.
2. The ice cream cone was introduced at the World's Fair in St Louis Missouri in celebration of the anniversary of the Louisiana Purchase.
3. In Virginia it was once illegal to sell soda drinks on Sunday so a druggist who wanted to attract customers on that day invented the ice cream sundae as a substitute.
4. The ancient Arabs and Chinese knew how to make flavored ices, however, the Italians who also invented the pizza were the first to recognize that a combination of ice and salt would make a mixture freeze.
5. Around 1550 fortunately for ice cream lovers everywhere the Italians added milk or cream to this frozen liquid mixture and invented ice cream.
6. By the seventeenth century the cool delicious fattening dessert was served at most royal courts in Europe.
7. Bruce said "Linda did you know that ice cream didn't appear in the US until the early 1700s"
8. No I didn't know that but I knew that ice cream parlors were first built in America along the Atlantic coast around 1800.
9. Today America leads the world in ice cream consumption, Australia is second.
10. For many people ice cream is their favorite food, however, they should know that two scoops of the creamy rich dessert have I believe about 140 calories.

THE SEMICOLON (;)   P

1. Use a semicolon to link two closely related independent clauses.

Examples: Belinda sold shoes as an undergraduate; she earned enough money to buy her own sorority house.

The antique piggybank contained thirty-seven cents; only Jules needed money badly enough to break it.

2. Use a semicolon to avoid a comma splice when connecting two independent clauses with words like "however," "moreover," "thus," "therefore," and "consequently."

Examples: All Esmeralda's plants die shortly after she gets them home from the store; consequently, she has the best compost heap in town.
This town is not big enough for both of us; therefore, I suggest we expand the city limits.
I don't like the way she dresses, talks, walks, sings, or smiles; moreover, I dislike girls who are not infatuated with me.

3. Use a semicolon in a series between items that already contain internal punctuation.

Examples: Last year the Wildcats suffered enough injuries to keep them from winning the pennant, as Jake Pritchett, third baseman, broke his arm in a fight; Hugh Rosenbloom, starting pitcher, sprained his back on a trampoline; and Boris Baker, star outfielder, ate rotten clams and nearly died.
Her children were born a year apart: Moe, 1936; Curley, 1937; and Larry, 1938.

THE COLON (:)   P

1. Use a colon to introduce a long or formal list, but do not use one after "to be" verbs.

Correct: Please pick up these items at the store: garlic, wolfbane, mirrors, a prayer book, a hammer, and a wooden stake.
Incorrect: My uncle's three rules of success *are*: earn your money honestly, count your money nightly, and don't give your money away.
Correct: My uncle's three rules of success are the following: earn your money honestly, count your money nightly, and don't give your money away.

Avoid needless colons.

Incorrect: At the store I couldn't find: wolfbane or a wooden stake
Correct: At the store I couldn't find wolfbane or a wooden stake.

2. A colon may be used to introduce a formal or long quotation.

Examples: The ambassador explained that his country could not afford a revolution: "Our nation is in the midst of such an energy crisis that we've lowered the palace thermostats to save money."
The late statesman Hubert Humphrey once jokingly apologized to reporters about his having been born in a small apartment above a drugstore: "They were short on log cabins that year."

3. Use a colon to introduce a word, phrase, or sentence that explains, summarizes, or amplifies the preceding sentence.

Examples: Ann stayed up all night making her decision: she would return Frank's engagement ring on Saturday.
Of all the desserts I've ever eaten, I love one best of all: chocolate-covered grasshoppers.

Practicing What You've Learned

Errors with Semicolons and Colons

Correct the semicolon and colon errors below by adding, deleting, or substituting an appropriate mark of punctuation. Skip over any correct sentences.

1. Refrigerators are considered a luxury to many Eskimos, they use them to keep their food from freezing.
2. U.S. Presidents who never earned a college degree were: Washington, Jackson, Van Buren, Taylor, Fillmore, Lincoln, Andrew Johnson, Cleveland, and Truman.
3. In a Thurmont, Maryland, cemetery can be found this epitaph "Here lies an Atheist, all dressed up, and no place to go."
4. George Bernard Shaw, the famous playwright, claimed he wanted the following epitaph on his tombstone: "I knew if I stayed around long enough, something like this would happen."
5. The last president born in a log cabin was James A. Garfield, the first president born in a hospital was Jimmy Carter.
6. Some inventors who named weapons after themselves include Samuel Colt, the Colt revolver, Henry Deringer, Jr., the derringer pistol, Dr. Richard J. Gatling, the crank machine gun, Col. John T. Thompson, the submachine or "tommy" gun, and Oliver F Winchester, the repeating rifle.
7. William Kemmber, a convicted ax murderer, holds a special place in criminal history on August 6, 1890, he was the first man executed by electric chair.

8. As we drove down the highway we saw a sign that said "See the World's Largest Prairie Dog Turn Right at this Exit," therefore we stopped to look.
9. The next billboard read "See Live Rattlesnakes Pet Baby Pigs"; making us want to stop again.
10. Some people believe that the expression "OK" originated as an abbreviation for "oll korrect," however, others insist it arose from President Martin Van Buren's nickname of "Old Kinderhook."

THE APOSTROPHE(')   Ap

1. Use an apostrophe to indicate a contraction.

> Examples: *It's* too bad your car burned.[2]
> *Wouldn't* the insurance company believe your story?

2. Add an apostrophe plus "s" to a noun to show possession.

> Examples: *Jack's* dog ate the *cat's* dinner.
> The *veterinarian's* assistant later doctored the *puppy's* wounds.

3. Add only an apostrophe to a plural noun ending in "s" to show possession.

> Examples: Goldilocks invaded the *bears'* house.
> She ignored her *parents'* warning about breaking and entering.

4. In some cases you may add an apostrophe plus "s" to a singular word ending in "s," especially when the word is a proper name.

> Examples: Bill Jones's car
> Goldilocks's chair
> the boss's checkbook

5. To avoid confusion, you may use an apostrophe plus "s" to form the plurals of letters, figures, and words discussed as words.

> Examples: He made four "*C's*" last fall. [or "*Cs*"]
> The right to resist the draft was a major issue in the *1960's*. [or *1960s*]
> You use too many "*and's*" in your sentence. [or "*ands*"]

---

[2]Don't confuse the contraction "it's" (for "it is") with the possessive pronoun "its," which never takes an apostrophe (The car was old, but *its* coat of paint was new)

QUOTATION MARKS   P

1. Use quotation marks to enclose someone's spoken or written words.

> Examples: The reporter wrote, "Senator Raycough is, without a doubt, the most conceited politician I've ever encountered."
> "I am the humblest man in the world," retorted the senator proudly.

2. Use quotation marks around the titles of essays,[3] articles, chapter headings, short stories, short poems, and songs.

> Examples: "How To Paint Ceramic Ashtrays"
> "The Fall of the House of Usher"
> "Stopping by Woods on a Snowy Evening"
> "Moon River"

3. You may either underline or place quotation marks around a word, phrase, or letter used as the subject of discussion.

> Examples: Never use "however" as a coordinating conjunction.
> The "which" clause in your sentence is misplaced.
> Is your middle initial "X" or "Y"?
> Her use of such words as "drab," "bleak," and "musty" gives the poem a somber tone.

4. Place quotation marks around uncommon nicknames and words used ironically. Do not, however, try to apologize for slang or clichés by enclosing them in quotation marks; instead, substitute specific words.

> Examples: "Scat-cat" Malone takes candy from babies.
> Her "friend" was an old scarecrow in an abandoned barn.

> Slang: He discovered his tricycle had been "ripped off."
> Specific: He discovered his tricycle had been stolen.

5. The period and the comma go inside quotation marks; the semicolon and the colon go outside. If the quoted material is a question, the question mark goes inside; if quoted material is a phrase of a whole sentence that is a question, the mark goes outside. The same is true for exclamation points.

---

[3] Do not, however, put quotation marks around your own essay's title on either the title page or the first page of your theme.

Examples: "Please wait outside until I finish pouting."

"Please wait outside until I finish pouting," Joe said with a quivering lip.

"Please wait outside until I finish pouting"; he closed the door and left us on the porch.

"Will you please wait until I finish pouting?" Joe repeated angrily as we knocked on the door.

Did he really say, "until I finish pouting"?

6. Material requiring quotation marks (quotations, poems, stories, etc.) within a quotation is enclosed with single quotation marks.

Example: "Did T. S. Eliot write a poem called 'The Love Song of J. Edgar Hoover'?" asked Seymour.

Practicing What You've Learned

Errors with Apostrophes and Quotation Marks

Correct the errors below by adding, changing, or deleting apostrophes and quotation marks; skip any correct sentences.

1. Its true that when famous wit Dorothy Parker was told that President Coolidge, also known as Silent Cal, was dead, she exclaimed, How can they tell?
2. When a woman seated next to Coolidge at a dinner party once told him she had made a bet with a friend that she could get more than two words out of him, he replied You lose.
3. Twenty-one of Elvis Presleys albums have sold over a million copies; twenty of the Beatles albums have also done so.
4. Leslies mother was pleased that her daughter received As on her quizzes about Edgar Allen Poes famous detective story The Purloined Letter.
5. Wasnt it essayist William Hazlitt who said, Man is the only animal that laughs and weeps, for he is the only animal that is struck with the difference between what things are and what they ought to be? asked David.
6. The most popular song ever recorded is not White Christmas, as some people think, but Happy Birthday.
7. Sarah's favorite stories are Peter Pan, The Three Bears, and Little Red Riding Hood; its hard for her to pick just one to hear at bedtime.
8. Despite both her lawyers advice, she used the words terrifying, hideous, and unforgettable to describe her latest flight on Golden Fleece Airways, piloted by Jack One-Eye Marcus.

9. A scholars research has revealed that the five most commonly used words in written English are the, of, and, a, and to.
10. Shakespeares' signature is worth thousands of dollars to collectors because theres only seven of them in existence.

PARENTHESES ()   P

1. Use parentheses to set off statements that give additional information, explain, or qualify the main thought.

Examples: The executive pulled over to the side of the road (a decision he would later regret) and held open the door for the hitchhiker.
Many states (including Texas) still have laws that prohibit persons from remarrying until their divorces have been final for one month.

2. The period comes inside the close parenthesis if a complete sentence is enclosed; it occurs after the close parenthesis when the enclosed matter comes at the end of the main sentence and is only a part of the main sentence.

Examples: Use the subjunctive tense when you need to express a wish. (See pp. 213–214 for more information.)
Avoid comma splices by using a comma and a coordinating conjunction (such as "and," "or," "yet," "but," and "so").

3. If you are confused trying to distinguish whether information should be set off by commas, parentheses, or dashes, here are three general guidelines:

a. Use commas to set off information closely related to the rest of the sentence.

Example: When Billy Clyde married Maybelle, his brother's young widow, the family was shocked. [The information identifies Maybelle and tells why the family was shocked.]

b. Use parentheses to set off information loosely related to the rest of the sentence or material that would disturb the grammatical structure of the main sentence.

Examples: Billy Clyde married Maybelle (his fourth marriage, her second) in Las Vegas on Friday. [The information is merely additional comment not closely related to the meaning of the sentence.]
Billy Clyde married Maybelle (she was previously married to his brother) in Las Vegas on Friday. [The information is an additional comment that would also disturb the grammatical structure of the main sentence were it not enclosed in parentheses.]

c. Use dashes to set off information dramatically or emphatically.

Example: Billy Clyde eloped with Maybelle—only three days after her husband's funeral—without saying a word to anyone in the family.

BRACKETS [   ]   P

1. Use brackets to set off editorial explanations in quoted material.

Examples: The Countess ended the legend by saying, "The original castle [completed in 1434] was built of inferior quality and melted in a rainstorm in the late fifteenth century."
According to the old letter, the treasure map could be found "in the library taped to the back of the portrait [of Gertrude the Great] that faces north."

2 Use brackets to set off editorial corrections in quoted material. By placing the bracketed word "sic" (meaning "thus") next to an error, you indicate that the mistake appeared in the original text and that *you* are not misquoting or misspelling.

Examples: The student wrote, "I think it's unfair for teachers to count off for speling [sic]." ["Sic" in brackets indicates that the student who is quoted misspelled the word "spelling."]
The highway advertisement read as follows: "For great stakes [sic], eat at Joe's, located right behind Daisy's Glue Factory." [Here, "sic" in brackets indicates an error in word choice; the restaurant owner incorrectly advertised "stakes" instead of "steaks."]

THE DASH (—)   P

1. Use a dash to indicate a strong or sudden break in thought.

Examples: We toil hard upon this earth—but not for long.
Now let's be reasonable—wait, put down that ice pick!

2. Use dashes to set off parenthetical matter that deserves more emphasis than parentheses denote.

Example   Sue began dating Bubba's uncle—the president of the local

bank—in an effort to overcome her poor background.
He was amazed to learn his test score—a pitiful 43.

(To clear up any confusion over the uses of dashes, commas, and parentheses, see the guidelines on pp. 239–240.)

3. Use a dash before a summarizing statement.

> Example: Wine, food, someone else picking up the check—the dinner was perfect.

THE HYPHEN (-)   P

1. Use a hyphen to join words into a single adjective before the noun.

> Examples: a wind-blown wig
> the mud-caked sneakers
> a made-for-television movie
> a middle-aged hippie
> a five-year-old boy

2. Some compound words use a hyphen; always check your dictionary when you're in doubt.

> Examples: mother-in-law
> President-elect
> runner-up
> good-for-nothing
> twenty-one

3. Some words with prefixes use a hyphen; again, check your dictionary if necessary.

> Examples: all-American
> ex-wife
> self-hypnosis
> pre-law

4. Use a hyphen to mark the separation of syllables when you divide a word at the end of a line. Do not divide one-syllable words; do not leave one or two letters at the end of a line. (In most dictionaries, dots are used to indicate the division of syllables. Example: va·ca·tion)

> Examples: In your essays you should avoid using frag-
> ment sentences.
> Did your father try to help you with your home-
> work?

ITALICS (UNDERLINING) (_____)   **Ital**

1. Underline or place quotation marks around a word, phrase, or letter used as the subject of discussion. Whether you underline or use quotation marks, always be consistent. (See also pp. 237–238.)

> Examples: Never use <u>however</u> as a coordinating conjunction.
> Is your middle initial <u>X</u> or <u>Y</u>?
> Her use of such words as <u>drab, bleak,</u> and <u>musty</u> give the poem a somber tone.

2. Underline the title of books, magazines, newspapers, movies, works of art, television programs (but use quotes for individual episodes), airplanes, trains, and ships.

> Examples: <u>Moby Dick</u>
> <u>The Reader's Digest</u>
> <u>Texarkana Gazette</u>
> <u>Gone With the Wind</u>
> <u>Mona Lisa</u>
> <u>Sixty Minutes</u>
> <u>Spirit of St. Louis</u>
> <u>Queen Mary</u>

Exceptions: Do not underline the Bible or the titles of legal documents, including the United States Constitution, or the name of your own essay when it appears on your title page. Do not underline the city in a newspaper title unless the city's name is actually part of the newspaper's title.

3. Underline foreign words that are not commonly regarded as part of the English language.

> Examples: He shrugged and said, <u>"C'est la vie."</u>
> Under the "For Sale" sign on the old rusty truck, the farmer had written the words <u>"caveat emptor,"</u> meaning "let the buyer beware."

4. Use underlining sparingly to show emphasis.

> Examples: Everyone was surprised to discover that the butler <u>didn't</u> do it.
> "Do you realize that <u>your</u> son just ate a piece of a priceless Bamzant sculpture?" the man screamed at his wife.

THE ELLIPSIS MARK (. . . or . . . .)   **P**

1. To show an omission in quoted material within a sentence, use three periods, with spaces before and after each one.

Example: The secret of living a reasonably long life is not to grow old.
The secret of . . . long life is not to grow old.

2. Three periods with spaces may be used to show an incomplete or interrupted thought.

Example: My wife is an intelligent, beautiful woman who wants me to live a long time. On the other hand, Harry's wife . . .

3. If you omit any words at the end of a sentence, use four periods with spaces between each one.

Example: "Four score and seven years ago our fathers brought forth upon this continent, a new nation . . . ."

4. If the omission of one or more sentences occurs at the end of a sentence, use four periods with no space before the first dot.

Example: "The Lord is my shepherd; I shall not want. . . . he leadeth me in the paths of righteousness for his name's sake."

Practicing What You've Learned

Errors with Parentheses, Brackets, Dashes, Hyphens, Italics, and Ellipses

Correct the errors below by adding, changing, or deleting parentheses, brackets, dashes, hyphens, italics, and ellipses. Skip any correct sentences.

1. Meet the Press holds the record for the longest run on television a remarkable 35 years.
2. In 1948 Gertrude Rogallo with an assist from her husband invented the hang glider.
3. In mystery stories the detective often advises the police to cherchez la femme. Editor's note: "Cherchez la femme" means "look for the woman."
4. With a death defying leap Annie Edson Taylor she was a Michigan schoolteacher at the time became the first person to go over Niagara Falls in a barrel back in 1901.
5. Few people know that James Arness later Matt Dillon in the long running television series Gunsmoke got his start by playing the vegetable creature in the postwar monster movie The Thing 1951.
6. Similarly, well known T.V. star Michael Landon played the leading role in the 1957 classic I Was a Teenage Werewolf what a terrible movie!

7. When Lucille Ball, star of I Love Lucy, became pregnant with her first child, the network executives decided that the word expecting could be used on the air to refer to her condition, but not the word pregnant.

8. In a face to face interview the fifty five year old ex champion swore "to tell the truth . . . . and nothing but the truth" about the trans Atlantic phone calls he made while pretending to be hard at work at his nine to five job.

9. A French chemist named Georges Claude invented the first neon sign in 1910. For additional information on his unsuccessful attempts to use seawater to generate electricity, see pp. 200–205.

10. As the principal hated by everyone for his anti intellectual attitude strode into the room, the children dropped their books and began reciting "I pledge allegiance to the flag . . ."

Chapter

14

A Concise Guide to Mechanics

CAPITALIZATION   Cap

1. Capitalize the first word of every sentence.

> Example: The lazy horse leans against a tree all day.

2. Capitalize proper names and proper adjectives.

> Examples: John Doe, Miami, France, Japanese cars, Havana cigars

3. Capitalize titles when they are accompanied by proper names.

> Examples: President Jones, Major Smith, Governor Brown, Judge
> Wheeler

4. Capitalize all the principal words in titles of books, articles, stories, plays, movies, and poems. Prepositions, articles, and conjunctions are not capitalized unless they begin the title or contain more than four letters.

> Examples: "The Face on the Barroom Floor"
> *A Short History of the War Between the States*
> *For Whom the Bell Tolls*

5. Capitalize the first word of a direct quotation.

Examples: The clerk frowned and said, "Please take your business elsewhere, sir."
The customer replied, "Don't speak to your father that way."

6. Capitalize "east," "west," "north," and "south" when they refer to particular
sections of the country but not when they merely indicate direction.

Examples: The South may or may not rise again. ["South" here refers to a
section of the country.]
If you travel south for ten miles, you'll see the papier-mâché
replica of the world's largest hamburger. [In this case, "south" is
a direction.]

7. Capitalize a title when referring to a particular person;[1] do not capitalize a title if
a pronoun precedes it.

Examples: The General ate lentils for breakfast every morning.
Even though I hate them, Mother wants me to eat lentils, too.
We gave our mother a lentil cooker for her birthday.

ABBREVIATIONS   Ab

1. Abbreviate the titles "Mr.," "Mrs.," "Ms.," "St.," and "Dr." when they
precede names.

Examples: Dr. Scott, Ms. Steinham, Mrs. Morgan, St. Jude

2. Abbreviate titles and degrees when they follow names.

Examples: Charles Byrd, Jr.; Andrew Gordon, Ph.D.; Joe Bucks, C.P.A.

3. You may abbreviate the following in even the most formal writing: A.M. (*ante
meridiem*, before noon), P.M. (*post meridiem*, after noon), A.D. (*anno Domini*, in
the year of our Lord), B.C. (before Christ), etc. (*et cetera*, and others), i.e. (*id est*,
that is), and e.g. (*exempli gratia*, for example).

4. In formal writing do *not* abbreviate the names of days, months, centuries,
states, countries, or units of measure. Do *not* use an ampersand ("&"), unless it is
an official part of a title.

Incorrect: Tues., Sept., 18th century, Ark., Mex., lbs.
Correct: Tuesday, September, eighteenth century, Arkansas, Mexico,
pounds

---

[1]Some authorities disagree; others consider such capitalization optional.

Incorrect: Tony & Gus went to the store to buy ginseng root.
Correct: Tony *and* Gus went to the A & P to buy ginseng root. [The "&" in "A & P" is correct because it is part of the store's official name.]

5. Do *not* abbreviate the words for page, chapter, volume, and so forth, except in footnotes and bibliographies, which have prescribed rules of abbreviation. (For additional information on proper abbreviation, consult your dictionary.)

NUMBERS

1. Use figures for dates, street numbers, page numbers, telephone numbers, and hours with A.M. and P.M.[2]

Examples: April 22, 1946
             710 West 14th Street
             page 242
             476-1423
             10 A.M.

2. Some authorities say spell out numbers that can be expressed in one or two words; others say spell out numbers under one hundred.

Examples: Ten thousand dollars or $10,000
             Twenty-four hours
             Five partridges
             $12.99 per pair
             1,294 essays

3. When several numbers are used in a short passage, use figures.

Examples: On the punctuation test, Jennifer made 82, Juan made 91, Pete made 86, and I made 60.
             The hole in the ground was 12 feet long, 10 feet wide, and 21 feet deep.

4. Never begin a sentence with a figure.

Incorrect: 600 men applied for the job of bouncer at the health club.
Correct: Six hundred men applied for the job of bouncer at the health club.

[2]*8 a.m.* but *eight o'clock.*

Practicing What You've Learned

Errors with Capitalization, Abbreviations, and Numbers

Correct the errors below by adding, deleting, or changing capitals, abbreviations, and numbers. Skip any correct sentences.

1. According to legend, catherine the great, empress of russia, was so vain she kept her hairdresser locked in an iron cage in her room so he wouldn't reveal that she wore a wig.
2. At last count China had 20,000 newspaper reporters, 382 newspapers, 99 radio stations, and 38 television stations.
3. When a political opponent once called Lincoln "two-faced,' the president retorted, "if I had another face, do you think I would wear this one?"
4. On p. 14 of my history text professor Sara N. Dipity, ph.d., is quoted as saying that king Mongut of siam, the 19th-century monarch who was the inspiration for the play *the king and I,* had over 9,000 wives.
5. I agree that english muffins are wonderful, but french pastries are still my favorite breakfast treat on Sat. mornings before I leave at 9 A.M. for my lesson in southern cooking.
6. 2 of our presidents have been buried in Arlington national cemetery: president William H. Taft, who died in 1930 at age seventy-two, and president John F. Kennedy, who died in 1963 at age forty-six.
7. In 1883, when american aviator Orville Wright was in the 6th grade, he was expelled from his Richmond, Ind., school for mischievous behavior.
8. The most people—30,472—ever to attend a U.S. tennis match assembled in Houston, Tex., at the astrodome on Sept. 20, 1973, to watch Billie Jean King beat Bobby Riggs in the "Tennis Match Of The Century" in straight sets.
9. My Brother, a Doctor who went to medical school in the east, won't believe that Theodore J. Coombs of Hermosa Beach, Calif., once roller-skated 5,193 miles from Los Angeles, Calif., to New York and then back to Yates Center, Kan., from May thirtieth to Sept. fourteenth, 1979.
10. The british soldier T. E. Lawrence, better known as "lawrence of arabia," stood less than 5 ft. 6 in. tall.

Appendix

Using Source Material

Many writing assignments call for documented source material. Citing sources in your essays or reports shows the reader that you have researched and found support for your ideas. The steps listed below will help you write a research paper that is carefully and effectively documented.

Step One: After you have narrowed your subject matter and have a focused thesis, you should become familiar with the school or public library where you will begin your research. Most libraries will have handouts or librarians who will help you locate the pertinent sources in the area you are studying. Once you are comfortable in the library, begin to compile a *working bibliography*, a list of possible sources, by noting on an index card the following information for each source: author's name, title of work, publisher, date and city of publication, page numbers of the material you're interested in, and library call number.

Step Two: Begin to look up and take notes from the sources listed in your working bibliography. Most authorities recommend that you take notes on index cards rather than on notebook paper because the cards may be shuffled around more easily when you are organizing your material. Each card should contain the author's name, title of the book, publisher, date and city of publication (as found on the book's title page and/or copyright page), and the page numbers on which the information is found. If the notes are from a periodical, the card should contain the author's name, journal's name, article's name, volume number, date of the issue, page numbers of the article, and the page numbers on which the information is found.

Your notes will probably be of three kinds:

1. Direct quotations: When you use other people's direct words, you must always credit them as the sources. If you omit any material within a direct quotation, use the proper ellipsis dots (see pp. 242–243).
2. Paraphrase: You paraphrase when you put into your own words what someone else has said or written. Please note: *Paraphrased ideas that are borrowed ideas and not your original thoughts must also be credited!* Writers occasionally plagiarize unintentionally because they believe only direct quotations and statistics must be attributed.
3. Summary: You may wish to condense a piece of writing so that you may

offer it as support to your own ideas. Using your own words, you should condense the original work, presenting in shorter form the writer's thesis and supporting ideas. In addition, you may find it helpful to include a few direct quotations in your summary to retain the flavor of the original work. Of course, you will tell your readers what you are summarizing and by whom it was written.

Your note cards may also contain your personal comments that occur to you as you read. It might be helpful to jot these down in a different colored pen or put them in brackets that you've initialed, so that you will recognize them later as your own responses.

Step Three: As you write your rough drafts, you must decide which sources to use. You wish to persuade your reader to accept your opinion; using the facts, figures, and ideas of others can help you win your case by supporting your views or by refuting the views of your opposition. Make sure, however, that your source is *reliable.* Is the author an authority on the subject? Is he/she unreasonably biased in some way? Is the material recent enough? Is the reasoning valid? Is the material directly related to your topic? You, the writer, must decide which sources are dependable and what material is persuasive.

Here are a few hints for effectively using your source material:

1. Do not overuse direct quotations. It's best to use a direct quotation *only* when it expresses or emphasizes a point in a far more impressive or succinct way than you could say it yourself.

2. Don't merely drop in your quotations. Lead into them smoothly so that they obviously support or clarify what you are saying (see examples below).

Poor: Scientists have been studying the ill effects of nitrites on test animals since 1961. "Nitrites produced malignant tumors in 62 percent of the test animals within six months."

Better: Scientists have been studying the ill effects of nitrites on test animals since 1961. According to Dr. William Smith, head of the Farrell Institute of Research, "Nitrites produced malignant tumors in 62 percent of the test animals within six months."

3. Don't use the same pattern again and again to introduce your quotations. Here are some sample lead-in phrases for quotations:

As drama critic William Smith observed last year in *The Saturday Review*, the play was "a rousing failure."

In his introduction to *The Great Gatsby*, William Smith points out that "Fitzgerald wrote about himself and produced a narcissistic masterpiece."

William Smith, author of *Impact*, summarized the situation this way: "Eighty-eight percent of the sales force threaten a walkout."

Perhaps the well-known poet William Smith expressed the idea best when he wrote, "Love is a spider waiting to entangle its victims."

Congressman William Smith presented the opposing view when he claimed, "Employment figures are down ten percent from last year."

In other words, don't simply repeat "William Smith said," "John Jones said," "Mary Brown said."

4. Direct quotations more than five lines long should be block indented on the left side and single spaced, without quotation marks. Remember that periods and commas go inside quotation marks; semicolons and colons go outside. The titles of books and journals are underlined; the titles of articles, essays, and chapters are enclosed in quotation marks.

Step Four: Each idea you borrow and each quotation you include must be attributed to its author(s) in a *footnote* that appears at the bottom of the appropriate page.* Number your footnotes consecutively throughout the essay (do not start over with "1" on each new page), and place the number in the text to the right of and slightly above the end of the passage, whether it is a direct quotation, a paraphrase, or a summary. Place the corresponding number, indented (five spaces) and slightly raised, before the footnote at the bottom of the page. Single space each entry and double space after each footnote if more than one appears on the same page. See below for sample footnote entries.

Once you have provided a first full reference, subsequent footnotes for that source may only include the author's last name and the page number. However, some authorities still require the use of Latin abbreviations such as *ibid.* ("in the same place") and *op. cit.* ("in the work cited"), so please consult the proper style manual for your writing assignment. If your assignment requires these Latin abbreviations, use *Ibid.* immediately after the original footnote to substitute for the author's name, the title, and the publication information; add a page number only if it differs from the one in the original footnote. Use *op. cit.* with the author's name to substitute for the title in later references.

First reference: [5]Barbara Tuchman, A *Distant Mirror: The Calamitous Fourteenth Century* (New York: Knopf, 1978), p. 77.

Next footnote: [6]*Ibid.*, p. 82.

Later reference: [12]Tuchman, *op. cit.*, p. 120.

Step Five: At the end of your essay include a *bibliography*, a formal list of the sources in your essay. Arrange the entries alphabetically by the authors' last names; single space within each entry and double space after each one. If an entry takes more than one line, indent the subsequent lines five spaces. See the sample bibliographic entries on pp. 254–257.

[*]Some writing situations permit the use of endnotes, a list of your footnotes that appears following the essay or report. Consult your teacher or the person (or publication) for whom you are writing to see if endnotes are permissible or even preferred.

For a sample student essay with footnotes and a bibliography, see pp. 177–180.

Sample Footnote Forms

Books

Book with one author:

[1]Barbara Tuchman, *A Distant Mirror: The Calamitous Fourteenth Century* (New York: Alfred A. Knopf, Inc., 1978), p. 77.

Book with an editor:

[2]Albert C. Baugh, ed., *A Literary History of England* (New York: Appleton-Century-Crofts, 1974), p. 1236.

Book with author and editor:

[3]Geoffrey Chaucer, *The Tales of Canterbury,* ed. Robert Pratt (Boston: Houghton Mifflin Company, 1974), p. 156.

Book with two or three authors:

[4]Ben Weider and David Hapgood, *The Death of Napoleon* (New York: Congdon and Weed, 1982), p. 228.

Book with more than three authors:

[5]Wilfred L. Guerin, et al., *A Handbook of Critical Approaches to Literature* (New York: Harper & Row, Publishers, 1979), p. 271.

Selection or chapter from anthology or collection with an editor:

[6]Kate Chopin, "La Belle Zoraïde," in *Classic American Women Writers,* ed. Cynthia Griffin Wolff (New York: Harper & Row, Publishers, 1980), p. 255.

Work in more than one volume:

[7]Harold Sharp, *Handbook of Pseudonyms and Personal Nicknames* (New York: Scarecrow Press, Inc., 1972), II, p. 1179.

Later edition:

[8]C. Hugh Holman, *A Handbook to Literature,* 3rd edition (Indianapolis: The Bobbs-Merrill Company, Inc., 1972), p. 754.

Book with corporate authorship:

[9]Editors of *Sunset, Alaska* (Menlo Park, Calif.: Lane Books, 1975), p. 45.

Work in a series:

[10]Barbara L. Berg, *The Remembered Gate: Origins of American Feminism,* Urban Life in America Series (New York: Oxford University Press, 1978), p. 98.

Translation:

[11]Marcel Proust, *Remembrance of Things Past,* trans. by C. K. S. Moncrieff (New York: Random House, Inc., 1970), p. 77.

Reprint:

[12]Celia Thaxter, *Among the Isles of Shoals* (Boston, 1873; rpt. Hampton, N.H.: Heritage Books, 1978), p. 55.

Newspapers, Magazines, Periodicals

Signed article in a newspaper:

[1]Art Branscombe, "American Students Not Getting 'Basics,'" *Denver Post,* Sept. 19, 1982, p. 17, col. 2.

Unsigned article in newspaper:

[2]"Soviet Union Buys 7.6 Million Metric Tons of Grain from Canada," *The Wall Street Journal,* Oct. 14, 1982, sec. 1, p. 18, col. 4.

Signed article in magazine:

[3]Walter Dellinger, "Another Route to the ERA," *Newsweek,* Aug. 2, 1982, p. 8.

Unsigned article in magazine:

[4]"Men's and Women's Trenchcoats," *Consumer Reports,* Oct. 1982, p. 491.

Signed article in periodical:

[5]Thomas Lockwood, "Divided Attention in *Persuasion,*" *Nineteenth Century Fiction,* 33 (Dec. 1978), 309.

Encyclopedias

Signed article:

[1]Ernst Langlotz, "Greek Art," *Encyclopedia of World Art,* 1963 ed., vol. 7, p. 115.

Unsigned article:

[2]"Sailfish," *The International Wildlife Encyclopedia,* 1970 ed., vol. 15, p. 2008.

Pamphlets and Government Documents

[1]*The Essentials of Education: A Call for Dialog and Action* (Urbana, Ill.: Organization for the Essentials of Education, 1982), p. 2.

[2]U.S. Dept. of Health's National Institute on Drug Abuse, "Drug Abuse Prevention" (Washington, D.C.: Government Printing Office, 1980), p. 15.

Unpublished Dissertations and Theses

[1]Gail A. Harmon, "Poor Writing Skills at the College Level: A Program for Correction," Thesis University of Colorado, 1982, p. 19.

Films, Television, Records, Plays, Concerts, Interviews

[1]Edouard Molinaro, dir., *La Cage aux Folles,* with Ugo Tognazzì and Michel Serrault, United Artists, 1979.

[2]*20/20,* prod. Av Westin, Oct. 14, 1982.

[3]The Willows, *Protest Songs of the Sixties,* Capitol, GH 17033, 1975.

[4]Howard Davies, dir., *Good,* by C. P. Taylor, with the Royal Shakespeare Company, Booth Theatre, New York, Oct. 13, 1982.

[5]Maxim Shostakovich, cond., New York Philharmonic Orchestra Concert, Avery Fisher Hall, New York, Oct. 12, 1982.

[6]Interview with Professor Henry Johns, Department of Political Science, Colorado State University, Sept. 4, 1982.

Sample Bibliographical Entries

Books

Book with one author:

Tuchman, Barbara. *A Distant Mirror: The Calamitous Fourteenth Century.* New York: Alfred A. Knopf, Inc., 1978.

Book with an editor:

Baugh, Albert C., ed. *A Literary History of England.* New York: Appleton-Century-Crofts, 1974.

Book with author and editor:

> Chaucer, Geoffrey. *The Tales of Canterbury*. Ed. Robert Pratt. Boston: Houghton-Mifflin Company, 1974.

Book with two or three authors:

> Weider, Ben, and David Hapgood. *The Death of Napoleon*. New York: Congdon and Weed, 1982.

Book with more than three authors:

> Guerin, Wilfred L., et al. *A Handbook of Critical Approaches to Literature*. New York: Harper & Row, Publishers, 1979.

Selection or chapter from an anthology or collection with an editor:

> Chopin, Kate. "La Belle Zoraïde." In *Classic American Women Writers*. Ed. Cynthia Griffin Wolff. New York: Harper & Row, Publishers, 1980.

Work in more than one volume:

> Sharp, Harold. *Handbook of Pseudonyms and Personal Nicknames*. Vol. 2. New York: Scarecrow Press, 1972.

Later edition:

> Holman, C. Hugh. *A Handbook to Literature*. 3rd edition. Indianapolis: The Bobbs-Merrill Company, Inc., 1972.

Book with corporate authorship:

> Editors of *Sunset, Alaska*. Menlo Park, Calif.: Lane Books, 1975.

Work in a series:

> Berg, Barbara L. *The Remembered Gate: Origins of American Feminism*. Urban Life in America Series. New York: Oxford University Press, 1978.

Translation:

> Proust, Marcel. *Remembrance of Things Past.* Trans. C. K. S. Moncrieff. New York: Random House, Inc., 1970.

Reprint:

> Thaxter, Celia. *Among the Isles of Shoals.* Boston, 1873; rpt. Hampton, N.H.: Heritage Books, 1978.

Newspapers, Magazines, Periodicals

Signed article in newspaper:

> Branscombe, Art. "American Students Not Getting 'Basics.'" *Denver Post,* Sept. 19, 1982, p. 17, col. 2.

Unsigned article in newspaper:

> "Soviet Union Buys 7.6 Million Metric Tons of Grain from Canada." *The Wall Street Journal,* Oct. 14, 1982, sec. 1, p. 18, col. 4.

Signed article in magazine:

> Dellinger, Walter. "Another Route to the ERA." *Newsweek,* Aug. 2, 1982, p. 8.

Unsigned article in magazine:

> "Men's and Women's Trenchcoats." *Consumer Reports,* Oct. 1982, p. 491–97.

Signed article in periodical:

> Lockwood, Thomas, "Divided Attention in *Persuasion.*" *Nineteenth Century Fiction, 33* (Dec. 1978), 309–323.

Encyclopedias

Signed article:

> Langlotz, Ernst. "Greek Art." *Encyclopedia of World Art,* 1963.

Unsigned article:

"Sailfish." *The International Wildlife Encyclopedia*, 1970.

Pamphlets and Government Documents

The Essentials of Education: A Call for Dialog and Action. Urbana, Ill.: Organizations for the Essentials of Education, 1982.

"Drug Abuse Prevention." Department of Health, National Institute on Drug Abuse. Washington, D.C.: Government Printing Office, 1980

Unpublished Dissertations and Theses

Harmon, Gail A. "Poor Writing Skills at the College Level: A Program for Correction." Thesis University of Colorado, 1982.

Films, Television, Records, Plays, Concerts, Interviews

Molinaro, Edouard, dir. *La Cage aux Folles.* With Ugo Tognazzi and Michel Serrault. United Artists, 1979.

Westin, Av, producer. *20/20.* Oct. 14, 1982.

The Willows. *Protest Songs of the Sixties.* Capitol. GH17033, 1975.

Davies, Howard, dir. *Good.* Written by C. P. Taylor. With Royal Shakespeare Company. New York, Booth Theater, Oct. 13, 1982.

Shostakovich, Maxim, cond. New York Philharmonic Orchestra Concert. New York, Avery Fisher Hall, Oct. 12, 1982.

Johns, Professor Henry. Department of Political Science, Colorado State University. Interview, Sept. 4, 1982.

Index

259